32.00

THE AMERICAN FAMILY

REFLECTING A CHANGING NATION

THE AMERICAN FAMILY

REFLECTING A CHANGING NATION

Linda Regensburger

INFORMATION PLUS® REFERENCE SERIES
Formerly published by Information Plus, Wylie, Texas

 GALE GROUP

Detroit
New York
San Francisco
London
Boston
Woodbridge, CT

THE AMERICAN FAMILY: REFLECTING A CHANGING NATION
Linda Regensburger, *Author*

The Gale Group Staff:

Editorial: John F. McCoy, *Project Manager and Series Editor*; Andrew Claps, *Series Associate Editor*; Jason M. Everett, *Series Associate Editor*; Michael T. Reade, *Series Associate Editor*; Rita Runchock, *Managing Editor*; Luann Brennan, *Editor*

Image and Multimedia Content: Barbara J. Yarrow, *Manager, Imaging and Multimedia Content*; Robyn Young, *Project Manager, Imaging and Multimedia Content*

Indexing: Lynne Maday, *Indexing Specialist*; Amy Suchowski, *Indexing Specialist*

Permissions: Julie Juengling, *Permissions Specialist*; Maria Franklin, *Permissions Manager*

Product Design: Michelle DiMercurio, *Senior Art Director*; Kenn Zorn, *Product Design Manager*

Production: Evi Seoud, *Assistant Manager, Composition Purchasing and Electronic Prepress*; NeKita McKee, *Buyer*; Dorothy Maki, *Manufacturing Manager*

ISBN 0-7876-5103-6 (set)
ISBN 0-7876-5399-3 (this volume)
ISSN 1534-164X (this volume)
Printed in the United States of America
10 9 8 7 6 5 4 3 2 1

TABLE OF CONTENTS

Drawing a general profile of the American family is a daunting task, especially given the wide variety of living arrangements in the United States. But this chapter does just that, using Census Bureau statistics to trace trends in the number of births, divorces, and married-couple, single-parent, and same-sex households.

The shape of the American family has been drastically altered by three significant trends: a declining fertility rate; an increase in the number of births among young, unmarried women; and a growing desire by women—especially working women—to put off having children until later in life. These and other trends, such as the changing family roles of men and women, are discussed here.

This chapter presents an overview of the U.S. child population. Some of the topics discussed include trends in the age, racial, and ethnic composition of America's children; different types of living arrangements, such as one- and two-parent households and grandparent-maintained families; adoption and foster care; and the numerous challenges posed by child care, including cost and availability.

American children face a lot of challenges today. This chapter explores some of those challenges, including poverty, lack of health insurance, teen sexuality, pregnancy, substance abuse, divorce, and school violence.

This chapter analyzes the issues of employment, income, and poverty, as they pertain to the American family. Some of the topics explored here include the increasing number of wives and mothers in the work force; the wage gap between men and women; trends in U.S. household income; and the disturbing rise in the number of homeless families.

The American family has undergone numerous changes in the last 50 years. Many of these changes are discussed here, including the "suburban flight" that began in the late 1940s and continues today; the increasing racial and ethnic diversity of the suburbs; the shortage of affordable housing, and what the federal government is attempting to do about it; artificial reproduction and multiple births; and single-parent and same-sex adoptions.

Using results from various polls, this chapter analyzes Americans' feelings on a variety of family-related issues, including marriage, divorce, adultery, parenting, religion, and family values.

PREFACE

The American Family: Reflecting a Changing Nation is the latest volume in the ever-growing *Information Plus Reference Series*. Previously published by the Information Plus company of Wylie, Texas, the *Information Plus Reference Series* (and its companion set, the *Information Plus Compact Series*) became a Gale Group product when Gale and Information Plus merged in early 2000. Those of you familiar with the series as published by Information Plus will notice a few changes from the 1999 edition. Gale has adopted a new layout and style that we hope you will find easy to use. Other improvements include greatly expanded indexes in each book, and more descriptive tables of contents.

While some changes have been made to the design, the purpose of the *Information Plus Reference Series* remains the same. Each volume of the series presents the latest facts on a topic of pressing concern in modern American life. These topics include today's most controversial and most studied social issues: abortion, capital punishment, care for the elderly, crime, health care, the environment, immigration, minorities, social welfare, women, youth, and many more. Although written especially for the high school and undergraduate student, this series is an excellent resource for anyone in need of factual information on current affairs.

By presenting the facts, it is Gale's intention to provide its readers with everything they need to reach an informed opinion on current issues. To that end, there is a particular emphasis in this series on the presentation of scientific studies, surveys, and statistics. This data is generally presented in the form of tables, charts, and other graphics placed within the text of each book. Every graphic is directly referred to and carefully explained in the text. The source of each graphic is presented within the graphic itself. The data used in these graphics is drawn from the most reputable and reliable sources, in particular from the various branches of the U.S. government and from major independent polling organizations. Every effort was made to secure the most recent information available. The reader should bear in mind that many major studies take years to conduct, and that additional years often pass before the data from these studies is made available to the public. Therefore, in many cases the most recent information available in 2001 dated from 1998 or 1999. Older statistics are sometimes presented as well, if they are of particular interest and no more-recent information exists.

Although statistics are a major focus of the *Information Plus Reference Series* they are by no means its only content. Each book also presents the widely held positions and important ideas that shape how the book's subject is discussed in the United States. These positions are explained in detail and, where possible, in the words of those who support them. Some of the other material to be found in these books includes: historical background; descriptions of major events related to the subject; relevant laws and court cases; and examples of how these issues play out in American life. Some books also feature primary documents, or have pro and con debate sections giving the words and opinions of prominent Americans on both sides of a controversial topic. All material is presented in an even-handed and unbiased manner; the reader will never be encouraged to accept one view of an issue over another.

HOW TO USE THIS BOOK

Throughout history, the family has been seen as the basic social and economic unit of American life. Most people would agree that it continues to hold this status today. However, exactly what constitutes a family has changed dramatically over the last half of the twentieth century. Some people believe that these changes have been for the worse, and conflict has arisen over different people's opinions on what makes a "good" family. This book presents the latest information available on America's families. Trends in American family size and structure are explored, and their effects examined. The significant racial and ethnic differences in family structure are also presented. There are many theories to explain these trends and differences, some of the most widely accepted are discussed. This includes coverage of such controversial topics as unwed mothers, same-sex couples, the roles of fathers and mothers in child care, and other issues.

The American Family: Reflecting a Changing Nation consists of seven chapters and three appendices. Each chapter covers a major issue related to families in America; for a summary of the information covered in each chapter, please see the synopses provided in the Table of Contents at the front of the book. Chapters generally begin with an overview of the basic facts and background information on the chapter's topic, then proceed to examine sub-topics of particular interest.

For example, Chapter 2: Women, Men, and the Family begins by listing some of the major changes that have taken place since the 1950s in the roles that men and women play in family life. It then moves on to examine these changes in detail, starting with the decline in the overall fertility rate and changes in when women were most likely to have children. Differences between the fertility rates of women of varying races and ethnicities are discussed. Moving on, the chapter examines the increasing number of women who work outside the home, and the impact this has had on families. Next comes a discussion of the roles women have historically played as caregivers, and how these roles have changed in recent years. This is followed by a similar examination of the care-giving roles of men. The chapter concludes with a section on the child support system in the United States. Readers can find their way through a chapter by looking for the section and sub-section headings, which are clearly set off from the text. Or, they can refer to the book's extensive index, if they already know what they are looking for.

Statistical Information

The tables and figures featured throughout *The American Family: Reflecting a Changing Nation* will be of particular use to the reader in learning about this topic. These tables and figures represent an extensive collection of the most recent and valuable statistics on American families; for example: the number of married couples in America,

the percentage of single-parent families that live below the poverty line, how many children are born out of wedlock, and the opinions of Americans on marriage and child-rearing. Gale believes that making this information available to the reader is the most important way in which we fulfill the goal of this book: To help readers understand the topic of family life in America and reach their own conclusions about controversial issues related to it.

Each table or figure has a unique identifier appearing above it, for ease of identification and reference. Titles for the tables and figures explain their purpose. At the end of each table or figure, the original source of the data is provided.

In order to help readers understand these often complicated statistics, all tables and figures are explained in the text. References in the text direct the reader to the relevant statistics. Furthermore, the contents of all tables and figures are fully indexed. Please see the opening section of the index at the back of this volume for a description of how to find tables and figures within it.

In addition to the main body text and images, *The American Family: Reflecting a Changing Nation* has three appendices. The first is the Important Names and Addresses directory. Here the reader will find contact information for a number of organizations that study families. The second appendix is the Resources section, which is provided to assist the reader in conducting his or her own research. In this section, the author and editors of *The American Family: Reflecting a Changing Nation* describe some of the sources that were most useful during the compilation of this book. The final appendix is this book's index. It has been greatly expanded from previous editions, and should make it even easier to find specific topics in this book.

COMMENTS AND SUGGESTIONS

The editor of the *Information Plus Reference Series* welcomes your feedback on *The American Family: Reflecting a Changing Nation*. Please direct all correspondence to:

Editor
Information Plus Reference Series
27500 Drake Rd.
Farmington Hills, MI, 48331-3535

ACKNOWLEDGEMENTS

The editors wish to thank the copyright holders of the excerpted graphics included in this volume and the permissions managers of many book and magazine publishing companies for assisting us in securing reproduction rights. We are also grateful to the staffs of the Detroit Public Library, the Library of Congress, the University of Detroit Mercy Library, Wayne State University Purdy/Kresge Library Complex, and the University of Michigan Libraries for making their resources available to us. Following is a list of the copyright holders who have granted us permission to reproduce material in American Family. Every effort has been made to trace copyright, but if omissions have been made, please let us know.

COPYRIGHTED MATERIAL IN THE AMERICAN FAMILY: REFLECTING A CHANGING NATION WAS REPRODUCED FROM THE FOLLOWING PERIODICALS:

Family Caregiving in the U.S.: Findings from a National Survey, illustrations. Copyright © by The National Alliance for Caregiving and The American Association of Retired Persons. All reproduced by permission of the National Alliance for Caregiving.

The Gallup Poll Monthly, illustrations. Copyright © 2000 by The Gallup Organization. All reproduced by the permission of The Gallup Organization.

Involving Males in Preventing Teen Pregnancy, tables. The Urban Institute, 1999. Copyright © 1999 by The Urban Institute. Reproduced by permission.

Kids These Days: What Americans Really Think About the Next Generation, table, Spring, 1999. Copyright © 1999 by Public Agenda. Reproduced by permission.

National Adoption Information Clearinghouse, illustrations, 1996, 1998, March, 1999. Copyright © 1996, 1998, 1999 by National Adoption Information Clearinghouse. Reproduced by permission of the National Adoption Information Clearinghouse.

Out of Reach: The Growing Gap Between Housing Costs and Income of Poor People in the United States, illustrations. Copyright © by National Low Income Housing Coalition. All reproduced by permission.

Out of Reach: Rental Housing at What Cost, tables. Copyright © by the National Low Income Housing Coalition. All reproduced by permission.

Public Agenda, 1998, illustration. Copyright © 1998 by Public Agenda. Reproduced by permission.

The Relationship between Family Structure and Adolescent Substance Use, table. Copyright © by Substance Abuse and Mental Health Services Administration. Reproduced by permission.

Teens and Religion, table, October, 2000. Barna Research, 2000. Copyright © 2000 by Barna Research. Reproduced by permission of Barna Research.

U.S. Conference of Mayors, illustrations. Copyright © by the U.S. Conference of Mayors. Both reproduced by permission of the United States Conference of Mayors.

Whatever Happened to Childhood? The Problem of Teen Pregnancy in the United States, illustrations. Copyright © by The National Campaign to Prevent Teen Pregnancy. All reproduced by permission.

Women: The New Providers, tables. Whirlpool Foundation, 1999. Copyright © 1999 by the Whirlpool Foundation. All reproduced by permission.

YOUTHviews, tables. Copyright © 2000 by The Gallup Organization. Both reproduced by the permission of The Gallup Organization.

CHAPTER 1
AMERICA'S FAMILIES

In virtually all cultures the family is considered the basic societal unit. Because the U.S. Census Bureau provides the most comprehensive statistics available on families in America, this book uses the Bureau's terms and definitions as they concern the American family.

To understand the Census Bureau's definition of the family, one must first understand its terminology describing the wide variety of living arrangements in the United States. In gathering its statistics the Census Bureau starts with the American household. An individual in a household is designated as the "householder"—the person who owns or rents (maintains) the home. Households are then divided into "family households" and "nonfamily" households. Family households are further divided into "families maintained by married couples," and "other families," which are maintained by men or women with no spouse at home.

The Census Bureau defines a family household as a group of two or more people living together who are related by birth, marriage, or adoption. Traditionally, this has meant a man, his wife, and their children—referred to as the "nuclear" or "elementary" family. However, a single parent living with a child or children, siblings sharing a home, and any combination of relatives (except when the spouse of the householder lives in the same home) are all considered family households.

A nonfamily household consists of a person living alone or living only with nonrelatives, such as boarders or roommates.

HOUSEHOLDS

In 1998 the Bureau of the Census counted 102.5 million households in the United States. About 70.8 million were family households and 31.6 million were nonfamily households. (See Table 1.1.) Traditionally, family households comprised a large majority of all households. In 1940, 9 of 10 households were families. By 1970, however, families accounted for 81 percent of households, further dropping to 74 percent in 1980. In 1998 just 69.1 percent of all households were families. (See Table 1.1.)

The number of households is projected to climb to 103 million by the 2000 census and to nearly 115 million by 2010. (See Figure 1.1.) During the 1980s and 1990s the large cohorts of Baby Boomers (children born from 1946 to 1964) swelled the numbers of households. In contrast the relatively smaller groups of young adults who will form new households during the decade of 2010 will account for a slower growth in household numbers. (See Figure 1.2.)

MARRIED-COUPLE FAMILIES

World War II's Impact on Marriages

World War II (1939–45), following close on the heels of the Great Depression, forever changed the dynamics of the American family. The uncertainties of the future drove many young couples to rush into marriage, sometimes after a very short courtship. Some draft-age men married to get an exemption from military service. Others, fearing they might not come back from the war alive, wanted a last chance at some happiness. Ronald H. Bailey, in *The Home Front: U.S.A.* (Time-Life Books, Inc., Alexandria, Virginia, 1977), reported that, during the first 5 months after Pearl Harbor (December 7, 1941), an estimated 1,000 servicemen were married every day.

The number of marriages in the United States peaked at the end of the war. Returning soldiers, happy to have survived, wanted to resume a normal life and start a family. The number of marriages climbed from 1.6 million in 1945 to 2.3 million in 1946, a figure not surpassed until 1979. (See Table 1.2.) Between 1940 and 1947 the number of married-couple families rose by more than 4 million. (See Table 1.1.)

In the 1950s getting married became the norm for young people. Eager to forget the economic crisis of the Depression

TABLE 1.1

Households, by type: 1940 to 1998

(Numbers in thousands)

Year	Total households	Family households				Nonfamily households		
		Total	Married couples	Other family		Total	Male householder	Female householder
				Male householder	Female householder			
1998	102,528	70,880	54,317	3,911	12,652	31,648	14,133	17,516
1997	101,018	70,241	53,604	3,847	12,790	30,777	13,707	17,070
1996	99,627	69,594	53,567	3,513	12,514	30,033	13,348	16,685
1995	98,990	69,305	53,858	3,226	12,220	29,686	13,190	16,496
1994	97,107	68,490	53,171	2,913	12,406	28,617	12,462	16,155
1993r	96,426	68,216	53,090	3,065	12,061	28,210	12,297	15,914
1993	96,391	68,144	53,171	3,026	11,947	28,247	12,254	15,993
1992	95,669	67,173	52,457	3,025	11,692	28,496	12,428	16,068
1991	94,312	66,322	52,147	2,907	11,268	27,990	12,150	15,840
1990	93,347	66,090	52,317	2,884	10,890	27,257	11,606	15,651
1989	92,830	65,837	52,100	2,847	10,890	26,994	11,874	15,120
1988a	91,124	65,204	51,675	2,834	10,696	25,919	11,282	14,637
1988	91,066	65,133	51,809	2,715	10,608	25,933	11,310	14,624
1987	89,479	64,491	51,537	2,510	10,445	24,988	10,652	14,336
1986	88,458	63,558	50,933	2,414	10,211	24,900	10,648	14,252
1985	86,789	62,706	50,350	2,228	10,129	24,082	10,114	13,968
1984b	85,290	62,015	50,081	2,038	9,896	23,276	9,689	13,587
1984	85,407	61,997	50,090	2,030	9,878	23,410	9,752	13,658
1983	83,918	61,393	49,908	2,016	9,469	22,525	9,514	13,011
1982	83,527	61,019	49,630	1,986	9,403	22,508	9,457	13,051
1981	82,368	60,309	49,294	1,933	9,082	22,059	9,279	12,780
1980c	80,776	59,550	49,112	1,733	8,705	21,226	8,807	12,419
1980	79,108	58,426	48,180	1,706	8,540	20,682	8,594	12,088
1979	77,330	57,498	47,662	1,616	8,220	19,831	8,064	11,767
1978	76,030	56,958	47,357	1,564	8,037	19,071	7,811	11,261
1977	74,142	56,472	47,471	1,461	7,540	17,669	6,971	10,698
1976	72,867	56,056	47,297	1,424	7,335	16,811	6,548	10,263
1975	71,120	55,563	46,951	1,485	7,127	15,557	5,912	9,645
1974	69,859	54,917	46,787	1,421	6,709	14,942	5,654	9,288
1973	68,251	54,264	46,297	1,432	6,535	13,986	5,129	8,858
1972	66,676	53,163	45,724	1,331	6,108	13,513	4,839	8,674
1971	64,778	52,102	44,928	1,254	5,920	12,676	4,403	8,273
1970	63,401	51,456	44,728	1,228	5,500	11,945	4,063	7,882
1969	62,214	50,729	44,086	1,221	5,422	11,485	3,890	7,595
1968	60,813	50,012	43,507	1,195	5,310	10,801	3,658	7,143
1967	59,236	49,086	42,743	1,190	5,153	10,150	3,419	6,731
1966	58,406	48,399	42,263	1,163	4,973	10,007	3,299	6,708
1965	57,436	47,838	41,689	1,167	4,982	9,598	3,277	6,321
1964	56,149	47,381	41,341	1,204	4,836	8,768	2,965	5,803
1963	55,270	46,872	40,888	1,295	4,689	8,398	2,838	5,560
1962	54,764	46,262	40,404	1,268	4,590	8,502	2,932	5,570
1961	53,557	45,383	39,620	1,199	4,564	8,174	2,779	5,395
1960	52,799	44,905	39,254	1,228	4,422	7,895	2,716	5,179
1959	51,435	43,971	38,410	1,285	4,276	7,464	2,449	5,015
1958	50,474	43,426	37,911	1,278	4,237	7,047	2,329	4,718
1957	49,673	43,262	37,718	1,241	4,304	6,411	2,038	4,374
1956	48,902	42,593	37,047	1,408	4,138	6,309	2,058	4,250
1955	47,874	41,732	36,251	1,328	4,153	6,142	2,059	4,083
1954	46,962	40,998	35,926	1,315	3,757	5,964	1,925	4,039
1953	46,385	40,540	35,577	1,206	3,757	5,845	1,902	3,943
1952	45,538	40,235	35,164	1,119	3,952	5,303	1,757	3,546
1951	44,673	39,502	34,391	1,154	3,957	5,171	1,732	3,439
1950	43,554	38,838	34,075	1,169	3,594	4,716	1,668	3,048
1949	42,182	38,080	33,257	1,197	3,626	4,102	1,308	2,794
1948	40,532	36,629	31,900	1,020	3,709	3,903	1,198	2,705
1947	39,107	34,964	30,612	1,129	3,223	4,143	1,388	2,755
1940d	34,949	31,491	26,571	1,510	3,410	3,458	1,599	1,859

r Revised using population controls based on the 1990 census.
a Data based on 1988 revised processing.
b Incorporates Hispanic-origin population controls.
c Revised using population controls based on the 1980 census.
d Based on 1940 census.

SOURCE: *Household and Family Characteristics: March 1998*, U.S. Bureau of the Census, Washington, D.C., 1999

FIGURE 1.1

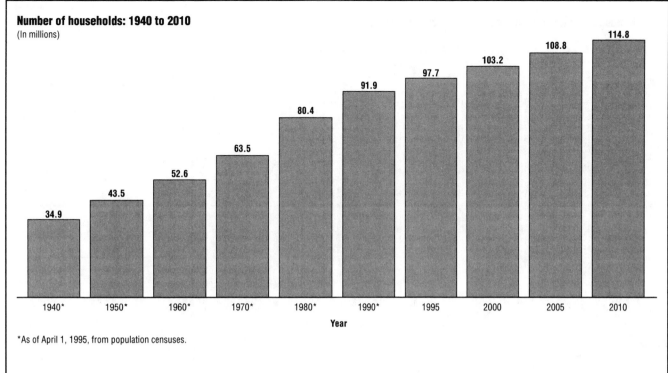

Number of households: 1940 to 2010
(In millions)

34.9   43.5   52.6   63.5   80.4   91.9   97.7   103.2   108.8   114.8

1940*   1950*   1960*   1970*   1980*   1990*   1995   2000   2005   2010

Year

*As of April 1, 1995, from population censuses.

SOURCE: Jennifer Cheeseman Day, *Projections of the Number of Households and Families in the United States: 1995 to 2010*, U.S. Bureau of the Census, Washington, D.C., 1996

and the horrors and uncertainties of war, many Americans sought the security of family. The "American Dream" was to have a family where the father earned a good living, the mother kept house, and the children were lovingly cared for. In 1950 the estimated average age at first marriage for men was 22.8 years, down from 24.3 years in 1940. Meanwhile, the average age at first marriage for women was 20.3, down from 21.5 years in 1940. (See Table 1.3.)

The popular culture of the 1950s promoted marriage as the normal state. Those who chose to stay single were generally considered unusual or eccentric, especially if they were female. In 1950, out of a total male population of 54.6 million 15 years old and older, 36.9 million (67.5 percent) were married. Of 57.1 million women, 37.6 million (66 percent) were married. Just 20 percent of women and 26 percent of men never married. (See Table 1.4.)

The Baby Boom

According to the U.S. Census Bureau, married couples of the 1950s generally started a family immediately; women spaced their childbearing closer together and bore more children than the previous generation. Many had three or four children. The 77 million children born during the years 1946–64 would comprise the future Baby Boomers, the single largest generation in U.S. history.

The fertility rate (the number of live births per 1,000 women of reproductive ages 15–44 years) reached 106.2

live births per 1,000 women in 1950 and peaked at 118 live births per 1,000 women in 1960. (See Table 1.5.)

In 1965, among families with their own children under the age of 18 years, married-couple families had an average of 2.44 children. Families maintained by men with no wife present had an average of 2.13 children, while families maintained by women with no husband present had an average of 2.42 children. (See Table 1.6.)

A CHANGING WORLD

The 1960s heralded the beginning of a moral and cultural transformation largely precipitated by young people, particularly college students. Many were the Baby Boomers who had grown up under circumstances dramatically different from those experienced by their parents who had been raised during the Depression. The 1960s was also a period of rapid economic growth. Rebelling against their parents' more conformist culture, many American youths launched a "counterculture" that included the loosening of sexual mores. Searching for personal growth and self-fulfillment, they challenged the family values of the 1950s.

According to information reported by the Alan Gutmacher Institute in December 2000, birth control pills—first approved for marketing and use by the Food and Drug Administration (FDA) in 1960—were being used by more than 10 million women, or 26.5 percent of the female population using contraceptives, in 1995. The

FIGURE 1.2

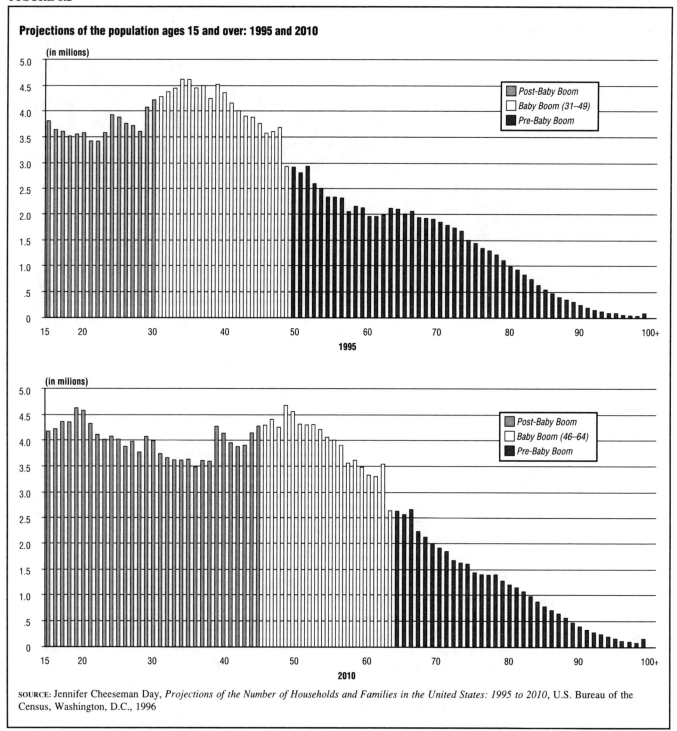

Projections of the population ages 15 and over: 1995 and 2010

(in milions)

Post-Baby Boom
Baby Boom (31–49)
Pre-Baby Boom

1995

(in milions)

Post-Baby Boom
Baby Boom (46–64)
Pre-Baby Boom

2010

SOURCE: Jennifer Cheeseman Day, *Projections of the Number of Households and Families in the United States: 1995 to 2010*, U.S. Bureau of the Census, Washington, D.C., 1996

introduction of intrauterine devices (IUDs) in 1961 gave women another option in family planning. In 1965 the U.S. Supreme Court, in its landmark case *Griswold v. Connecticut* (381 U.S. 479), held that married couples had the right to privacy, specifically the right to marital privacy, or the right to use contraception.

Married-Couple Families Had Fewer Children

By 1970 the overall fertility rate plummeted from a high of 118 live births per 1,000 women (1960) to 87.9 live births per 1,000 women. By 1998 live births per 1,000 women dropped to 65.6. (See Table 1.5.) By 1977 the average married-couple family had two children. This trend has continued; in 1998 the typical married couple with children under the age of 18 years had 1.90 children. (See Table 1.6.)

Delaying Marriage

Between 1960 and 1970 the marriage rate increased from 8.5 to 10.6 per 1,000 population. (See Table 1.2.) However, young people were waiting longer to marry than

TABLE 1.2

Marriages and marriage rates: 1940–93

Year	Number	Rate per 1,000 population				
		Total population	Men 15 years of age and over [1]	Women 15 years of age and over [1]	Unmarried women 15 years of age and over	Unmarried women 15–44 years of age
Provisional:						
1993	2,334,000	9.0	...	...	52.3	86.8
1992	2,362,000	9.3	...	...	53.3	88.2
1991	2,371,000	9.4	...	...	54.2	89.0
Final:						
1990	2,443,489	9.8	26.0	24.1	54.5	91.3
1989	2,403,268	9.7	25.8	23.9	54.2	91.2
1988	2,395,926	9.8	26.0	24.0	54.6	91.0
1987	2,403,378	9.9	26.3	24.3	55.7	92.4
1986	2,407,099	10.0	26.6	24.5	56.2	93.9
1985	2,412,625	10.1	27.0	24.9	57.0	94.9
1984	2,477,192	10.5	28.0	25.8	59.5	99.0
1983	2,445,604	10.5	28.0	25.7	59.9	99.3
1982	2,456,278	10.6	28.5	26.1	61.4	101.9
1981	2,422,145	10.6	28.4	26.1	61.7	103.1
1980	2,390,252	10.6	28.5	26.1	61.4	102.6
1979	2,331,337	10.4	28.1	25.8	63.6	107.9
1978	2,282,272	10.3	28.0	25.7	64.1	109.1
1977	2,178,367	9.9	27.2	25.0	63.6	109.8
1976	2,154,807	9.9	27.4	25.2	65.2	113.4
1975	2,152,662	10.0	27.9	25.6	66.9	118.5
1974	2,229,667	10.5	29.4	27.1	72.0	128.4
1973	2,284,108	10.8	30.7	28.2	76.0	137.3
1972	2,282,154	10.9	31.3	28.8	77.9	141.3
1971	2,190,481	10.6	30.7	28.2	76.2	138.9
1970	2,158,802	10.6	31.1	28.4	76.5	140.2
1969	2,145,000	10.6	31.4	28.9	80.0	149.1
1968	2,069,000	10.4	30.8	28.3	79.1	147.2
1967	1,927,000	9.7	29.1	26.9	76.4	145.2
1966	1,857,000	9.5	28.4	26.4	75.6	145.1
1965	1,800,000	9.3	27.9	26.0	75.0	144.3
1964	1,725,000	9.0	27.1	25.3	74.6	146.2
1963	1,654,000	8.8	26.4	24.7	73.4	143.3
1962	1,577,000	8.5	25.5	23.9	71.2	138.4
1961	1,548,000	8.5	25.5	24.0	72.2	145.4
1960	1,523,000	8.5	25.4	24.0	73.5	148.0
1959	1,494,000	8.5	25.2	23.8	73.6	149.8
1958	1,451,000	8.4	24.8	23.5	72.0	146.3
1957	1,518,000	8.9	26.4	24.9	78.0	157.4
1956	1,585,000	9.5	27.8	26.4	82.4	165.6
1955	1,531,000	9.3	27.2	25.8	80.9	161.1
1954	1,490,000	9.2	26.9	25.4	79.8	154.3
1953	1,546,000	9.8	28.2	26.7	83.7	163.3
1952	1,539,318	9.9	28.3	26.8	83.2	159.9
1951	1,594,694	10.4	29.4	28.1	86.6	164.9
1950	1,667,231	11.1	30.7	29.8	90.2	166.4
1949	1,579,798	10.6	29.4	28.5	86.7	158.0
1948	1,811,155	12.4	34.0	33.0	98.5	174.7
1947	1,991,878	13.9	37.9	36.8	106.2	182.7
1946	2,291,045	16.4	44.5	42.8	118.1	199.0
1945	1,612,992	12.2	35.8	30.5	83.6	138.2
1944	1,452,394	10.9	31.2	27.8	76.5	124.5
1943	1,577,050	11.7	32.2	30.6	83.0	133.5
1942	1,772,132	13.2	35.6	34.8	93.0	147.6
1941	1,695,999	12.7	34.0	33.7	88.5	138.4
1940	1,595,879	12.1	32.3	32.3	82.8	122.4

[1] Rates for 1981–88 are revised and may differ from rates published previously.

Note: Data refer only to events occurring within the United States. Alaska included beginning 1959 and Hawaii beginning 1960. Beginning with 1978, data include nonlicensed marriages registered in California. Rates per 1,000 population enumerated as of April 1 for 1940, 1950, 1960, 1970, and 1980 and estimated as of July 1 for all other years.

SOURCE: Sally C. Clark, "Advance Report of Final Marriage Statistics, 1989 and 1990," *Monthly Vital Statistics Report,* vol. 43, no. 12(S), National Center for Health Statistics, 1995

did their parents. Between 1960 and 1980 the median age at first marriage rose from 22.8 to 24.7 years for men, and for women from 20.3 to 22 years. (See Table 1.3.)

The trend of young adults delaying marriage continued through the 1990s. In 1997 the average age of men at first marriage was 26.8 years and the average age of

TABLE 1.3

Estimated median age at first marriage, by sex: 1890 to 1997

Year	Men	Women	Year	Men	Women
1997	26.8	25.0	1969	23.2	20.8
1996	27.1	24.8	1968	23.1	20.8
1995	26.9	24.5	1967	23.1	20.6
1994	26.7	24.5	1966	22.8	20.5
1993	26.5	24.5	1965	22.8	20.6
1992	26.5	24.4	1964	23.1	20.5
1991	26.3	24.1	1963	22.8	20.5
1990	26.1	23.9	1962	22.7	20.3
1989	26.2	23.8	1961	22.8	20.3
1988	25.9	23.6	1960	22.8	20.3
1987	25.8	23.6	1959	22.5	20.2
1986	25.7	23.1	1958	22.6	20.2
1985	25.5	23.3	1957	22.6	20.3
1984	25.4	23.0	1956	22.5	20.1
1983	25.4	22.8	1955	22.6	20.2
1982	25.2	22.5	1954	23.0	20.3
1981	24.8	22.3	1953	22.8	20.2
1980	24.7	22.0	1952	23.0	20.2
1979	24.4	22.1	1951	22.9	20.4
1978	24.2	21.8	1950	22.8	20.3
1977	24.0	21.6	1949	22.7	20.3
1976	23.8	21.3	1948	23.3	20.4
1975	23.5	21.1	1947	23.7	20.5
1974	23.1	21.1	1940	24.3	21.5
1973	23.2	21.0	1930	24.3	21.3
1972	23.3	20.9	1920	24.6	21.2
1971	23.1	20.9	1910	25.1	21.6
1970	23.2	20.8	1900	25.9	21.9
			1890	26.1	22.0

Notes: Figures for 1947 to 1997 are based on Current Population Survey data. Figures for years prior to 1947 are based on decennial censuses. A standard error of 0.1 years is appropriate to measure sampling variability for any of the above estimated median ages at first marriage, based on Current Population Survey data.

SOURCE: *Marital Status and Living Arrangements: March 1997*, U.S. Bureau of the Census, Washington, D.C., 1998

women was 25 years—about half a decade later than during the 1950s. (See Table 1.3.) The overall marriage rate has been declining since 1987 (9.9 marriages per 1,000 population). For the 12 months ending January 1999 the marriage rate was down to 8.3 per 1,000 population. (See Tables 1.2 and 1.7.)

Children Out Of Wedlock

The postponement of marriage, along with the introduction of birth control and the relaxation of sexual mores, resulted in a rise in premarital sex. Despite the availability of contraceptive methods more women of all races and ethnic origins were having babies outside of marriage. In 1970 unmarried women accounted for 10.7 percent of all births; by 1980, 18.4 percent of all births; and by 1998, 32.8 percent of all births. (See Table 1.8.) The proportions of teenage pregnancies out of wedlock were increasing even more dramatically.

Nonmarital Cohabitation

In the 1960s many young people lived together without getting married—nearly 440,000 in 1960 according to Census Bureau estimates. Between 1960 and 1970 unmarried-

couple households increased only 19 percent, but between 1970 and 1980 the number tripled. In 1997 there were more than 4 million cohabiting unmarried couples. Nearly 36 percent of these couples had children younger than 15 years of age. These children may be the result of the union of the two people in the relationship, or they may be the products of an earlier marriage or relationship, or both. (See Table 1.9.)

DIVORCE

During World War II the separation of servicemen from their wives generally put a great strain on marriages. Some of these marriages were already tenuous to start with, having resulted from "war romances." Spouses sometimes suspected each other of infidelity. In many cases the chance of reconciliation was made more difficult by the husband's consternation over coming home to a newly self-sufficient wife who was now used to supporting the family. At the end of the war about half a million couples divorced. By 1950 a total of 2.4 million men and women were divorced. (See Table 1.4.) Because of the unique wartime situation, divorce began to lose much of its former stigma.

Divorce Is Here to Stay

The divorce rates during the 1950s and early 1960s were low, ranging from 2.1 to 2.6 per 1,000 population. Starting in 1967 it rose almost annually, peaking at 5.3 in 1979. After reaching 5.3 again in 1981, it began leveling off. (See Figure 1.3.)

The divorce rate for the 12-month period ending January 1999 was 4.2 divorces per 1,000 population. (See Table 1.7.) The National Center for Health Statistics reports that, based on these figures, one-half of all marriages will end in divorce. It should be noted, however, that a certain percentage of people get married and divorced multiple times, thus adding to the overall number of divorces. For those not among this group more than one-half of the marriages will not end in divorce.

STEPFAMILIES

According to a 1995 report by the Centers for Disease Control and Prevention/National Center for Health Statistics, even though Americans are waiting longer to get married and are more likely to get divorced, marriage is still a fundamental element of American society. With the exception of older Americans most people remarry after they divorce. About 75 percent of divorced men and 60 percent of divorced women eventually marry again. These marriages create situations in which adults and children become part of stepfamilies, or blended families, and approximately 20 percent of married-couple families have at least one stepchild under 18 years of age. It should be noted that, in the Census Bureau's count of "own children," stepchildren are included, along with biological and adopted children.

TABLE 1.4

Marital status of the population 15 years old and over by sex: 1950 to 1998
(Numbers in thousands)

			Males			
				Unmarried		
Years	Total	Married	Total	Never Married	Widowed	Divorced
All races						
1998	101,123	58,633	42,491	31,591	2,569	8,331
1997	100,159	57,923	42,236	31,315	2,690	8,231
1996	98,593	57,656	40,937	30,691	2,478	7,768
1995	97,704	57,570	39,953	30,286	2,284	7,383
1994	96,768	57,068	39,700	30,228	2,222	7,250
1993	94,854	56,833	38,021	28,775	2,468	6,778
1990	91,955	55,833	36,121	27,505	2,333	6,283
1980	81,947	51,813	30,134	24,227	1,977	3,930
1970	70,559	47,109	23,450	19,832	2,051	1,567
1960*	60,273	41,781	18,492	15,274	2,112	1,106
1950*	54,601	36,866	17,735	14,400	2,264	1,071

			Females			
				Unmarried		
Years	Total	Married	Total	Never Married	Widowed	Divorced
All races						
1998	108,168	59,333	48,835	26,713	11,029	11,093
1997	107,076	58,829	48,248	26,073	11,058	11,116
1996	106,031	58,905	47,127	25,528	11,078	10,521
1995	105,028	58,984	46,045	24,693	11,082	10,270
1994	104,032	58,185	45,847	24,645	11,073	10,129
1993	102,400	57,768	44,631	23,534	11,214	9,883
1990	99,838	56,797	43,040	22,718	11,477	8,845
1980	89,914	52,965	36,950	20,226	10,758	5,966
1970	77,766	48,148	29,618	17,167	9,734	2,717
1960*	64,607	42,583	22,024	12,252	8,064	1,708
1950*	57,102	37,577	19,525	11,418	6,734	1,373

*1950 and 1960 data are for the population 14 yrs old and over.

SOURCE: *Marital Status and Living Arrangements: March 1998*, U.S. Bureau of the Census, Washington, D.C., 1999

SINGLE-PARENT FAMILIES

Since the 1970s one of the most dramatic changes in the composition of family households has been the increase in single-parent families, most notably mother-child families. These single-parent families have resulted from the increase in both divorce and the number of out-of-wedlock births.

In 1970, 10 percent of all families with their own children under the age of 18 years were headed by mothers, compared with just 1 percent maintained by fathers. In 1990 the percentages doubled for single mothers and more than tripled for single fathers. By 1998, 22 percent of all families were headed by single mothers, a slight decline from previous years, while single-father families comprised 5 percent of all families. (See Table 1.10.)

LESBIAN AND GAY PARENTS

The sexual revolution of the 1960s, which changed society's attitudes about male and female relationships, also spearheaded the "coming out" of lesbians and gays. The

FIGURE 1.3

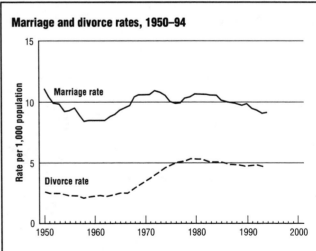

Marriage and divorce rates, 1950–94

SOURCE: Gopal K. Singh et al., "Annual Summary of Births, Marriages, Divorces, and Deaths: United States, 1994," *Monthly Vital Statistics Report*, vol. 43, no. 13, October 23, 1995

TABLE 1.5

Crude birth rates, fertility rates, and birth rates by age of mother, all races: selected years 1950–98

[Data are based on the National Vital Statistics System]

Race, Hispanic origin, and year	Crude birth rate[1]	Fertility rate[2]	10–14 years	15–19 years Total	15–17 years	18–19 years	20–24 years	25–29 years	30–34 years	35–39 years	40–44 years	45–54 years[3]
All races							Live births per 1,000 women					
1950	24.1	106.2	1.0	81.6	40.7	132.7	196.6	166.1	103.7	52.9	15.1	1.2
1960	23.7	118.0	0.8	89.1	43.9	166.7	258.1	197.4	112.7	56.2	15.5	0.9
1970	18.4	87.9	1.2	68.3	38.8	114.7	167.8	145.1	73.3	31.7	8.1	0.5
1980	15.9	68.4	1.1	53.0	32.5	82.1	115.1	112.9	61.9	19.8	3.9	0.2
1985	15.8	66.3	1.2	51.0	31.0	79.6	108.3	111.0	69.1	24.0	4.0	0.2
1990	16.7	70.9	1.4	59.9	37.5	88.6	116.5	120.2	80.8	31.7	5.5	0.2
1994	15.2	66.7	1.4	58.9	37.6	91.5	111.1	113.9	81.5	33.7	6.4	0.3
1995	14.8	65.6	1.3	56.8	36.0	89.1	109.8	112.2	82.5	34.3	6.6	0.3
1996	14.7	65.3	1.2	54.4	33.8	86.0	110.4	113.1	83.9	35.3	6.8	0.3
1997	14.5	65.0	1.1	52.3	32.1	83.6	110.4	113.8	85.3	36.1	7.1	0.4
1998	14.6	65.6	1.0	51.1	30.4	82.0	111.2	115.9	87.4	37.4	7.3	0.4

[1] Live births per 1,000 population.

[2] Total number of live births regardless of age of mother per 1,000 women 15–44 years of age.

[3] Prior to 1997 data are for live births to mothers 45–49 years of age per 1,000 women 45–49 years of age. Starting in 1997 data are for live births to mothers 45–54 years of age per 1,000 women 45–49 years of age.

SOURCE: *Health, United States, 2000,* National Center for Health Statistics, Hyattsville, MD, 2000

modern gay rights movement traces its beginning to New York City in the late 1960s. Previously, gays and lesbians had kept a low profile within their communities. However, in 1969, when the police raided the Stonewall Inn, a gay bar in Greenwich Village, New York, its patrons retaliated by rioting for several nights. More protest rallies followed, sparking the activist movement intended to end all discrimination and maltreatment based on sexual orientation.

The Lambda Legal Defense and Education Fund, an advocacy organization supporting the civil rights of lesbians and gays, seeks to have same-sex couples included in the popular definition of family. It claims there are

between 6 to 10 million same-sex parents in the United States who are the mothers and fathers to an estimated 6 to 14 million children. The Bureau of the Census estimates that, in 1998, nearly 3 percent (166,000) of the nation's 5.9 million households with two unrelated adults consisted of same-sex partners with children under the age of 15 years living with them. (See Table 1.11.)

An increasing number of same-sex couples are also forming new families through adoption, donor insemination, or other reproductive technologies. Some also act as foster parents in states that allow placement of foster children in same-sex households. (See Chapter 4.)

TABLE 1.6

Average number of own children under 18 per family, by type of family: selected years 1955–98

Year	All families				Families with own children under 18			
	Total	Married Couple	Male, no wife present	Female, no husband present	Total	Married Couple	Male, no wife present	Female, no husband present
1998	0.92	0.88	0.74	1.13	1.85	1.90	1.52	1.78
1997	0.91	0.89	0.69	1.08	1.84	1.89	1.55	1.75
1996	0.92	0.89	0.69	1.11	1.86	1.90	1.49	1.81
1995	0.91	0.89	0.66	1.10	1.84	1.89	1.49	1.76
1994	0.91	0.89	0.67	1.08	1.84	1.88	1.49	1.75
1993	0.90	0.87	0.65	1.07	1.84	1.88	1.48	1.76
1992	0.90	0.88	0.64	1.08	1.85	1.88	1.51	1.79
1991	0.90	0.88	0.61	1.05	1.84	1.88	1.50	1.74
1990	0.89	0.88	0.60	1.04	1.83	1.87	1.50	1.72
1989	0.90	0.88	0.58	1.04	1.82	1.86	1.55	1.74
1988	0.89	0.88	0.58	1.03	1.81	1.84	1.51	1.74
1987	0.90	0.88	0.58	1.05	1.81	1.84	1.51	1.74
1986	0.91	0.90	0.57	1.06	1.83	1.86	1.46	1.78
1985	0.92	0.90	0.62	1.06	1.85	1.88	1.53	1.79
1984	0.93	0.92	0.59	1.05	1.85	1.89	1.50	1.76
1983	0.94	0.92	0.53	1.09	1.87	1.89	1.46	1.81
1982	0.95	0.93	0.52	1.13	1.87	1.89	1.53	1.80
1981	0.97	0.96	0.55	1.11	1.88	1.91	1.59	1.79
1980r	1.00	0.98	0.55	1.17	1.91	1.93	1.55	1.87
1979	1.01	1.00	0.56	1.16	1.93	1.95	1.63	1.86
1978	1.04	1.03	0.55	1.22	1.96	1.98	1.63	1.93
1977	1.07	1.06	0.54	1.23	2.01	2.02	1.66	1.99
1976	1.10	1.09	0.49	1.26	2.04	2.05	1.59	2.03
1975	1.13	1.12	0.60	1.27	2.09	2.09	1.85	2.10
1974	1.15	1.16	0.52	1.27	2.14	2.14	1.90	2.12
1973	1.18	1.19	0.50	1.26	2.17	2.18	1.87	2.20
1972	1.22	1.24	0.52	1.28	2.22	2.22	1.93	2.20
1971	1.28	1.30	0.53	1.32	2.31	2.31	2.00	2.33
1970r	1.27	1.30	0.54	1.20	2.28	2.29	1.93	2.29
1965	1.38	1.43	0.45	1.20	2.44	2.44	2.13	2.42
1960	1.33	1.39	0.35	1.04	2.33	2.34	1.88	2.24
1955	1.21	1.27	0.39	0.96	2.19	2.20	1.98	2.17

r Revised based on population from the decennial census for that year.

SOURCE: *Household and Family Characteristics: March 1998*, U.S. Bureau of the Census, Washington, D.C., 1999

TABLE 1.7

Provisional vital statistics for the United States
[Rates for infant deaths are deaths under 1 year per 1,000 live births; fertility rates are live births per 1,000 women aged 15–44 years; all other rates are per 1,000 total population. Data are subject to monthly reporting variation]

Item	January				12 months ending with January				
	Number		Rate		Number		Rate		
	1999	1998	1999	1998	1999	1998	1999	1998	1997
Live births	325,000	308,000	14.1	13.5	3,960,000	3,885,000	14.7	14.5	14.6
Fertility rate	. . .	. . .	63.7	60.8	. . .	. . .	66.3	65.1	65.2
Deaths	214,000	225,000	9.3	9.8	2,320,000	2,301,000	8.6	8.6	8.7
Infant deaths	2,200	2,400	6.8	7.4	27,500	27,300	6.9	7.0	7.2
Natural increase	111,000	83,000	4.8	3.7	1,640,000	1,584,000	6.1	5.9	5.9
Marriages	131,000	135,000	6.0	6.2	2,251,000	2,414,000	8.3	9.0	8.9
Divorces[1]	- - -	- - -	- - -	- - -	- - -	- - -	4.2	4.3	4.3
Population base (in millions)	. . .	. . .	271.6	268.9	. . .	. . .	270.3	267.8	265.4

- - - Data not available.
. . . Category not applicable.

[1]Divorce rates exclude data for California, Colorado, Indiana, and Louisiana.

Notes: Figures include revisions received from the States. Twelve-month figures for the current year reflect revisions received for previous months, and figures for earlier years may differ from those previously published.

SOURCE: "Births, Marriages, Divorces, and Deaths: Provisional Data for January 1999," *National Vital Statistics Reports*, vol. 48, no. 1, January 25, 2000

TABLE 1.8

Nonmarital childbearing according to detailed race of mother, Hispanic origin of mother, and maternal age and birth rates for unmarried women by race of mother and Hispanic origin of mother: selected years 1970–98

[Data are based on the National Vital Statistics System]

Race of mother, Hispanic origin of mother, and maternal age	1970	1975	1980	1985	1990	1992	1993	1994	1995	1996	1997	1998
					Percent of live births to unmarried mothers							
All races	10.7	14.3	18.4	22.0	28.0	30.1	31.0	32.6	32.2	32.4	32.4	32.8
White	5.5	7.1	11.2	14.7	20.4	22.6	23.6	25.4	25.3	25.7	25.8	26.3
Black	37.5	49.5	56.1	61.2	66.5	68.1	68.7	70.4	69.9	69.8	69.2	69.1
American Indian or Alaska Native	22.4	32.7	39.2	46.8	53.6	55.3	55.8	57.0	57.2	58.0	58.7	59.3
Asian or Pacific Islander	- - -	- - -	7.3	9.5	13.2	14.7	15.7	16.2	16.3	16.7	15.6	15.6
Chinese	3.0	1.6	2.7	3.0	5.0	6.1	6.7	7.2	7.9	9.2	6.5	6.4
Japanese	4.6	4.6	5.2	7.9	9.6	9.8	10.0	11.2	10.8	11.4	10.1	9.7
Filipino	9.1	6.9	8.6	11.4	15.9	16.8	17.7	18.5	19.5	19.4	19.5	19.7
Hawaiian and part Hawaiian	- - -	- - -	32.9	37.3	45.0	45.7	47.8	48.6	49.0	49.9	49.1	51.1
Other Asian or Pacific Islander	- - -	- - -	5.4	8.5	12.6	14.9	16.1	16.4	16.2	16.5	15.6	15.2
Hispanic origin (selected states)[1,2]	- - -	- - -	23.6	29.5	36.7	39.1	40.0	43.1	40.8	40.7	40.9	41.6
Mexican	- - -	- - -	20.3	25.7	33.3	36.3	37.0	40.8	38.1	37.9	38.9	39.6
Puerto Rican	- - -	- - -	46.3	51.1	55.9	57.5	59.4	60.2	60.0	60.7	59.4	59.5
Cuban	- - -	- - -	10.0	16.1	18.2	20.2	21.0	22.9	23.8	24.7	24.4	24.8
Central and South American	- - -	- - -	27.1	34.9	41.2	43.9	45.2	45.9	44.1	44.1	41.8	42.0
Other and unknown Hispanic	- - -	- - -	22.4	31.1	37.2	37.6	38.7	43.5	44.0	43.5	43.6	45.3
White, non-Hispanic (selected states)[1]	- - -	- - -	9.6	12.4	16.9	18.5	19.5	20.8	21.2	21.5	21.5	21.9
Black, non-Hispanic (selected states)[1]	- - -	- - -	57.3	62.1	66.7	68.3	68.9	70.7	70.0	70.0	69.4	69.3
					Number of live births, in thousands							
Live births to unmarried mothers	399	448	666	828	1,165	1,225	1,240	1,290	1,254	1,260	1,257	1,294
					Percent distribution of live births to unmarried mothers							
Maternal age												
Under 20 years	50.1	52.1	40.8	33.8	30.9	29.8	29.7	30.5	30.9	30.4	30.7	30.1
20–24 years	31.8	29.9	35.6	36.3	34.7	35.6	35.4	34.8	34.5	34.2	34.9	35.6
25 years and over	18.1	18.0	23.5	29.9	34.4	34.6	34.9	34.6	34.7	35.3	34.4	34.3
					Live births per 1,000 unmarried women 15–44 years of age[3]							
All races and origins	26.4	24.5	29.4	32.8	43.8	45.2	45.3	46.9	45.1	44.8	44.0	44.3
White[4]	13.9	12.4	18.1	22.5	32.9	35.2	35.9	38.3	37.5	37.6	37.0	37.5
Black[4]	95.5	84.2	81.1	77.0	90.5	86.5	84.0	82.1	75.9	74.4	73.4	73.3
Hispanic origin (selected states)[1,2]	- - -	- - -	- - -	- - -	89.6	95.3	95.2	101.2	95.0	93.2	91.4	90.1
White, non-Hispanic	- - -	- - -	- - -	- - -	- - -	- - -	- - -	28.5	28.2	28.3	27.0	27.4

- - - Data not available.

[1] Trend data for Hispanics and non-Hispanics are affected by expansion of the reporting area for an Hispanic-origin item on the birth certificate and by immigration. These two factors affect numbers of events, composition of the Hispanic population, and maternal and infant health characteristics. The number of states in the reporting area increased from 22 in 1980, to 23 and the District of Columbia (D.C.) in 1983 –87, 30 and D.C. in 1988, 47 and D.C. in 1989, 48 and D.C. in 1990, 49 and D.C. in 1991–92, and 50 and D.C. in 1993 and later years.

[2] Includes mothers of all races.

[3] Rates computed by relating births to unmarried mothers, regardless of age of mother, to unmarried women 15–44 years of age.

[4] For 1970 and 1975, birth rates are by race of child.

Notes: National estimates for 1970 and 1975 for unmarried mothers based on births occurring in states reporting marital status of mother. The race groups, white, black, American Indian or Alaska Native, and Asian or Pacific Islander, include persons of Hispanic and non-Hispanic origin. Conversely, persons of Hispanic origin may be of any race. In 1995 procedures implemented in California to more accurately identify the marital status of Hispanic mothers account for some of the decline in measures of nonmarital childbearing for women of all races, white women, and Hispanic women between 1994 and 1995. Other reporting changes implemented in California, Nevada, New York City, and Connecticut in 1997 and 1998 have affected trends for all groups.

SOURCE: *Health, United States, 2000*, National Center for Health Statistics, Hyattsville, MD, 2000

TABLE 1.9

Unmarried-couple households, by presence of children: 1960–97

(Numbers in thousands. Data based on Current Population Survey (CPS) unless othewise specified)

Year	Total	Without children under 15 yrs.	With children under 15 yrs.
1997	4,130	2,660	1,470
1996	3,958	2,516	1,442
1995	3,668	2,349	1,319
1994	3,661	2,391	1,270
1993	3,510	2,274	1,236
1992	3,308	2,187	1,121
1991	3,039	2,077	962
1990	2,856	1,966	891
1989	2,764	1,906	858
1988	2,588	1,786	802
1987	2,334	1,614	720
1986	2,220	1,558	662
1985	1,983	1,380	603
1984	1,988	1,373	614
1983	1,891	1,366	525
1982	1,863	1,387	475
1981	1,808	1,305	502
1980	1,589	1,159	431
1979	1,346	985	360
1978	1,137	865	272
1977	957	754	204
1970 Census	523	327	196
1960 Census	439	242	197

SOURCE: *Marital Status and Living Arrangements: March 1997,* U.S. Bureau of the Census, Washington, D.C., 1998

TABLE 1.10

Family groups, with own children under 18, and head of household

Years	Total with own children under 18	Two-parent	One parent Maintained by Total	One parent Maintained by Mother	One parent Maintained by Father
All Races					
1998	34,760	25,269	10,429	7,693	1,798
1997	34,665	25,083	9,583	7,874	1,709
1996	34,203	24,920	9,284	7,656	1,628
1995	34,296	25,241	9,055	7,615	1,440
1994	34,018	25,058	8,961	7,647	1,314
1993	33,257	24,707	8,550	7,226	1,324
1992	32,746	24,420	8,326	7,043	1,283
1991	32,401	24,397	8,004	6,823	1,181
1990	32,289	24,537	7,752	6,599	1,153
1989	32,322	24,735	7,587	6,519	1,068
1988	31,920	24,600	7,320	6,273	1,047
1987	31,898	24,645	7,252	6,297	955
1986	31,607	24,630	7,040	6,105	935
1985	31,112	24,210	6,902	6,006	896
1984	31,046	24,339	6,706	5,907	799
1983	30,818	24,363	6,455	5,718	737
1982	31,012	24,465	6,547	5,868	679
1981	31,227	24,927	6,300	5,634	666
1980	31,022	24,961	6,061	5,445	616
1970	28,731	25,532	3,199	2,858	341

SOURCE: *Household and Family Characteristics: March 1998,* U.S. Bureau of the Census, Washington, D.C., 1999

TABLE 1.11

Households with two unrelated adults, by marital status, age, and sex: March 1998

[Numbers in thousands.]

Subject	Households with two unrelated adults	Age of householder					Marital status of householder				
		Under 25 years	25 to 34 years	35 to 44 years	45 to 64 years	65 years and over	Never married	Married, spouse absent		Widowed	Divorced
								Separated	Other		
All Householders											
Total	5,911	1,183	2,190	1,196	1,059	283	3,516	268	137	253	1,738
Partner of opposite sex	4,236	776	1,618	857	797	188	2,270	210	111	179	1,466
No children under 15 years in household	2,716	452	883	509	695	177	1,439	110	77	158	932
Age of partner:											
Under 25 years	487	287	157	20	14	9	422	2	12	7	45
25 to 34 years	944	154	614	141	33	1	713	38	18	–	175
35 to 44 years	502	4	92	224	170	11	168	28	14	10	281
45 to 64 years	621	–	18	122	418	63	109	35	29	70	379
65 years and over	163	6	2	1	59	93	28	7	5	71	53
Marital status of partner:											
Never married	1,482	391	715	202	152	22	1,138	43	16	17	268
Married, spouse absent	198	13	43	55	63	24	34	16	54	13	81
Separated	117	9	25	40	39	5	30	16	–	6	65
Widowed	114	3	8	4	43	56	15	11	1	54	33
Divorced	922	45	117	248	438	74	251	40	7	73	551
With children under 15 years in household	1,520	325	735	348	102	11	831	100	34	21	534
Age of partner:											
Under 25 years	419	222	168	29	–	–	319	15	3	8	74
25 to 34 years	683	97	435	129	21	–	367	52	13	4	247
35 to 44 years	330	5	108	152	61	5	120	30	16	3	161
45 to 64 years	83	–	24	39	17	3	25	3	1	3	50
65 years and over	5	–	–	–	3	3	–	–	–	3	2
Marital status of partner:											
Never married	878	267	452	134	26	–	600	41	21	9	206
Married, spouse absent	134	13	60	47	11	3	64	30	10	3	27
Separated	99	10	42	35	10	3	41	28	7	2	22
Widowed	23	–	8	6	6	3	11	–	–	3	9
Divorced	485	45	215	162	58	5	156	29	2	6	292
Partner of same sex	1,674	407	571	339	263	95	1,245	58	26	74	271
No children under 15 years in household	1,508	387	484	301	243	93	1,165	41	25	72	205
Age of partner:											
Under 25 years	423	302	82	22	15	2	386	1	4	8	23
25 to 34 years	544	80	318	82	59	6	429	16	11	8	80
35 to 44 years	271	–	57	144	56	13	194	10	2	15	50
45 to 64 years	211	2	24	45	105	35	116	14	5	28	48
65 years and over	58	3	2	7	9	37	40	–	2	13	4
Marital status of partner:											
Never married	1,189	370	413	211	146	50	1,008	18	7	28	128
Married, spouse absent	80	13	15	13	30	9	26	17	13	8	15
Separated	54	8	8	9	25	4	18	16	2	6	13
Widowed	21	–	2	–	4	14	2	–	–	11	7
Divorced	218	4	53	76	64	21	128	7	4	24	56
With children under 15 years in household	167	20	88	38	19	2	81	17	2	2	66
Age of partner:											
Under 25 years	47	12	23	4	9	–	21	4	–	–	23
25 to 34 years	74	7	46	18	3	–	42	8	2	–	23
35 to 44 years	27	1	10	11	4	–	12	1	–	–	14
45 to 64 years	15	–	7	6	3	–	6	3	–	–	7
65 years and over	3	–	1	–	–	2	–	1	–	2	–
Marital status of partner:											
Never married	118	18	60	28	12	–	57	13	–	–	47
Married, spouse absent	10	2	8	–	–	–	6	3	2	–	–
Separated	9	1	8	–	–	–	6	3	–	–	–
Widowed	2	–	–	–	–	2	–	–	–	2	–
Divorced	37	–	19	11	7	–	18	1	–	–	19

SOURCE: *Marital Status and Living Arrangements: March 1998*, U.S. Bureau of the Census, Washington, D.C., 1999

CHAPTER 2

WOMEN, MEN, AND THE FAMILY

CHILDBEARING

Beginning around the early 1960s three growing trends—a lower fertility rate; women (especially working women) delaying childbearing; and the increase in the number of births among young, unmarried women—have greatly changed the composition of the American family. (See Chapter 4.)

Fertility Rates

The fertility rate (the number of live births per 1,000 women of reproductive age 15–44 years) increased dramatically during the postwar Baby Boom of the late 1940s, 1950s, and early 1960s. After peaking at 118 in 1960, the fertility rate has been dropping ever since. (See Table 1.5 in Chapter 1.)

In 1999 the overall fertility rate was 65.8 live births per 1,000 women. Women ages 20–29 years accounted for the highest fertility rate: 111 for those 20–24 years, and 117.8 for those 25–29 years. (See Table 2.1.)

RACIAL AND ETHNIC DIFFERENCES. Preliminary data for 1999 show that the fertility rate for Hispanic (who may be of any race) women (101.8 live births per 1,000 Hispanic women of childbearing age) was significantly higher than for black (70.2), white (65), Asian/Pacific Islander (65.7), and American Indian (69.4) women. (See Table 2.1.)

Childbearing Among Older Women

Before the 1960s, when larger families were more common, it was not unusual for a woman to continue having babies well into her 30s or even her 40s. However, as families became smaller it became more common to have the typical two or three children during the first years of marriage when the woman was generally in her 20s. As a result the fertility rate for women in their 30s dropped significantly between 1960 and 1980. However, as a growing number of women continued their education beyond high school, entered careers that required greater commitment, or simply chose to hold off having a child, the fertility rate among older women began to increase.

While most women still give birth while in their 20s a significant proportion now wait until their 30s. The difference between women in the 1950s and women in the 1990s who had children in their 30s was that the former were generally having their third and fourth child, while the latter were typically having their first or second.

In 1999, among women ages 40–44, the birth rate was highest for women of Asian/Pacific Islander origin (11.5 per 1,000 women)—nearly twice the rate for white, black, and American Indian women. Hispanic women also had a high birth rate, at 10.7 live births per 1,000 women. (See Table 2.1.)

Nonmarital Childbearing

The proportion of children born to parents who were not married has increased dramatically. In 1970, 1 of every 9 children (10.7 percent) was born to an unmarried mother. (See Table 1.8 in Chapter 1.) By 1998, 1 of every 3 children (32.8 percent) was born to an unmarried mother, a huge increase in a relatively short time. (See Table 2.2.)

There were also significant differences among racial and ethnic groups. In 1998, among Asian/Pacific Islanders, about 1 of 5 children (15.6 percent) were born to unmarried mothers; among whites, 1 of 4 children (26.3 percent) were born to unmarried mothers; among Hispanics, 2 of 5 (41.6 percent); and among blacks, more than two-thirds (69.1 percent). (See Table 2.2, and Table 1.8 in Chapter 1.)

FEWER FAMILIES NOW HAVE THEIR OWN CHILDREN UNDER 18 YEARS OF AGE

According to the U.S. Census Bureau, by the late 1990s, fewer families had their own children under 18

TABLE 2.1

Births and birth rates, by age, race and Hispanic origin of mother, final 1998 and preliminary 1999

[Data for 1999 are based on a continuous file of records received from the states. Figures for 1999 are based on weighted data rounded to nearest individual, so categories may not add to totals]

Age and race/ Hispanic origin	1999 Number	1999 Rate	1998 Number	1998 Rate
All races				
Total [1]	3,957,829	65.8	3,941,553	65.6
10-14 years	9,049	0.9	9,462	1.0
15-19 years	475,745	49.6	484,895	51.1
15-17 years	163,559	28.7	173,231	30.4
18-19 years	312,186	80.2	311,664	82.0
20-24 years	981,207	111.0	965,122	111.2
25-29 years	1,078,350	117.8	1,083,010	115.9
30-34 years	892,478	89.6	889,365	87.4
35-39 years	433,793	38.3	424,890	37.4
40-44 years	82,875	7.4	81,027	7.3
45-54 years [2]	4,330	0.4	3,782	0.4
White, total [3]				
Total [1]	3,130,100	65.0	3,118,727	64.6
10-14 years	4,723	0.6	4,801	0.6
15-19 years	337,323	44.5	340,694	45.4
15-17 years	111,481	24.8	116,623	25.9
18-19 years	225,842	73.4	224,071	74.6
20-24 years	747,217	106.8	736,664	107.2
25-29 years	873,586	121.1	880,688	119.1
30-34 years	739,967	93.2	737,532	90.5
35-39 years	356,546	38.7	349,799	37.8
40-44 years	67,228	7.3	65,485	7.2
45-54 years [2]	3,509	0.4	3,064	0.4
White, non-Hispanic				
Total [1]	2,349,536	57.9	2,361,462	57.7
10-14 years	2,046	0.3	2,132	0.3
15-19 years	213,223	34.1	219,169	35.2
15-17 years	63,659	17.1	68,619	18.4
18-19 years	149,564	59.0	150,550	60.6
20-24 years	515,026	90.1	511,101	90.7
25-29 years	665,018	111.3	678,227	109.7
30-34 years	601,676	90.4	603,639	88.0
35-39 years	294,585	37.3	291,202	36.4
40-44 years	55,037	6.8	53,480	6.7
45-54 years [2]	2,802	0.4	2,388	0.4
Black, total [3]				
Total [1]	606,720	70.2	609,902	71.0
10-14 years	3,981	2.6	4,289	2.9
15-19 years	121,262	81.1	126,937	85.4
15-17 years	45,979	52.1	50,103	56.8
18-19 years	75,283	122.9	76,834	126.9
20-24 years	193,483	141.9	189,088	141.9
25-29 years	139,175	102.2	139,302	101.8
30-34 years	91,596	64.5	93,785	64.7
35-39 years	47,244	30.7	46,657	30.5
40-44 years	9,562	6.5	9,496	6.7
45-54 years [2]	417	0.3	348	0.3
American Indian, total [3,4]				
Total [1]	40,015	69.4	40,272	70.7
10-14 years	203	1.7	197	1.6
15-19 years	7,905	67.7	8,201	72.1
15-17 years	2,980	41.3	3,167	44.4

TABLE 2.1

Births and birth rates, by age, race and Hispanic origin of mother, final 1998 and preliminary 1999 [CONTINUED]

[Data for 1999 are based on a continuous file of records received from the States. Figures for 1999 are based on weighted data rounded to nearest individual, so categories may not add to totals]

Age and race/ Hispanic origin	1999 Number	1999 Rate	1998 Number	1998 Rate
American Indian, total [3,4]				
18-19 years	4,925	110.4	5,034	118.4
20-24 years	13,203	136.9	13,046	139.3
25-29 years	9,549	101.4	9,529	102.2
30-34 years	5,695	64.3	5,930	66.3
35-39 years	2,822	30.5	2,795	30.2
40-44 years	613	7.0	555	6.4
45-54 years [2]	26	0.4	19	*
Asian or Pacific Islander, total [3]				
Total [1]	180,993	65.7	172,652	64.0
10-14 years	142	0.4	175	0.4
15-19 years	9,255	22.8	9,063	23.1
15-17 years	3,119	12.6	3,338	13.8
18-19 years	6,135	38.8	5,725	38.3
20-24 years	27,304	70.4	26,324	68.8
25-29 years	56,040	116.3	53,491	110.4
30-34 years	55,220	109.2	52,118	105.1
35-39 years	27,182	54.6	25,639	52.8
40-44 years	5,472	11.5	5,491	12.0
45-54 years [2]	379	0.9	351	0.9
Hispanic [5]				
Total [1]	762,364	101.8	734,661	101.1
10-14 years	2,721	2.0	2,716	2.1
15-19 years	124,352	93.1	121,388	93.6
15-17 years	48,127	61.2	48,234	62.3
18-19 years	76,226	139.0	73,154	140.1
20-24 years	230,881	178.3	223,113	178.4
25-29 years	203,399	162.6	196,012	160.2
30-34 years	131,134	102.1	125,702	98.9
35-39 years	57,926	46.2	54,195	44.9
40-44 years	11,430	10.7	11,056	10.8
45-54 years [2]	519	0.6	479	0.6

* Figure does not meet standards of reliability or precision.

[1] The total number includes births to women of all ages, 10-54 years. The rate shown for all ages is the fertility rate, which is defined as the total number of births, regardless of age of mother, per 1,000 women aged 15-44 years.

[2] The number of births shown is the total for women aged 45-54 years. The birth rate is computed by relating the number of births to women aged 45-54 years to women aged 45-49 years, because most of the births in this group are to women aged 45-49.

[3] Race and Hispanic origin are reported separately on the birth certificate. Data for persons of Hispanic origin are also included in the data for each race group, according to the mother's reported race.

[4] Includes births to Aleuts and Eskimos.

[5] Includes all persons of Hispanic origin of any race.

Note: Data are subject to sampling and/or random variation. For information on the relative standard errors of the data and further discussion.

SOURCE: Sally C. Curtain and Joyce A. Martin, "Births: Preliminary Data for 1999", *National Vital Statistics Reports,* vol. 48, no. 13, August 8, 2000

TABLE 2.2

Total number of births, rates, and percent of births with selected demographic characteristics, by specified race of mother and place of birth of mother, 1998

Characteristic	All races	White	Black	American Indian[1]	Asian or Pacific Islander					
					Total	Chinese	Japanese	Hawaiian	Filipino	Other
Number										
Births	3,941,553	3,118,727	609,902	40,272	172,652	28,058	8,893	6,025	31,170	98,506
Rate										
Birth rate [2]	14.6	14.0	17.7	17.1	16.4	—	—	—	—	—
Fertility rate [3]	65.6	64.6	71.0	70.7	64.0	—	—	—	—	—
Total fertility rate [4]	2,058.5	2,041.0	2,171.0	2,090.5	1,867.5	—	—	—	—	—
Sex ratio [5]	1,047	1,049	1,034	1,038	1,061	1,067	1,030	1,044	1,067	1,061
Percent										
All births										
Births to mothers under 20 years	12.5	11.1	21.5	20.9	5.4	0.9	2.4	18.8	6.2	5.8
4th- and higher-order births	10.5	9.7	14.9	19.5	7.7	2.4	4.3	14.7	7.2	9.2
Births to unmarried mothers	32.8	26.3	69.1	59.3	15.6	6.4	9.7	51.1	19.7	15.2
Mothers completing 12 years or more of school	78.1	78.8	73.1	67.3	87.1	88.6	97.6	81.5	93.1	84.1
Mothers born in the 50 States and D.C.	80.5	82.2	89.1	95.8	16.6	9.8	43.7	97.9	19.4	10.2
Mothers born in the 50 States and D.C.										
Births to mothers under 20 years	13.6	11.4	23.3	21.4	16.0	3.7	4.7	19.0	17.6	21.0
4th- and higher-order births	9.9	8.7	15.0	19.8	8.1	3.9	5.5	14.8	7.5	6.5
Births to unmarried mothers	33.8	25.3	72.2	60.5	33.8	11.1	15.7	51.5	51.5	39.0
Mothers completing 12 years or more of school	82.2	84.5	72.2	67.2	86.5	97.0	96.2	81.4	88.0	81.9
Mothers born outside the 50 States and D.C.										
Births to mothers under 20 years	8.1	9.6	6.8	9.3	3.2	0.6	0.5	10.5	3.5	4.1
4th- and higher-order births	12.8	14.1	13.3	11.4	7.6	2.2	3.4	6.5	7.1	9.5
Births to unmarried mothers	28.5	31.1	42.7	31.0	11.9	5.8	5.0	31.5	15.1	13.1
Mothers completing 12 years or more of school	61.0	51.7	81.2	70.4	87.1	87.7	98.6	86.8	94.2	84.3

— Data not available.

[1] Includes births to Aleuts and Eskimos.
[2] Rate per 1,000 population.
[3] Rate per 1,000 women aged 15-44 years.
[4] Rates are sums of birth rates for 5-year age groups multiplied by 5.
[5] Male live births per 1,000 female live births.

Note: Race and Hispanic origin are reported separately on birth certificates. In this table all women (including Hispanic women) are classified only according to their race.

SOURCE: Stephanie J. Ventura et al., "Births: Final Data for 1998," *National Vital Statistics Report*, vol. 48, no. 3, March 28, 2000

years of age living with them at home. In Census terms, "own children under 18" are never-married sons and daughters, including stepchildren and adopted children. As of March 1998, 51 percent (36.1 million) of all families (70.9 million) had no own children under the age of 18 years. (See Table 2.3.) This was an increase of 7 percentage points from 1970 (44 percent). However, this does not necessarily mean that such families are childless. Some contain other related children (for example, nieces, nephews, or grandchildren) or unrelated foster children. Other families may have sons and daughters over the age of 18 years still living at home. The vast majority, however, are "empty nesters"—adults whose grown children now live away from home.

Another significant change reported by the Census Bureau is that, in 1998, younger families were more likely to be without children than in 1970. Among married-couple families with a householder younger than 35 years old, 27 percent had no "own children," compared with 23 percent in 1970. This is attributable to younger couples delaying childbirth and fewer couples choosing to have children at all.

WOMEN REDEFINE THEIR ROLE

Despite the nostalgia associated with the 1950s, many sociologists agree that the stereotypical family of the era, taken in the context of the historical American family, was

TABLE 2.3

Families by type, race and Hispanic[1] origin and selected characteristics: 1998
(Numbers in thousands, except averages)

Characteristics	All families	Married couple families				Other Families							
						Female householder				Male householder			
	All races	All races	White	Black	Hispanic	All races	White	Black	Hispanic	All races	White	Black	Hispanic
All families	70,880	54,317	48,066	3,921	4,804	12,652	8,308	3,926	1,612	3,911	3,137	562	545
Own children under 18													
Without own children under 18	36,120	29,048	26,156	1,865	1,683	4,960	3,396	1,357	491	2,113	1,623	339	312
With own children under 18	34,760	25,269	21,910	2,055	3,121	7,693	4,912	2,569	1,121	1,798	1,514	223	233
One own child under 18	14,363	9,507	8,231	723	1,001	3,739	2,539	1,104	445	1,117	945	133	140
Two own children under 18	13,122	10,241	8,913	830	1,174	2,425	1,498	865	384	456	385	53	58
Three or more own children under 18	7,277	5,521	4,766	502	945	1,529	875	600	292	225	184	36	35
Average per family with own children under 18	1.85	1.90	1.88	1.94	2.19	1.78	1.72	1.85	2.10	1.52	1.50	1.66	1.70
Householder's marital status													
Married, Spouse present	54,317	54,317	48,066	3,921	4,804	x	x	x	x	x	x	x	x
Married, spouse absent	2,506	x	x	x	x	1,977	1,269	617	399	529	430	69	95
Separated	1,905	x	x	x	x	1,586	1,032	502	317	319	267	38	53
Other	601	x	x	x	x	392	236	116	82	209	164	31	42
Widowed	2,698	x	x	x	x	2,325	1,767	493	200	373	289	64	13
Divorced	5,910	x	x	x	x	4,518	3,486	914	457	1,391	1,213	125	113
Never married	5,449	x	x	x	x	3,831	1,787	1,901	557	1,618	1,204	305	323

[1] People of Hispanic origin may be of any race.
(x) Not Applicable

SOURCE: *Household and Family Characteristics: March 1998*, U.S. Bureau of the Census, Washington, D.C., 1999

TABLE 2.4

Women and educational attainment, 1960–97

	1960	1965	1970	1975	1980	1985	1990	1995	1997
Percentage of bachelor degrees awarded to women (includes first professional degrees)	35.3	42.8	43.1	45.3	49.0	50.5	53.2	52.6	55.4
Percentage of masters degrees awarded to women	31.6	32.9	39.7	44.8	49.2	50.1	52.6	55.1	52.7
Percentage of 1st professional degrees awarded to women	n.a.	3.6	5.3	12.4	24.8	32.8	38.1	40.8	39.3

SOURCE: *Equal Pay: A Thirty-five Year Perspective,* Women's Bureau, U.S. Department of Labor, Washington, D.C., 1998

more an exception than the rule. This "nuclear" family became insulated—and often, isolated—with women molding the children and doing more housework than women of past generations did.

While the husband's main role was as the breadwinner, by the 1960s many women were looking to redefine their own roles as homemakers. Many women who had experienced the economic independence of a paying job during World War II and who had attained personal satisfaction from working re-entered the labor force. The availability of contraceptives enabled many young married women to postpone childbearing. The mothers of Baby Boomers, most of whom had given birth at a young age, saw the last of their children leave the nest. (Baby Boomers are defined as people who were born between 1946 and 1964.) These mothers were now ready to start a new chapter in life.

More Education

Unlike older women who performed service-oriented jobs traditionally held by females, such as secretaries and sales clerks, many young women aspired to a different career. Realizing that higher education meant better wages, these young women pursued post-secondary education. In 1960 women earned about one-third of both bachelor's (35.3 percent) and master's degrees (31.6 percent). By 1985 they were earning fully half of these degrees. The increase in the attainment of first professional degrees, such as medicine and law, was even more dramatic, doubling between 1975 (12.4 percent) and 1980 (24.8 percent) and soaring to 32.8 percent by 1985. By 1997 more than half of bachelor's and master's degrees, and 4 of 10 first professional degrees, went to women. (See Table 2.4.)

Into the Labor Force

In 1960 about 1 of every 4 (27.6 percent) married women with children were employed outside the home.

By 1980 more than one-half (54.1 percent) were in the labor force. According to *Women's Jobs 1964–1999: More Than 30 Years of Progress,* (U.S. Department of Labor, Women's Bureau, December 2000), in 1999, 7 of 10 married women with children worked. The U.S. Department of Labor predicts that women's labor participation rates will continue to rise for all age groups into the year 2005. (See Figure 2.1.)

Family Formation and Mothers' Labor Force Participation

Women's participation in the labor force varies according to the age and number of children in the family. In *Gender Differences in Earnings Among Young Adults Entering the Labor Market* (National Center for Education Statistics, U.S. Department of Education, Washington, D.C., 1998), the National Education Longitudinal Studies (NELS) program examined, among other things, the work consistency of the 1980 sophomore class for 12 years as it related to family formation.

The NELS, based on the *High School and Beyond* (HS&B) study by the National Center for Education Statistics (NCES), which followed high school seniors and sophomores between 1980 into their work experiences through 1992, found that marriage and having children are closely associated with women leaving their jobs or working less than full time. Women who were either married (33.3 percent) or had never married (36 percent) by June 1992 were more likely to work consistently than those who were no longer married (26.3 percent) by June 1992. (See Table 2.5.)

Mothers with multiple children were also less likely to work consistently than those without children. In 1992 just 17.1 percent of mothers with two or more children worked consistently, while 35.3 percent of mothers with

FIGURE 2.1

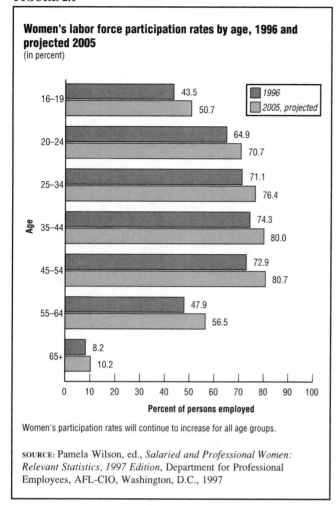

Women's labor force participation rates by age, 1996 and projected 2005
(in percent)

Age (vertical axis); Percent of persons employed (horizontal axis, 0–100)

Age	1996	2005, projected
16–19	43.5	50.7
20–24	64.9	70.7
25–34	71.1	76.4
35–44	74.3	80.0
45–54	72.9	80.7
55–64	47.9	56.5
65+	8.2	10.2

Women's participation rates will continue to increase for all age groups.

SOURCE: Pamela Wilson, ed., *Salaried and Professional Women: Relevant Statistics, 1997 Edition*, Department for Professional Employees, AFL-CIO, Washington, D.C., 1997

TABLE 2.5

Percentage of 1980 high school sophomores working consistently[1] according to gender, by marital status and number of children, June 1992

	Women	Men
Total	**32.8**	**45.7**
Marital status, June 1992		
Married	33.3	54.1
Never married	36.0	38.6
No longer married	26.3	48.9
Number of children, June 1992		
None	45.1	43.6
One	35.3	48.7
Two or more	17.1	49.7

[1] Consistent employment was defined as working 91.67 percent of the total months in the labor force after highest degree attainment to the end of the data collection period.

SOURCE: Suzanne B. Clery et al., *Gender Differences in Earnings Among Young Adults Entering the Labor Market,* National Center for Education Statistics, Washington, D.C., 1998

one child and 45.1 percent of women with no children worked consistently. In contrast men with more than one child were more likely to work consistently than men with no children. In 1992 half (49.7 percent) of men with two or more children worked consistently, compared with 43.6 percent of childless men. (See Table 2.5.)

Society's Opinion Divided About Working Mothers

Many people believe that women cannot balance work and family without the family suffering in the long run. Some blame mothers if anything goes wrong in the family. Others feel that if a mother does not need the extra income she should not work outside the home, even on a part-time basis. (See Chapter 7.)

Some high-profile court cases have propelled this issue into the forefront of public opinion. In 1997 Dr. Deborah Eappen was severely criticized for working part time after her baby died while being cared for by the British nanny Louise Woodward. (Woodward was later released from jail after serving a short sentence.)

Another high-profile case involved 54-year-old attorney Alice Hector who lost her two daughters to their stay-at-home father in a custody battle that drew national attention. In 1999 Hector regained custody of the two girls after appealing to a higher court. The case made advocates of both working mothers and supporters of fathers' rights question whether women must choose between career and children, and whether fathers can nurture as well as mothers.

WOMEN AS CAREGIVERS

A somewhat unexpected result of better medical care and increased longevity is the phenomenon of the "Sandwich Generation"—adults who still have children living at home but who are also attending to the needs of their aging parents. While an increasing number of men have parental responsibility, women remain the traditional caregivers. In most cases these women are employed and must meet the challenge of both family and work obligations.

According to a survey conducted by the National Alliance for Caregiving and the American Association of Retired Persons (*Family Caregiving in the U.S.: Findings from a National Survey,* Bethesda, Maryland and Washington, D.C., 1997), approximately 22.4 million U.S. households—nearly 1 in 4—were involved in caring for elderly relatives or friends. The survey found that the typical caregiver was a woman employed full-time, had a mean age of 46 years, and a mean annual household income of $35,000. Overall, more than 7 in 10 (72.5 percent) caregivers were women, although, among Asians, the caregiving responsibility was more evenly split among males (47.7 percent) and females (52.3 percent). (See Table 2.6.)

Marital Status and Presence of Children

Nearly two-thirds (65.7 percent) of caregivers were married or living with a partner, 13 percent were separat-

TABLE 2.6

Caregiver Profile
(Base = Total Caregivers)

	Total	White	Black	Hispanic	Asian
Number interviewed (unweighted)	n=1,509	n=623	n=306	n=307	n=264
Number in U.S. population (weighted)*	n=2,241	n=1,829	n=238	n=105	n=40
Gender					
Female	72.5%	73.5%	76.8%	67.4%	52.3%
Male	27.5	26.5	23.2	32.6	47.7
Age of caregiver					
Under 35	22.3%	20.5%	23.5%	37.1%	38.6%
35-49	39.4	39.0	44.4	37.5	43.6
50-64	26.0	26.8	22.5	21.2	14.4
65 or older	12.4	13.6	9.5	4.2	3.4
Mean (years)	46.15	46.93	44.75	40.01	39.01
Marital status					
Married or living with partner	65.7%	67.8%	50.9%	63.8%	64.4%
Single, never married	12.6	11.1	19.3	18.2	26.1
Separated or divorced	13.0	12.1	19.0	15.7	6.0
Widowed	8.0	8.3	9.8	2.0	3.0
Children under age 18 in household					
Yes	41.3%	38.8%	51.0%	58.3%	51.1%
No	57.8	60.2	48.4	41.7	48.1
Educational attainment					
Less than high school	9.0%	8.2%	16.3%	11.1%	2.3%
High school graduate	35.3	36.0	32.0	35.2	18.2
Some college	22.5	22.2	26.8	26.7	17.0
College graduate	20.1	20.4	15.4	18.2	39.0
Graduate School +	8.8	8.8	5.6	6.5	20.8
Technical school	3.5	3.5	3.3	2.3	1.9
Ever on active duty/ U.S. armed forces	11.5%	11.1%	11.1%	11.4%	7.2%
Current employment					
Employed full-time	51.8%	51.0%	55.6%	51.8%	63.3%
Employed part-time	12.3	12.7	10.5	13.4	14.0
Retired	15.9	17.0	13.7	6.8	4.2
Not employed	19.7	18.9	20.3	28.0	18.2
Household income					
Under $15,000	14.0%	11.7%	29.1%	21.1%	8.3%
$15K-24.9K	18.0	17.3	24.8	22.5	11.0
$25K-29.9K	9.3	9.5	9.8	7.8	8.0
$30K-39.9K	14.0	14.0	12.4	16.3	13.3
$40K-49.9K	10.3	10.4	7.8	11.1	14.0
$50K-74.9K	14.0	14.4	9.5	10.4	15.5
$75K or higher	10.9	12.1	3.0	6.2	19.7
Median	$35K	$35K	$22.5K	$27.5K	$45K

Note: Column percentages may not total 100% because of refusals.

¹ Weighted numbers refer to numbers of caregiving households in the U.S. population. Each number must be multiplied by 10,000 to determine the U.S. population prevalence for that cell. For example, 2,241 means 22,410,000 (i.e., there are an estimated 22,410,000 caregiving households in the U.S.). All percentages are based on weighted data.

SOURCE: *Family Caregiving in the U.S.: Findings from a National Survey,* The National Alliance for Caregiving and The American Association of Retired Persons, Bethesda, MD, and Washington, D.C., 1997

ed or divorced, 12.6 percent were single, and 8 percent were widowed. Black caregivers were less likely to be married or living with a partner (50.9 percent) than whites (67.8 percent), Asians (64.4 percent), or Hispanics (63.8 percent). (See Table 2.6.)

About 41 percent of caregivers were caring for children at the same time they were tending to the elderly. More than one-half of black (51 percent), Asian (51.1 percent), and Hispanic (58.3 percent) caregivers had one or more children in their households, compared with 38.8 percent of white caregivers. (See Table 2.6.)

Demands on Work

The demands of caregiving usually require some adjustments at work. Nearly two-thirds (64.1 percent) of caregivers surveyed were employed, most (51.8 percent) full time. (See Table 2.6.) About one-half (54.2 percent) reported having to make some type of adjustments at work as a result of caregiving responsibilities. (See Table 2.7.) The survey categorized the nature of care given into five levels, with Level 1 being the lowest in caregiving demand and intensity and Level 5 being the highest.

TABLE 2.7

Work-related adjustments by level of care
(Base = caregivers ever employed while providing care to this care recipient)
[percentages]

	Total	Level 1	Level 2	Level 3	Level 4	Level 5
Total unweighted[1]	(N=1,193)	(n=330)	(n= 174)	(n=240)	(n=277)	(n= 113)
Total weighted[1]	(N=1,716)	(n=530)	(n=245)	(n=331)	(n=363)	(n= 166)
Made any changes listed below	54.2	40.8	45.1	58.2[2]	66.5[2]	75.0[2]
Changed daily schedule: go in late, leave early, take time off during work	49.4	36.3	44.0	54.0[2]	61.5[2]	64.0[2]
Took leave of absence	10.9	5.5	5.9	9.1	17.8[2]	26.0[2]
Worked fewer hours, took less demanding job	7.3	2.0	3.8	6.5	11.7[2]	25.0[2]
Lost any job benefits	4.2	2.4	3.4	1.7	7.5	11.0[2]
Turned down a promotion	3.1	1.2	2.1	0.7	6.0	10.4[2]
Chose early retirement	3.6	1.2	0.3	3.0	5.1	14.8[2]
Gave up work entirely	6.4	1.3	0.2	4.4	10.2[2]	30.3[2]

[1] Unweighted numbers refer to numbers of caregivers in the sample, while weighted numbers refer to numbers of caregiving households in the U.S. population nationwide.
[2] Differences in percentages are significant at the .05 level.

SOURCE: *Family Caregiving in the U.S.: Findings from a National Survey,* The National Alliance for Caregiving and The American Association of Retired Persons, Bethesda, MD, and Washington, D.C., 1997

Overall, nearly half (49.4 percent) of caregivers had to make changes to their daily work schedule, such as going in late, leaving early, or taking time off during the day. Some caregivers reported giving up their job either temporarily or permanently—about one-tenth (10.9 percent) took a leave of absence, 3.6 percent took early retirement, and 6.4 percent gave up their jobs altogether. About 7 percent worked fewer hours or took a less demanding job. A smaller percentage reported having lost some job benefits (4.2 percent) or having turned down a promotion (3.1 percent) due to caregiving. Not surprisingly, as the level of care became more demanding, the adjustments required became greater. (See Table 2.7.) In 1997 the National Alliance for Caregiving and The American Association of Retired Persons reported that Asian (22 percent) and Hispanic (18 percent) caregivers were more likely to take a leave of absence from work than were white (10 percent) caregivers.

WOMEN WHO MAINTAIN FAMILIES

The U.S. Census Bureau defines a female-headed family as a family consisting of two or more persons living together who are related by birth, marriage, or adoption and in which the householder is a woman without a spouse present. Female-headed households may or may not have children present. Those that do not have children may consist of any combination of related persons, such as parents, grandparents, aunts, uncles, and in-laws.

Since 1970 the number of female-headed families (5.5 million, or 11 percent of all families) in the United States has grown considerably, almost doubling in number to 10.9 million, or 16 percent of all families, in 1990. This trend continues reflecting the rising numbers of divorces, marital separations, and out-of-wedlock births. By 1998 there were 12.7 million female-headed families—17.8 percent of all families. At the same time, there were 3.9 million male-headed families—6 percent of all families. (See Table 2.3.)

Marital Status

In 1998 women headed approximately 12.7 million (17.8 percent) of all families (70.9 million). Of those female-headed households almost 2 million (15. 6 percent) were married with an absent spouse, with 1.6 million (80 percent) being separated while other situations accounted for 392,000 (19.8 percent). Divorced female heads of households numbered 4.5 million (35.7 percent), those widowed 2.3 million (18.4 percent), and those never married 3.8 million (30.3 percent). (See Table 2.3.)

In comparison male heads of households totaled 3.9 million, or barely 6 percent of all households. Of these, 529,000 (13.5 percent) had absent spouses, with 319,000 (60 percent) being separated and 209,000 (39.5 percent) accounting for other absentee situations. Divorced male heads of households totaled 1.4 million (36 percent), widows 373,000 (10 percent), and those never married 1.6 million (41 percent). (See Table 2.3.)

Race and Ethnicity

Black women were more likely to head a family without a spouse present. In 1998, 3.9 million (46.6 percent) of the 8.4 million black families in the United States were maintained by women. Of the 59.5 million white families, 8.3 million (13.9 percent) were maintained by women. Among the 6.9 million Hispanic-origin families, 1.6 million (23 percent) were maintained by women. In comparison black male-headed families accounted for 7.7 percent of all black families, white male-headed families 5 percent of all white families, and Hispanic male-headed families 9 percent of all Hispanic families. (See Table 2.3.)

Families Maintained by Women with Children

The U.S. Census Bureau predicts that one-half of all children born in the first decade of the twenty-first century will live with a single parent at some point by the time they turn 18 years of age. In 1998 women maintained 7.7 million families with children under the age of 18 years, or 22 percent of all families (34.7 million) with children under the age of 18. Among female-headed families with children under 18 years of age, 64 percent were white, 33 percent were black, and 15 percent were Hispanic. In comparison, 1.8 million (5 percent) of all families with children younger than 18 years of age were maintained by men. Of these, 84 percent were white, 12 percent black, and 13 percent Hispanic. (See Table 2.3.)

MEN'S CHANGING ROLE

Traditional Role

Until the twentieth century fathers in the United States were legally responsible for the supervision and development of children, with mothers generally deferring to fathers on matters concerning the children's upbringing. Following divorce or parental separation, fathers were typically granted custody of the children.

The Provider

During the first decades of the nineteenth century the shift from an agricultural to an industrial economy led to a dramatic change in the father's role in the family. With the family no longer functioning as a self-sufficient farming production unit, many fathers began conducting business or earning their living away from the home. This marked the start of the father's distinct role as the family provider, separated from the family during much of the day.

During the early 1900s raising children, previously the province of the father, was turned over to the mother whose parenting skills were now considered more suited to molding the young. This resulted in the weakening of the father-child relationship, as the father appeared to focus upon earning the family income while the mother focused on raising the children. This stereotype of parental roles was held well into the twentieth century, even if the mother was working outside the home as well as raising the children.

Contemporary Fathers

In June 1998 Vice President Al Gore released the report *Nurturing Fatherhood: Improving Data and Research on Male Fertility, Family Formation and Fatherhood* (U.S. Department of Health and Human Services, Washington, D.C.). This report was in answer to President Bill Clinton's challenge to all federal agencies to promote paternal involvement in the lives of their children.

Nurturing Fatherhood observes that "the contemporary picture of fatherhood as reflected by the current research is one of Dr. Jekyl and Mr. Hyde." On one hand is the father who cares for his children, participating in their activities while at the same time financially providing for the family. On the other hand is the father who denies his paternity, is absent from his children's lives, or who refuses to provide child support.

The Future of Fatherhood

The researchers believe that more changes will occur in the roles of men and women as the American family enters the twenty-first century. If mothers of young children continue to join the labor force, fathers may have to assume more child care tasks. The researchers ask whether modern fathers would accept an increasing share of childrearing responsibilities or flee from them. (See Chapter 7.) A bigger issue concerns the role and/or the commitment of the non-custodial father in the divorced family and the fathers of children born out of wedlock.

FATHERS' ROLE IN CHILD CARE

Lynne M. Casper, in "My Daddy Takes Care of Me! Fathers as Care Providers" (Current Population Reports, U.S. Bureau of the Census, Washington, D.C., 1997), reported on married fathers' child care involvement. In 1993, 1 out of 8 fathers (12.9 percent) were the primary care providers for their children during the mothers' working hours outside the home. Almost one-fifth (19.6 percent) provided some child care. (See Table 2.8.)

In 1993 almost 2 in 10 (18.5 percent) fathers were primary care providers for their children under 5 years of age, compared with fewer than 1 in 10 (9.1 percent) for 5- to 14-year-olds. Almost one-quarter (24.8 percent) of fathers took some care of their preschoolers, and 15.6 percent took some care of their 5- to 14-year-olds. (See Table 2.8.)

Employment Status and Work Schedule Influence Provision of Care

In 1993 fathers who were not employed were more likely to provide child care for their preschoolers. Unemployed fathers were far more likely to be primary care providers (50.2 percent) than employed fathers (16.3 percent). More than half (57.6 percent) of unemployed fathers provided some care, compared with almost one-quarter (22.5 percent) of employed fathers. (See Table 2.9.)

TABLE 2.8

Fathers providing care for children while mothers are working: 1993

(Numbers in thousands)

Fathers providing care	1993	
	Number	Percent
Caring for children 0-14		
Total number of fathers[1]	14,849	100.0
Providing some care	2,914	19.6
Primary provider of care	1,915	12.9
Caring for children Under 5		
Total number of fathers	6,274	100.0
Providing some care	1,554	24.8
Primary provider of care	1,164	18.5
Caring for children 5-14		
Total number of fathers	11,412	100.0
Providing some care	1,780	15.6
Primary provider of care	1,034	9.1

[1] The number of fathers of children under 5 combined with the number of fathers of children 5-14 does not sum to the total number of fathers of children 0-14 because some fathers have children in both age groups.

Note: Limited to married fathers whose wives are employed.

SOURCE: Lynne M. Casper, "My Daddy Takes Care of Me! Fathers as Care Providers," *Current Population Reports,* P70-59, Spetember 1997

In 1993 part-time working fathers were nearly twice as likely (27.4 percent) to be the children's primary care providers than full-time working fathers (15.4 percent). Overall, fathers who worked part time were more likely (32.3 percent) to take some care of their children while the mother worked outside the home than full-time working fathers (21.7 percent). (See Table 2.9.)

The type of shift a father works also determines his availability to provide child care. Non-dayshift workers were twice as likely (25.7 percent) as dayshift workers (12.8 percent) to be primary care providers. Overall, non-dayshift workers were more likely to take care of their children (33.6 percent) than were dayshift workers (18.3 percent). (See Table 2.9.)

Poor and Nonpoor Fathers as Child Care Providers

In 1993 poor fathers were almost twice as likely (43 percent) as nonpoor fathers (24 percent) to care for their preschoolers. Poor fathers were also more likely (36.6 percent) than nonpoor fathers (17.7 percent) to be primary child-care providers while the mothers worked outside the home. (See Figure 2.2 and Table 2.10.)

Fathers' Occupations and Income Affect Provision of Care

Fathers in service occupations, such as policemen and firemen, were about twice as likely (42.1 percent) as those in managerial/professional occupations (18.1 percent) and technical/sales positions (20.1 percent) to care for their children while the mothers were at work. Fathers in ser-

TABLE 2.9

Fathers providing care for preschoolers while mothers are working, by employment status of fathers: 1993

(Numbers in thousands)

Employment status of father	1993		
	Total	Number of providers	Percent providing
All providers	6,274	1,554	24.8
Employment Status			
Not employed[1]	412	238	57.6
Employed[2]	5,862	1,316	22.5
Full time	5,428	1,176	21.7
Part time	434	141	32.3
Type of Work Shift[3]			
Day shift	4,275	784	18.3
Nonday shift	1,586	533	33.6
Primary care providers	6,274	1,164	18.5
Employment Status			
Not employed[1]	412	207	50.2
Employed[2]	5,862	957	16.3
Full time	5,428	838	15.4
Part time	434	119	27.4
Type of Work Shift[3]			
Day shift	4,275	549	12.8
Nonday shift	1,586	408	25.7

[1] Includes persons who were unemployed, enrolled in school, or not in the labor force the month prior to the survey.

[2] In the month prior to the survey.

[3] For fathers who were employed in the month prior to the survey.

Note: Limited to married fathers whose wives are employed.

SOURCE: Lynne M. Casper, "My Daddy Takes Care of Me! Fathers as Care Providers," *Current Population Reports,* P70-59, Spetember 1997

FIGURE 2.2

Fathers caring for their preschoolers by poverty status: 1988 to 1993

(As a percent of married fathers within the same poverty status whose wives are employed)

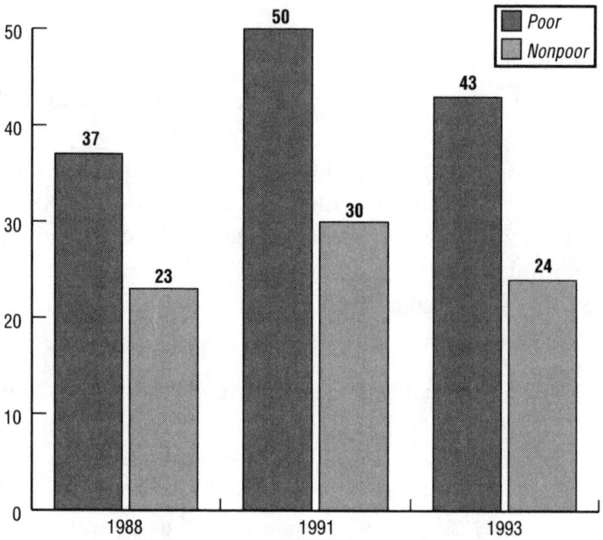

SOURCE: Lynne M. Casper, "My Daddy Takes Care of Me! Fathers as Care Providers," *Current Population Reports,* P70-59, September 1997

TABLE 2.10

Fathers providing care for preschoolers while mothers are working, by various characteristics: 1993

(Numbers in thousands)

		1993	
	Number of fathers	Percent providing care	
Characteristics		All providers	Primary providers
All fathers	6,274	24.8	18.5
Father's occupation			
Manager/professional	1,619	18.1	12.9
Technical/sales	1,189	20.1	15.0
Service	508	42.1	29.0
Other	2,547	22.4	16.6
Not employed last month	412	57.6	50.2
Poverty status[1]:			
Below poverty	286	43.0	36.6
Above poverty	5,975	23.9	17.7
Husband's monthly income:			
Less than $1,500	1,619	30.1	25.1
$1,500 to $2,999	2,706	24.6	17.5
$3,000 to $4,499	1,182	19.7	13.1
$4,500 and over	651	15.7	10.3

[1] Omits fathers with no income.

Note: Limited to married fathers whose wives are employed.

SOURCE: Lynne M. Casper, "My Daddy Takes Care of Me! Fathers as Care Providers," *Current Population Reports*, P70-59, Spetember 1997

FIGURE 2.4

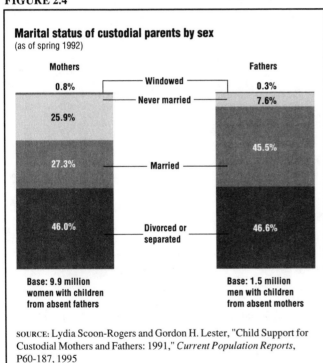

Marital status of custodial parents by sex
(as of spring 1992)

SOURCE: Lydia Scoon-Rogers and Gordon H. Lester, "Child Support for Custodial Mothers and Fathers: 1991," *Current Population Reports*, P60-187, 1995

vice occupations were also more likely (29 percent) to be primary care providers. (See Table 2.10.)

Since child care can be quite expensive, not surprisingly, low-income fathers were about twice as likely to care for their children than were higher-income fathers. In

FIGURE 2.3

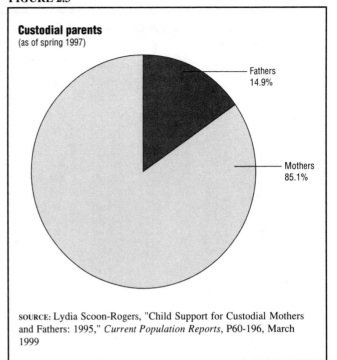

Custodial parents
(as of spring 1997)

SOURCE: Lydia Scoon-Rogers, "Child Support for Custodial Mothers and Fathers: 1995," *Current Population Reports*, P60-196, March 1999

FIGURE 2.5

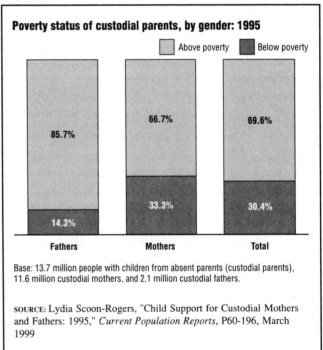

Poverty status of custodial parents, by gender: 1995

Base: 13.7 million people with children from absent parents (custodial parents), 11.6 million custodial mothers, and 2.1 million custodial fathers.

SOURCE: Lydia Scoon-Rogers, "Child Support for Custodial Mothers and Fathers: 1995," *Current Population Reports*, P60-196, March 1999

1993 fathers who made less than $1,500 a month were twice as likely (30.1 percent) as fathers who made more than $4,500 a month (15.7 percent) to care for their children. (See Table 2.10.)

CHILD SUPPORT

Inadequate, or lack of, financial support from noncustodial parents contributes to the high incidence of

TABLE 2.11

Child support payments agreed to or awarded custodial parents

(Numbers in thousands. Parents living with own children under 21 years of age whose other parent is absent from the home. Amounts in dollars)

		Child support agreed to or awarded							Child support not awarded	
			Supposed to receive child support payments in 1995							
			Received payments in 1995				Received no payments in 1995			
Characteristic	Number	Number	Number	Number	Average child support	Average total money income	Number	Average total money income	Number	Average total money income
All custodial parents										
Total	13,739	7,967	6,966	4,769	$3,732	$22,543	2,198	$17,398	5,772	$18,927
Standard error	287	222	208	173	$187	$546	118	$577	190	$591
Custodial mothers	11,634	7,123	6,233	4,353	$3,767	$21,829	1,880	$16,093	4,511	$14,068
Standard error	265	210	197	165	$200	$539	109	$575	168	$375
Custodial fathers	2,105	844	733	416	$3,370	$30,030	318	$25,122	1,261	$36,312
Standard error	116	73	69	52	$471	$2,628	45	$1,917	90	$2,141
Poverty status in 1995:										
Family income below poverty level	4,172	2,103	1,761	1,067	$2,531	$6,855	694	$6,043	2,069	$5,660
Standard error	162	116	106	83	$510	$202	67	$272	115	$147
Visitation and joint custody Arrangements with non-custodial parents in 1995:										
Visitation privileges only	7,469	4,683	4,074	2,924	$3,297	$21,110	1,150	$17,460	2,555	$20,084
Joint custody only[1]	121	95	73	39	(B)	(B)	35	(B)	26	(B)
Visitation and joint custody	3,044	2,089	1,901	1,487	$4,592	$26,836	414	$21,082	908	$29,404
Neither	3,105	1,100	917	318	$3,770	$15,630	599	$14,767	1,953	$13,012
Custodial mothers										
Race and Hispanic origin:										
White	7,970	5,403	4,782	3,488	$4,100	$23,067	1,294	$17,642	2,567	$15,517
White, not Hispanic origin	6,545	4,709	4,191	3,149	$4,274	$23,958	1,041	$19,083	1,836	$17,965
Black	3,323	1,509	1,273	749	$2,116	$16,614	524	$12,376	1,814	$11,916
Hispanic origin[2]	1,530	725	613	354	$2,420	$14,801	259	$11,744	806	$9,567
Current marital status:										
Married	2,216	1,516	1,368	981	$3,546	$19,968	387	$16,289	699	$15,418
Divorced	4,003	3,028	2,692	2,044	$3,990	$26,521	648	$21,257	975	$19,243
Separated	1,791	942	798	552	$4,182	$18,432	246	$13,157	850	$14,881
Widowed[3]	316	178	163	94	$9,624	$21,641	69	(B)	138	$17,490
Never married	3,309	1,459	1,212	683	$2,271	$13,224	530	$10,862	1,850	$10,201
Educational attainment:										
Less than high school diploma	2,419	1,145	945	523	$2,106	$9,299	422	$8,368	1,274	$7,172
High school graduate	4,396	2,702	2,350	1,586	$3,179	$16,827	764	$15,385	1,694	$13,531
Some college, no degree	2,545	1,682	1,467	1,085	$3,932	$22,505	383	$16,492	863	$16,107
Associate degree	953	634	586	459	$4,899	$28,484	126	$22,935	318	$17,587
Bachelors degree or more	1,322	960	885	700	$5,338	$37,109	186	$31,086	362	$32,907

(B) Represents base less than 75,000.

[1] Joint custody may be physical, legal or both. Legal custody does not necessarily include visitation.

[2] Persons of Hispanic origin may be of any race.

[3] Widowed parents have children from a previous marriage that ended in divorce or from a previous nonmarried relationship.

SOURCE: Lydia Scoon-Rogers, "Child Support for Custodial Mothers and Fathers: 1995," *Current Population Reports*, P60-196, March 1999

poverty among children living in single-parent families. When custodial parents are not paid the child support due them, they often turn to public welfare. In 1975 Congress created the Child Support Enforcement (CSE) program under Title IV-D of the Social Security Act to enforce the financial obligations owed by noncustodial parents to their children.

Custodial Parents

According to *Child Support for Custodial Mothers and Fathers: 1997* (Timothy Grall, U.S. Bureau of the Census, Washington, D.C., 2000), a comprehensive report on child support, of the 13.7 million custodial parents the majority, 11.6 million (85.1 percent), of custodial parents were women, and 2.1 million (14.9 percent) were men. (See Figure 2.3.)

MARITAL STATUS AND RACE/ETHNICITY. In 1992 slightly more than one-quarter (27.3 percent) of custodial mothers were married, compared with nearly half (45.5 percent) of custodial fathers. Custodial mothers were nearly three-and-a-half-times as likely to be never-married as custodial fathers (25.9 percent versus 7.6 per-

TABLE 2.12

Child support collection: twenty years of progress

Year	Total child support collections (millions)
1976	$692
1977	$864
1978	$1,048
1979	$1,333
1980	$1,478
1981	$1,629
1982	$1,770
1983	$2,024
1984	$2,378
1985	$2,694
1986	$3,245
1987	$3,918
1988	$4,613
1989	$5,241
1990	$6,010
1991	$6,886
1992	$7,965
1993	$8,907
1994	$9,850
1995	$10,827
1996	$12,019
1997	$13,400

SOURCE: "The Basics of Child Support Enforcement," *Children Today*, vol. 24, no. 2, U.S. Department of Health and Human Services, 1997

cent). Both custodial mothers and custodial fathers were equally as likely to be divorced or separated—about 46 percent and 47 percent, respectively. (See Figure 2.4.)

In 1995 approximately 56.3 percent of all custodial mothers were non-Hispanic white, 28.6 percent were black, and 13 percent were Hispanic. (See Table 2.11.)

AGE AND EDUCATIONAL ATTAINMENT. According to *Child Support for Custodial Mothers and Fathers: 1991,* (U.S. Bureau of the Census, Washington, D.C., 1995), custodial fathers were generally older than custodial mothers, with about half (45.8 percent) being 40 years old or older, compared with 24.5 percent of custodial mothers. On the other hand custodial mothers were more likely to be under 30 years old (30.5 percent versus 11 percent of fathers). Custodial parents typically had not attended college (63 percent); however, custodial fathers were almost twice as likely (18.6 percent) to have received a bachelor's degree than were custodial mothers (9.8 percent).

Custodial Parents Living Below Poverty Level

In 1995 custodial mothers were approximately two-and-a-half times more likely (33.3 percent) than custodial fathers (14.3 percent) to live in poverty. (See Figure 2.5.)

RACE/ETHNIC ORIGIN AND EDUCATIONAL ATTAINMENT. According to *Child Support for Custodial Mothers and Fathers: 1991,* (U.S. Bureau of the Census, Washington, D.C., 1995), among all custodial mothers living below the poverty level (3.5 million), non-Hispanic white custodial mothers made up 41.4 percent (1.5 million), black mothers 40.8 percent (1.4 million), and Hispanic mothers 16 percent (563,000). In comparison non-Hispanic white fathers comprised 60.9 percent (126,000) of all custodial fathers living below the poverty level, black fathers 21.7 percent (45,000), and Hispanic fathers 13.5 percent (28,000).

The Census Bureau's survey also found that the poverty status of custodial parents differed by their level of education. Of all custodial mothers living below the poverty line, those mothers who did not finish high school had a poverty rate of 41.3 percent, as compared with those with at least a high school education (40.4 percent) and those with a bachelor's degree or more (2.4 percent). Among all custodial fathers living below the poverty line, the poverty rate for those without a high school education (47.3 percent) was significantly higher than for those who graduated from high school (33.8 percent). Custodial fathers with a bachelor's degree or more had a poverty rate of only 6.3 percent.

Child Support Enforcement

The Child Support Enforcement (CSE) program, a joint effort involving federal, state, and local governments, collected barely $700,000 in child support during its first year of operation in 1976. In 1997 CSE agencies collected $13.4 billion from noncustodial parents. Total child support collections for 1999 were $15.8 billion, up from $14.3 billion in 1998. (See Table 2.12.)

CHAPTER 3
THE CHILDREN OF AMERICA

In 1936, for the first time, the Gallup Poll asked respondents what they felt was the ideal number of children per family. Sixty-six percent considered three or more children the ideal number. (See Figure 3.1.) After World War II (1939–45) Americans still believed that three or more children made up the ideal family. The United States recorded its highest number of births in the years following World War II, a period that came to be known as the "baby boom" (1946–64).

After the war, the proportion of Americans who thought that the ideal family consisted of three or more children continued to rise, peaking in 1962, when 80 percent of Gallup Poll respondents felt this way. In 1965 married-couple families with their own children under the age of 18 had an average of 2.44 children. (See Table 1.6 in Chapter 1.) Since then, the proportion of respondents who favor three or more children has dropped. In 1997, when the Gallup Poll asked the same question, only 36 percent of respondents indicated that three or more was the ideal number of children in a family. (See Figure 3.1.) Most thought two children were about right.

THE NUMBER OF CHILDREN

Since the mid-1960s the number of children has been decreasing as a proportion of the total U.S. population. In 1999 children through the age of 19 made up 28.7 percent of the population, down from a peak of 36 percent at the end of the baby boom in 1964. (See Figure 3.2.) Federal

FIGURE 3.1

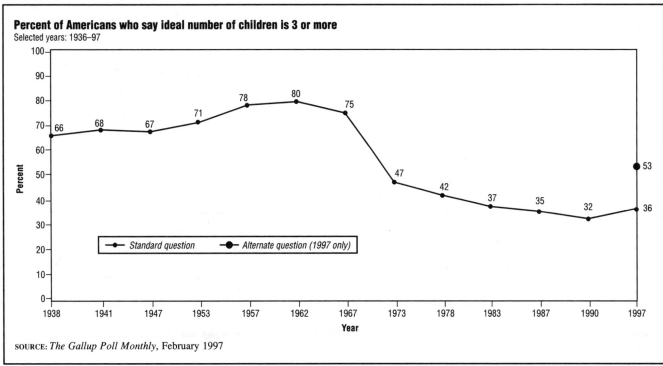

Percent of Americans who say ideal number of children is 3 or more
Selected years: 1936–97

SOURCE: *The Gallup Poll Monthly*, February 1997

estimates project that the total number of children will climb from 70.2 million in 1999 to 77.2 million in 2020. (See Figure 3.3.)

Racial and Ethnic Diversity

Over the past two decades, like the American population in general, America's children have become a more racially and ethnically diverse group. While the percentages of non-Hispanic black and American Indian/Alaskan Native children remained about the same from 1980 to 1999, the proportion of non-Hispanic white children declined from 74 percent in 1980 to 65 percent in that same period. (See Figure 3.4.)

Meanwhile, the proportions of Hispanic and Asian/Pacific Islander children continued to grow, with the proportion of Hispanic children growing faster than that of any other racial or ethnic group. Between 1980 and 1999 the proportion of Hispanic children rose from 9 percent to 16 percent of the child population, and that of Asian/Pacific Islander children doubled—from 2 percent to 4 percent of all American children. (See Figure 3.4.) In 1999 there were slightly more Hispanic children (16 percent) than non-Hispanic black children (15 percent). The U.S. Census Bureau attributes the rise in the percentages of Hispanic and Asian/Pacific Islander children to an increase in both the fertility rate and immigration. Also, Hispanic women tend to have more children than other racial and ethnic groups.

Projections

BY RACIAL AND ETHNIC ORIGIN. The U.S. Census Bureau predicts that, by 2050, children of Hispanic origin will make up nearly one-third of all children under the age of 18; blacks, almost one-fourth; Asian/Pacific Islanders, about one-tenth; and American Indians/Alaskan Natives, 1 percent.

FIGURE 3.2

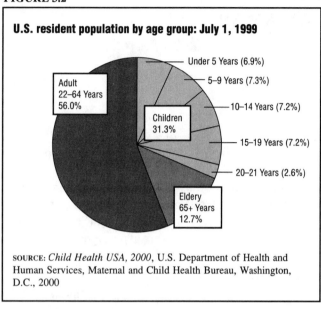

SOURCE: *Child Health USA, 2000*, U.S. Department of Health and Human Services, Maternal and Child Health Bureau, Washington, D.C., 2000

FIGURE 3.3

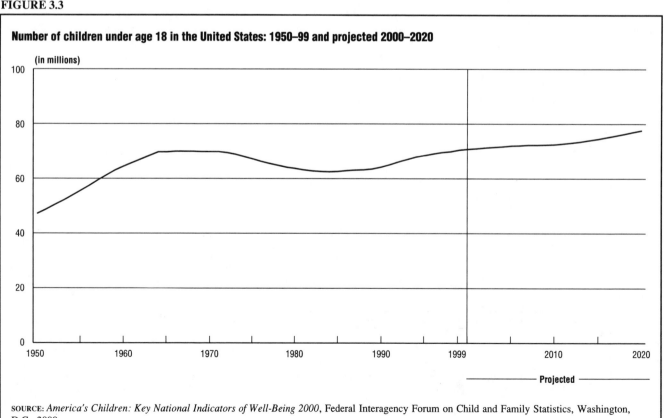

SOURCE: *America's Children: Key National Indicators of Well-Being 2000*, Federal Interagency Forum on Child and Family Statistics, Washington, D.C., 2000

FIGURE 3.4

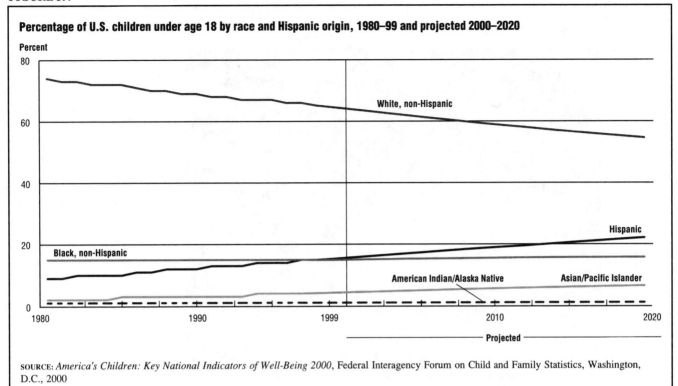

Percentage of U.S. children under age 18 by race and Hispanic origin, 1980–99 and projected 2000–2020

SOURCE: *America's Children: Key National Indicators of Well-Being 2000*, Federal Interagency Forum on Child and Family Statistics, Washington, D.C., 2000

TABLE 3.1

Population by age: 1990 to 2050
[In thousands. Resident population]

Year	Total	Under 5 years	5 to 13 years	14 to 17 years	18 to 24 years	25 to 34 years	35 to 44 years	45 to 64 years	65 years and over	85 years and over	100 years and over
Estimate											
1990	249,402	18,849	31,996	13,311	26,826	43,139	37,766	46,280	31,235	3,057	37
Projections											
Middle Series											
1995	262,820	19,591	34,378	14,773	24,926	40,863	42,514	52,231	33,543	3,634	54
2000	274,634	18,987	36,043	15,752	26,258	37,233	44,659	60,992	34,709	4,259	72
2005	285,981	19,127	35,850	16,986	28,268	36,306	42,165	71,113	36,166	4,899	101
2010	297,716	20,012	35,605	16,894	30,138	38,292	38,521	78,848	39,408	5,671	131
2020	322,742	21,979	38,660	16,965	29,919	42,934	39,612	79,454	53,220	6,460	214
2030	346,899	23,066	41,589	18,788	31,826	42,744	44,263	75,245	69,379	8,455	324
2040	369,980	24,980	43,993	19,844	34,570	45,932	44,159	81,268	75,233	13,552	447
2050	393,931	27,106	47,804	21,207	36,333	49,365	47,393	85,862	78,859	18,223	834

SOURCE: Jennifer Cheeseman Day, *Population Projections of the United States by Age, Sex, Race, and Hispanic Origin: 1995 to 2050*, U.S. Bureau of the Census, Washington, D.C., 1996

Non-Hispanic white youth, the only group predicted to decline in numbers, will comprise about 40% of the under-18 age group, down sharply from nearly 70% in 1990.

BY AGE. In 1995, children under 5 years of age made up 7.5 percent of the U.S. population. It is projected that, by 2050, this age group will comprise 6.9 percent of the population. It is also projected that, between 1995 and 2050, the number of children 5–13 years old will drop from 13.1 to 12.1 percent of the population, and the num-

ber of children ages 14–17 will stay almost unchanged—from 5.6 percent to 5.4 percent. (See Table 3.1.)

FAMILIES WITH CHILDREN

By Households

In 1970, despite the trend toward fewer children, married couples with children under the age of 18 made up 40 percent of all households. (See Figure 3.5.) (By Census Bureau definition, "nonfamily" households do not contain

FIGURE 3.5

Household composition: 1970 to 1997

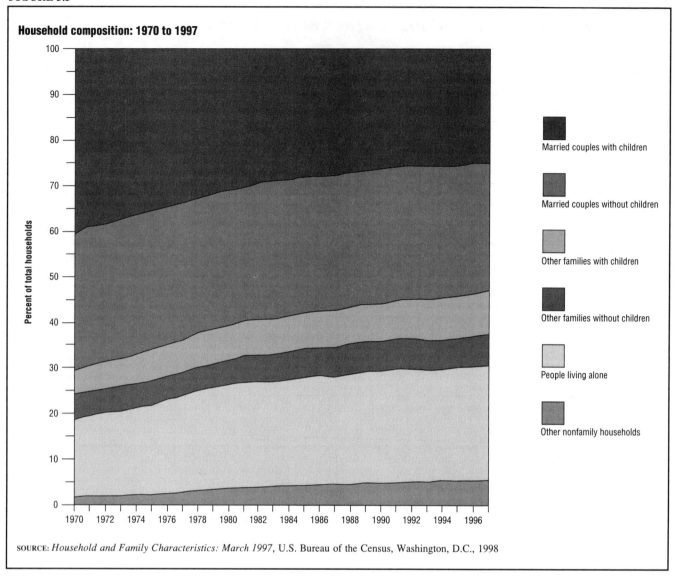

SOURCE: *Household and Family Characteristics: March 1997*, U.S. Bureau of the Census, Washington, D.C., 1998

"own children." However, the Census Bureau acknowledges that nonfamily households may contain persons under the age of 18 who are not relatives of the householder. These children are included in the total count of all children in the United States.)

From 1970 to 1990 the percentage of married couples with children under 18 years of age plummeted, from 40 percent to 26 percent. Since 1990 the decline has slowed, with a slight decrease to 25 percent in 1997. In 1970 "other families" (families maintained by men or women with no spouse at home) with their own children under 18 years of age comprised just 5 percent of all American households. The proportion rose to 8 percent in 1990, then to 9 percent in 1997. (See Figure 3.5.)

By Family Types

In 1950, of the different family types with children under the age of 18, approximately 93 percent (18.8 mil-lion) were married-couple families. By 1970 this proportion was down to 89 percent (25.5 million). With couples delaying marriage and women postponing childbirth, the proportion of married-couple families with children has steadily declined. By 1998 the rate had dropped to approximately 73% (25.3 million) of all family types with own children under the age of 18 (34.8 million), and 36 percent of all families with or without own children under 18 (70.9 million). (See Table 3.2.)

Meanwhile, the number of one-parent families with children continues to rise. In 1950 just 6 percent of families with own children under 18 years of age were headed by mothers only. This figure doubled to 12 percent by 1972, continuing upward through the 1980s, and by 1998 reached 22 percent (7.7 million). In 1950 father-only families made up just 1 percent of all families with own children under 18 years of age, doubling to 2 percent in 1980, and increasing to 5 percent in 1998. (See Table 3.2.)

TABLE 3.2

Families, by presence of own children under 18: 1950 to 1998

(Numbers in thousands)

Year	All families with or without own children under 18	Families with children under 18					
			One parent families				Married-couple families
		Total	Total	Mother only	Father only	
1998	70,880	34,760	9,491	7,693	1,798	25,269
1997	70,241	34,665	9,583	7,874	1,709	25,083
1996	69,594	34,203	9,284	7,656	1,628	24,920
1995	69,305	34,296	9,055	7,615	1,440	25,241
1994	68,490	34,018	8,961	7,647	1,314	25,058
1993	68,144	33,257	8,550	7,226	1,324	24,707
1992	67,173	32,746	8,326	7,043	1,283	24,420
1991	66,322	32,401	8,004	6,823	1,181	24,397
1990	66,090	32,289	7,752	6,599	1,153	24,537
1989	65,837	32,322	7,587	6,519	1,068	24,735
1988	65,133	31,920	7,320	6,273	1,047	24,600
1987	64,491	31,898	7,252	6,297	955	24,646
1986	63,558	31,670	7,040	6,105	935	24,630
1985	62,706	31,112	6,902	6,006	896	24,210
1984	61,997	31,046	6,706	5,907	799	24,340
1983	61,393	30,818	6,455	5,718	737	24,363
1982	61,019	31,012	6,547	5,868	679	24,465
1981	60,309	31,227	6,300	5,634	666	24,927
1980r	59,550	31,022	6,061	5,445	616	24,961
1980	58,426	30,517	5,949	5,340	609	24,568
1979	57,804	30,371	5,857	5,288	569	24,514
1978	57,215	30,369	5,744	5,206	539	24,625
1977	56,710	30,145	5,270	4,784	486	24,875
1976	56,245	30,177	5,067	4,621	446	25,110
1975	55,712	30,057	4,888	4,404	484	25,169
1974	55,053	29,750	4,472	4,081	391	25,278
1973	54,373	29,571	4,184	3,798	386	25,387
1972	53,296	29,445	3,963	3,598	365	25,482
1971	52,227	28,786	3,695	3,365	331	25,091
1970r	51,586	28,812	3,271	2,971	345	25,541
1970	51,237	28,665	3,260	2,925	335	25,406
1969	50,823	28,347	3,211	2,888	323	25,136
1968	50,111	27,964	3,069	2,772	297	24,895
1967	49,214	27,561	2,915	2,584	331	24,646
1966	48,509	27,004	2,728	2,450	278	24,276
1965	47,956	27,140	2,734	2,485	249	24,406
1964	47,540	27,068	2,629	2,361	268	24,439
1963	47,059	26,911	2,590	2,229	361	24,321
1962	46,418	26,271	2,483	2,229	254	23,788
1961	45,539	25,889	2,375	2,185	190	23,514
1960	45,111	25,690	2,332	2,099	232	23,358
1959	44,232	25,069	2,175	1,943	232	22,894
1958	43,696	24,541	2,115	1,822	293	22,426
1957	43,497	24,260	2,121	1,855	265	22,139
1956	42,889	23,743	2,112	1,814	298	21,631
1955	41,951	23,190	2,126	1,870	256	21,064
1954	41,263	22,544	1,899	1,615	283	20,645
1953	40,877	21,718	1,798	1,521	277	19,920
1952	40,608	21,353	1,747	1,514	233	19,606
1951	39,944	21,279	1,890	1,659	231	19,389
1950	39,303	20,324	1,500	1,272	229	18,824

Notes: Prior to 1980 the counts of families include unrelated subfamilies. Data for 1970 and 1980 are revised based on the 1980 decennial census.

r Revised based on population from the decennial census for that year.

SOURCE: *Household and Family Characteristics: March 1998,* U.S. Bureau of the Census, Washington, D.C., 1999

LIVING ARRANGEMENTS OF CHILDREN

One Parent, Two Parents, or No Parent

Not surprisingly, the increasing number of divorces, marital separations, and out-of-wedlock births has significantly reshaped the living arrangements of American children. In the year 2000 children under 18 were considerably more likely to be living with only one parent than they were 20 years earlier.

In 1960, toward the end of the baby boom, nearly 9 in 10 (87.7 percent) children under 18 lived with two parents. By 1980 this proportion declined to 77 percent, and dropped again, to 72.5 percent, by 1990. In 1998 the pro-

TABLE 3.3

Living arrangements of children under 18 years old: 1960 to 1998

(Numbers in thousands)

| | | | Living with: | | | | |
| | | | | One Parent | | | |
Year	Total children under 18 yrs.	Two parents	Total	Mother only	Father only	Other relatives	Non-relatives only
1998	71,377	48,642	19,777	16,634	3,143	2,125	833
1997	70,983	48,386	19,799	16,740	3,059	1,983	815
1996	70,908	48,224	19,752	16,993	2,759	2,137	795
1995	70,254	48,276	18,938	16,477	2,461	2,352	688
1994	69,508	48,084	18,590	16,334	2,257	2,150	684
1993	66,893	47,181	17,872	15,586	2,286	1,442	398
1992	65,965	46,638	17,578	15,396	2,182	1,334	415
1991	65,093	46,658	16,624	14,608	2,016	1,428	383
1990	64,137	46,503	15,867	13,874	1,993	1,421	346
1989	63,637	46,549	15,493	13,700	1,793	1,341	254
1988	63,179	45,942	15,329	13,521	1,808	1,516	392
1987	62,932	46,009	15,071	13,420	1,651	1,484	368
1986	62,763	46,384	14,759	13,180	1,579	1,348	272
1985	62,475	46,149	14,635	13,081	1,554	1,339	352
1984	62,139	46,555	14,025	12,646	1,378	1,226	333
1983*	62,281	46,632	14,006	12,739	1,267	1,349	294
1982*	62,407	46,797	13,702	12,512	1,189	1,556	352
1981	62,918	48,040	12,619	11,416	1,203	1,911	348
1980r	63,427	48,624	12,466	11,406	1,060	1,949	388
1980	61,744	47,286	12,162	11,131	1,031	1,912	384
1979	62,389	48,295	11,529	10,531	997	2,142	423
1978	63,206	49,132	11,711	10,725	985	1,940	423
1977	64,062	50,735	11,311	10,419	892	1,626	390
1976	65,129	52,101	11,121	10,310	811	1,500	407
1975	66,087	53,072	11,243	10,231	1,014	1,409	363
1974	67,047	54,561	10,489	9,647	842	1,532	465
1973	67,950	55,807	10,093	9,272	821	1,629	421
1972	68,811	57,201	9,634	8,838	796	1,593	383
1971	70,255	58,606	9,478	8,714	764	1,707	464
1970r	69,162	58,939	8,199	7,452	748	1,547	477
1970	70,213	59,694	8,438	7,678	760	1,599	482
1969	70,317	59,857	8,509	7,744	765	1,602	349
1968	70,326	60,030	8,332	7,556	776	1,660	304
1967	(NA)	(NA)	(NA)	(NA)	(NA)	(NA)	(NA)
1966	(NA)	(NA)	(NA)	(NA)	(NA)	(NA)	(NA)
1965	(NA)	(NA)	(NA)	(NA)	(NA)	(NA)	(NA)
1964	(NA)	(NA)	(NA)	(NA)	(NA)	(NA)	(NA)
1963	(NA)	(NA)	(NA)	(NA)	(NA)	(NA)	(NA)
1962	(NA)	(NA)	(NA)	(NA)	(NA)	(NA)	(NA)
1961	(NA)	(NA)	(NA)	(NA)	(NA)	(NA)	(NA)
1960 Census	63,727	55,877	5,829	5,105	724	1,601	420

Notes: Excludes householders, subfamily reference persons, and their spouses. Also excludes inmates of institutions. Based on Current Population Survey (CPS) unless otherwise indicated.

NA Not available.

r Revised based on population from the decennial census for that year.

* Introduction of improved data collection and processing procedures that helped to identify parent-child subfamilies.

SOURCE: *Marital Status and Living Arrangements: March 1998,* U.S. Bureau of the Census, Washington, D.C., 1999

portion of children living with two parents was down to 68 percent.

In comparison, the proportion of children in this age group living with one parent increased from just 9 percent in 1960 to 25 percent in 1990 and to 28 percent in 1998. About 4 percent lived with neither parent in 1998: 3 percent with other relatives and 1 percent with nonrelatives. (See Table 3.3.)

In 1998 nearly one-fourth (23 percent) of children under age 18 lived with their mother only, while 4 percent lived with their father only. The Census Bureau reported that, while, historically, children who stayed with one parent lived with their mother only, an increasing proportion were living with their father only. (See Table 3.3.)

BY SINGLE PARENT'S MARITAL STATUS. Census Bureau data show that, in 1998, a child in a single-parent situation was just as likely to be living with a parent who had never married (39 percent) as with a parent who was divorced (35 percent). Another 15 percent lived with a parent who was separated from the spouse, while 4 percent lived with a widowed parent.

FIGURE 3.6

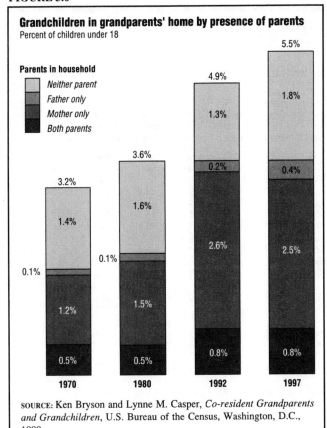

Grandchildren in grandparents' home by presence of parents
Percent of children under 18

Parents in household
- Neither parent
- Father only
- Mother only
- Both parents

SOURCE: Ken Bryson and Lynne M. Casper, *Co-resident Grandparents and Grandchildren*, U.S. Bureau of the Census, Washington, D.C., 1999

The government keeps track of the living arrangements of children, since the likelihood of getting financial aid depends upon the marital status of the parent with whom the child lives. According to the Census Bureau, about 75 percent of divorced mothers receive child support payments, compared with just 25 percent of never-married mothers.

RACIAL AND ETHNIC COMPARISON. The changing family structure has significantly affected black children. In 1980, 42 percent of black children lived with two parents and 46 percent lived with single parents. In 1997, 35 percent of black children lived in two-parent families and 57 percent lived in single-parent families. In comparison, most white children lived with two parents in 1980 (83 percent) and 1997 (75 percent). A large proportion of Hispanic children also lived with two parents (75 percent in 1980 and 64 percent in 1997).

Stepchildren

Many divorced parents eventually remarry and their children become part of stepfamilies, or blended families. The most common stepfamily situation is that of children living with a biological mother and a stepfather, with no other children present. The frequency of this arrangement is attributable to the large number of divorced women who gain custody of their children. Another type of step-

family consists of at least one stepchild and one biological child of the couple. According to the U.S. Census Bureau, approximately 15 percent of all children live in stepfamilies and are included in the Bureau's count of children in two-parent families.

Grandparents Raising Grandchildren

In *Coresident Grandparents and Their Grandchildren: Grandparent-Maintained Families* (U.S. Bureau of the Census, Washington, D.C., 1998) Lynne M. Casper and Kenneth R. Bryson reported on the rising trend of grandparents raising grandchildren. They reported that, in 1970, 3.2 percent (2.2 million) of all American children under the age of 18 lived in family households maintained by a grandparent. By 1980 this figure increased to 2.3 million, and rose to 3.3 million in 1992 and to 3.9 million (5.5 percent) in 1997. (See Table 3.4.)

According to Casper and Bryson, the proportion of grandchildren under the age of 18 living in grandparent-maintained families with just one parent present rose significantly from 1970 to 1997: by 118 percent for those with just the mother present, and by 217 percent with just the father present. In contrast, children living with their grandparents with both parents present rose 53 percent, and those with both parents absent, 37 percent. (See Figure 3.6.)

In 1997, 75 percent of coresident grandparent/grandchildren families were maintained by grandparents and 25 percent by parents. Casper and Bryson categorized these families into five basic types: both grandparents with some parents present (34 percent); both grandparents with no parents present (17 percent); grandmother-only with some parents present (29 percent); grandmother-only families with no parents present (14 percent); and grandfather-only families (6 percent). Overall, nearly two-thirds of grandparent-headed families had parents present. (See Figure 3.7.)

According to the authors, some researchers attribute the growing trend in coresident grandparent/grandchildren families to the continuing incidence of divorce, the rise in single-parent households, parental substance abuse, teen pregnancy, AIDS, child abuse and neglect, and other similar factors.

CHARACTERISTICS OF GRANDCHILDREN. In 1997, of the total of 3.9 million grandchildren living in grandparent-maintained families, 32 percent lived with both grandparents with some parents present; 15 percent with both grandparents with no parents present; 29 percent with their grandmother only with some parents present; and 17 percent with their grandmother only with no parent. Six percent lived with their grandfather only. (See Table 3.4.)

Among children living with their grandparents, there were marked sociological differences between those living in grandparent-maintained homes and in parent-maintained homes with coresident grandparents. Of the 3.9

TABLE 3.4

Characteristics of grandchildren who are co-resident with grandparents: 1997

(Numbers in thousands. Percent distribution of characteristics)

Characteristics	All co-resident grand-parent families	Grandparent-maintained families						Parent-maintained families				
		Total	Both grand-parents, some parents	Both grand-parents, no parent	Grand-mother only, some parents	Grand-mother only, no parent	Grand-father only	Total	Both grand-parents	Grand-mother only, two parents	Grand-mother only, one parent	Grand-father only
Grandchildren, total (number)	5,435	3,894	1,241	598	1,144	669	242	1,541	246	630	396	269
Percent distribution of grandchildren	100.0	100.0	100.0	100.0	100.0	100.0	100.0	100.0	100.0	100.0	100.0	100.0
Race and ethnicity												
White, non-Hispanic	42.5	42.4	51.7	58.0	35.6	19.3	52.3	42.6	38.7	49.0	26.6	54.9
Black, non-Hispanic	30.1	35.9	18.8	22.3	48.6	62.7	23.8	15.2	3.2	7.9	40.7	5.9
Hispanic	18.2	16.5	21.0	15.2	12.5	14.7	20.6	22.6	20.0	21.4	23.7	26.5
Other, non-Hispanic	9.2	5.1	8.5	4.6	3.2	3.3	3.2	19.5	38.2	21.7	9.0	12.7
Age												
Under 6	46.0	50.8	66.3	36.1	56.7	27.1	45.6	33.7	49.0	25.8	39.4	29.7
6 to 11	30.9	28.8	24.5	28.9	26.6	40.0	29.8	36.4	33.8	38.5	33.7	38.2
12 to 17	23.1	20.4	9.2	35.0	16.7	32.8	24.7	29.9	17.2	35.7	26.9	32.1
Gender												
Male	48.8	48.3	51.1	43.3	48.6	45.8	50.8	50.1	39.9	55.5	43.1	57.2
Female	51.2	51.7	48.9	56.7	51.4	54.2	49.2	49.9	60.1	45.5	56.9	42.8
Nativity												
U.S. born, U.S. parents	77.7	86.7	80.1	87.8	90.2	92.7	84.2	55.0	43.7	48.1	68.1	62.1
U.S. born, 1 foreign parent	6.7	6.0	9.1	4.3	4.7	4.2	5.5	8.3	7.7	10.0	6.2	8.1
U.S. born, 2 foreign parents	12.8	5.8	9.6	6.1	3.5	2.1	6.1	30.5	45.7	32.4	22.4	23.9
Foreign born	2.9	1.5	1.1	1.7	1.6	0.9	4.2	6.2	3.0	9.5	3.3	5.8
General state of health												
Excellent	40.7	39.6	42.2	40.4	42.3	34.6	24.9	43.4	53.4	42.1	35.7	48.8
Very good	29.0	27.8	28.1	30.3	25.7	26.5	33.0	32.2	26.9	35.1	27.0	38.2
Good	25.7	27.5	26.5	24.4	27.2	29.5	36.6	21.2	16.3	19.4	34.0	11.0
Fair or poor	4.6	5.2	3.3	4.9	4.8	9.4	5.5	3.1	3.5	3.4	3.2	2.1
Insurance coverage												
Private insurance	39.5	30.3	38.2	18.6	38.1	14.0	27.5	62.5	66.4	75.3	42.6	58.2
Public insurance only	31.3	36.3	31.7	27.2	36.8	52.8	34.3	18.8	16.3	9.2	37.0	17.0
No health insurance	29.2	33.4	30.1	54.2	25.2	33.2	38.2	18.7	17.3	15.5	20.4	24.7
Region of U.S.												
Northeast	20.1	18.7	19.1	17.6	15.5	24.2	18.9	23.7	20.8	25.6	25.5	19.1
Midwest	16.1	16.9	15.0	19.1	18.7	17.7	9.4	14.3	7.2	12.6	21.2	14.3
South	39.3	43.3	38.2	44.8	49.6	44.0	34.8	29.0	23.8	22.8	41.2	30.4
West	24.5	21.1	27.7	18.4	16.2	14.0	37.0	33.0	48.2	38.9	12.1	36.2
Metropolitan area status												
Central city	37.8	38.9	31.1	23.9	44.2	60.4	31.2	35.1	33.3	29.7	50.4	26.6
Suburbs	44.5	41.3	51.4	43.4	35.6	26.6	51.8	52.5	50.7	62.6	35.1	56.1
Nonmetropolitan area	17.7	19.8	17.5	32.6	20.2	13.0	16.9	12.5	16.0	7.7	14.6	17.3
Household members under 18												
One	29.2	31.9	32.4	48.2	27.6	24.6	30.0	22.3	32.1	21.1	24.4	12.9
Two	31.8	29.2	34.8	15.2	31.4	24.7	37.9	38.2	26.9	37.8	39.1	48.3
Three or more	39.0	38.9	32.9	36.6	41.0	50.7	32.1	39.5	41.0	41.1	36.5	38.8
Earners in household												
None	11.7	14.4	4.1	11.3	10.7	43.9	10.6	4.8	0.9	0.8	15.1	2.5
One	26.2	27.3	14.6	31.9	31.6	37.9	31.8	23.5	11.7	12.5	47.2	25.2
Two	32.4	28.0	22.7	35.1	37.7	11.3	37.1	43.5	38.9	57.3	27.3	39.4
Three or more	29.7	30.3	58.6	21.7	19.9	6.9	20.5	28.2	48.4	29.4	10.3	33.0
Family income/poverty level												
Under 50 percent of poverty level	9.2	10.7	1.5	6.8	11.5	29.4	12.0	5.4	2.1	0.0	17.4	3.6
50 to 99 percent of poverty level	14.9	16.2	10.1	8.2	18.0	33.4	11.1	11.8	9.6	8.0	21.4	8.4
100 to 149 percent of poverty level	13.7	14.6	11.2	15.8	17.5	16.8	9.6	11.5	10.7	7.6	19.1	10.4
150 to 199 percent of poverty level	12.9	13.5	14.8	14.5	15.0	7.6	13.7	11.4	3.9	11.7	15.7	11.2
200 percent or more of poverty level	49.2	45.0	62.4	54.7	38.0	12.8	53.7	59.9	73.7	72.7	26.4	66.4
Household public assistance												
No public assistance	48.1	43.8	58.7	50.7	39.8	15.6	47.2	59.1	69.7	68.1	32.3	67.9
Any public assistance program	51.9	56.2	41.3	49.3	60.2	84.4	52.8	40.9	30.3	31.9	67.7	32.1
School lunch program	37.5	40.0	26.0	34.1	40.3	73.5	32.5	31.1	20.4	24.4	52.4	25.2
Food stamps	26.6	30.3	20.3	20.0	37.6	48.3	22.5	17.3	10.1	10.8	37.9	8.7
AFDC, ADC, TANF, GA	20.6	24.5	18.1	20.8	26.4	40.3	14.1	10.5	2.5	4.1	30.4	3.5
SSI	14.9	15.5	9.9	13.2	16.9	28.1	8.7	13.4	5.3	12.7	22.2	9.7
Housing assistance	7.4	8.5	2.0	3.6	7.5	26.3	9.4	4.5	0.0	3.6	11.2	0.9
Energy assistance	5.2	6.7	3.8	2.9	7.0	17.4	0.0	1.3	0.0	1.3	2.9	0.1

SOURCE: Ken Bryson and Lynne M. Casper, *Co-resident Grandparents and Grandchildren*, U.S. Bureau of the Census, Washington, D.C., 1999

FIGURE 3.7

Families with co-resident grandparents and grandchildren: 1997
Percent distribution of family type

SOURCE: Ken Bryson and Lynne M. Casper, *Co-resident Grandparents and Grandchildren*, U.S. Bureau of the Census, Washington, D.C., 1999

FIGURE 3.8

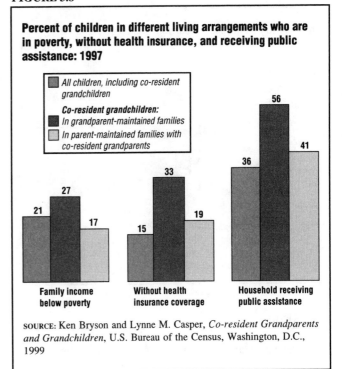

Percent of children in different living arrangements who are in poverty, without health insurance, and receiving public assistance: 1997

All children, including co-resident grandchildren
Co-resident grandchildren:
In grandparent-maintained families
In parent-maintained families with co-resident grandparents

SOURCE: Ken Bryson and Lynne M. Casper, *Co-resident Grandparents and Grandchildren*, U.S. Bureau of the Census, Washington, D.C., 1999

million children living in grandparent-maintained homes, 51 percent were under the age of six; 86.7 percent were born in the United States to U.S. parents; only 30.3 percent had private insurance coverage; and 14.4 percent had no income earner in the household. (See Table 3.4.)

In comparison, of the 1.5 million children living in parent-maintained homes with coresident grandparents, 33.7 percent were under the age of six; 55 percent were born in the United States to U.S. parents; 62.5 percent had private health insurance coverage; and only 5.4 percent had no income earner in the household. (See Table 3.4.) Children living in either grandmother-only homes with or without a parent present, or in parent-maintained homes with a grandmother and only one parent present, were more likely to be black, reside in the South, and live in central cities. (See Table 3.4.)

Children living in grandparent-maintained families had a higher incidence of living below poverty level (27 percent), being without any form of health insurance coverage (33 percent), and receiving public assistance (56 percent) than children living with grandparents in a parent-maintained home (17 percent, 19 percent, and 41 percent, respectively). (See Figure 3.8.)

ADOPTED AND FOSTER CHILDREN

Many American families who want to adopt a child consider two groups of available children:

- Children, primarily infants, whose parents voluntarily give them up for adoption. The parents generally deal with private adoption agencies or make private placements with adoptive families. The number of these adoptees is unknown.

- Children who have been placed in foster care based on court determination that they were abused or neglected, and for whom placement with adoptive families would serve the children's best interests.

Adopted Children

It is difficult to determine the actual number of adopted children in the United States because no comprehensive federal registry exists. Additionally, an unknown number of private adoptions occur each year. The National Center for State Courts provides the most recent reliable data, which are a compilation of 1992 statistics from state agencies. Of the 127,441 adopted children counted by state agencies, 42 percent were adopted by relatives or stepparents. Only 16 percent were adopted from the foster care system.

The National Council for Adoption (NCFA) estimates that nearly half of those children adopted by nonrelatives in 1992 were infants under the age of two. The rest were children with special needs—some had physical, mental, or emotional disabilities; others were part of sibling groups that did not want to be broken up.

In an attempt to make it easier for families to adopt, several laws have been enacted. In 1993 President Clinton signed into law the Family and Medical Leave Act (PL 103-3), enabling parents to take time off work to adopt a child without losing their jobs or health insurance.

In August 1996 he signed into law the Adoption Tax Credit and Gross Income Exclusion, part of the Small

FIGURE 3.9

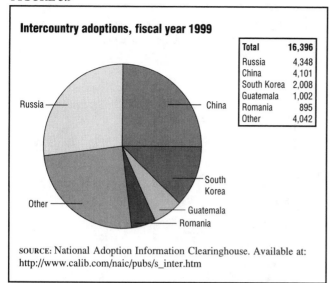

Intercountry adoptions, fiscal year 1999

Total	16,396
Russia	4,348
China	4,101
South Korea	2,008
Guatemala	1,002
Romania	895
Other	4,042

SOURCE: National Adoption Information Clearinghouse. Available at: http://www.calib.com/naic/pubs/s_inter.htm

FIGURE 3.10

Foreign-born adopted children, by sex, fiscal year 1998

Female 9,511 (64%)
Male 5,355 (46%)

SOURCE: National Adoption Information Clearinghouse. Available at: http://www.calib.com/naic/pubs/s_inter.htm

FIGURE 3.11

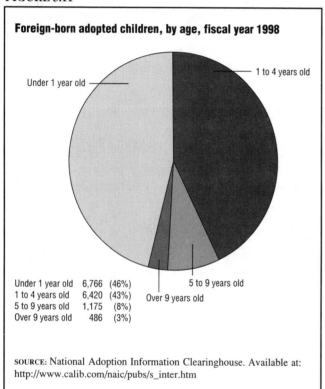

Foreign-born adopted children, by age, fiscal year 1998

Under 1 year old	6,766	(46%)
1 to 4 years old	6,420	(43%)
5 to 9 years old	1,175	(8%)
Over 9 years old	486	(3%)

SOURCE: National Adoption Information Clearinghouse. Available at: http://www.calib.com/naic/pubs/s_inter.htm

Business Job Protection Act of 1996 (PL 104-188). This law provides a $5,000 tax credit to families adopting children, and a $6,000 tax credit for families adopting children with special needs. The tax credit is designed to help middle-class families for whom adoption may be prohibitively expensive. Since 1993 the number of children with special needs who were adopted with federal assistance has increased by 60 percent.

The Inter-ethnic Adoption Provisions of the Small Business Job Protection Act of 1996 further amended the Multi-ethnic Placement Act of 1994 (PL 103-382) to ensure that the adoption process is free from discrimination and delays based on the race, culture, and ethnicity of the child or the prospective parents.

INTERCOUNTRY ADOPTION. Many American families choose to adopt children from other countries. In the 1970s most children adopted from outside the United States were Korean. By the late 1990s most were adopted from China and Russia. Because these foreign-born children require visas to enter the United States, the U.S. Department of State has current records of the numbers of foreign adoptees.

During fiscal year 1999 American households adopted 16,396 orphaned children from other countries. Twenty-seven percent were from Russia, 25 percent from China, 12 percent from South Korea, 6 percent from Guatemala, 5 percent from Romania, and 25 percent from other countries. (See Figure 3.9.)

In fiscal year 1998, 64 percent of the children adopted from overseas were female and 36 percent were male. (See Figure 3.10.) Forty-six percent of these children were under a year of age; 43 percent were 1–4 years old; and the rest were 5 or older. (See Figure 3.11.) The five primary states adopting foreign-born children were New York, California, Pennsylvania, New Jersey, and Illinois. (See Figure 3.12.)

In another effort to help adoptive parents, in October 2000 President Bill Clinton signed into law the Child Citizenship Act of 2000, which provides automatic citizenship to children adopted by U.S. citizens.

Children in Foster Care

Foster care is an integral part of the child welfare system, designed to provide temporary respite and some stability for children whose families are having difficulties parenting or are no longer able to care for them. Some

FIGURE 3.12

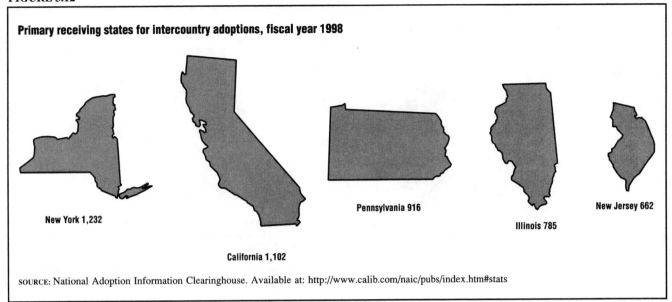

Primary receiving states for intercountry adoptions, fiscal year 1998

New York 1,232

California 1,102

Pennsylvania 916

Illinois 785

New Jersey 662

SOURCE: National Adoption Information Clearinghouse. Available at: http://www.calib.com/naic/pubs/index.htm#stats

children remain in foster care until their parents resolve the problems that led to the children's placement in foster care. Other children cannot safely return home and, therefore, wait with their foster family until they are permanently placed with an adoptive family.

According to the Children's Bureau of the U.S. Department of Health and Human Services, as of March 31, 1999, 547,000 children were in foster care, up from 340,000 in 1988. In fiscal year 1998, 36,000 children were adopted from the public foster care system and 117,000 foster children who could not return safely to their birth families awaited adoption.

AGE, SEX, AND RACE/ETHNICITY. In 1999 almost 63 percent of foster children were 6 or older; 35 percent were 1–5 years old; and only 2 percent were under a year old. (See Figure 3.13.) There were equally as many male (52 percent) as female (48 percent) children in foster care. (See Figure 3.14.) Almost 43 percent were black, and more than 36 percent were white. Hispanic children made up 15 percent, while Asian/Pacific Islander, American Indian children, and children of unknown ethnicity comprised 6 percent. (See Figure 3.15.)

LENGTH OF STAY AND REASON FOR DISCHARGE. A child's stay in foster care can vary from less than a month to 5 or more years. In 1999 about 27 percent were in foster care for 6–17 months. An almost equal proportion (23 percent) stayed in foster care 2.5–4 years. (See Figure 3.16.) In 1999 nearly 41 percent of foster children were reunited with their parent(s) or primary custodian; 4 percent went to live with other relative(s); and 20 percent were adopted—an increase of 8 percent from 1996. (See Figure 3.17.)

VICTIMS OF ABUSE AND NEGLECT. According to *Child Maltreatment 1998: Reports from the States to the Nation-*

al Child Abuse and Neglect Data System (Department of Health and Human Services, Administration for the Children and Families) many children entering the foster care system are victims of abuse and/or neglect—a majority coming from families with substance abuse problems. Fortunately, however, abuse and neglect statistics continue to decline. In 1998 child protective services agencies from 48 states reported that approximately 903,000 children were victims of maltreatment, a national rate of 12.9 victims per 1,000 children under the age of 18. This was a record low from the national high of just over 1 million in 1993.

Parents continue to be the main perpetrators of child maltreatment: More than 80 percent of all victims were abused or neglected by one or both parents. The most common pattern of maltreatment (45 percent) involved a child being victimized by a female parent acting alone. Compared with victims of neglect, victims of physical and sexual abuse were more likely to be maltreated by a male parent acting alone.

In 1998, 7.2 per 1,000 children suffered neglect; 2.9 per 1,000 were physically abused; 1.6 per 1,000 were sexually abused; and 0.6 per 1,000 were psychologically abused. (See Figure 3.18.) Most victims were younger children: 14.8 per 1,000 were 3 or younger, and 14.4 per 1,000 were 4–7. By the age of 16–17, the rate dropped to 6.6 per 1,000. (See Figure 3.19.)

ADOPTING FOSTER CHILDREN. In 1997 the Clinton Administration launched the "Adoption 2002" initiative, with the goal of doubling the number of foster children adopted each year—from approximately 27,000 in 1996 to a projected 54,000 in 2002. To this end, on November 19, 1997, President Clinton signed the Adoption and Safe Families Act of 1997 (PL 105-89), which requires, among other provisions, permanency hearings to be held no later

FIGURE 3.13

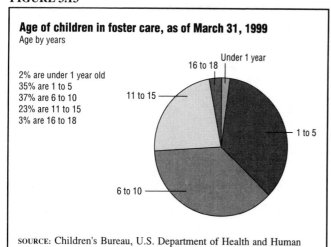

Age of children in foster care, as of March 31, 1999
Age by years

2% are under 1 year old
35% are 1 to 5
37% are 6 to 10
23% are 11 to 15
3% are 16 to 18

SOURCE: Children's Bureau, U.S. Department of Health and Human Services. Using data collected through the Adoption and Foster Care Analysis and Reporting System (AFCARS), January 2000

FIGURE 3.14

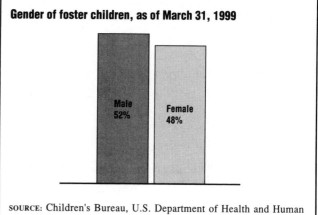

Gender of foster children, as of March 31, 1999

SOURCE: Children's Bureau, U.S. Department of Health and Human Services. Using data collected through the Adoption and Foster Care Analysis and Reporting System (AFCARS), January 2000

FIGURE 3.15

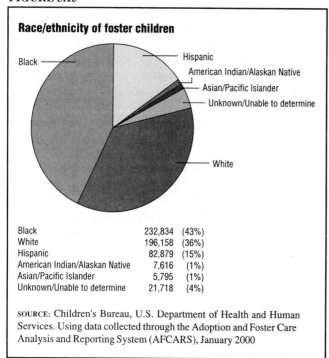

Race/ethnicity of foster children

Black	232,834	(43%)
White	196,158	(36%)
Hispanic	82,879	(15%)
American Indian/Alaskan Native	7,616	(1%)
Asian/Pacific Islander	5,795	(1%)
Unknown/Unable to determine	21,718	(4%)

SOURCE: Children's Bureau, U.S. Department of Health and Human Services. Using data collected through the Adoption and Foster Care Analysis and Reporting System (AFCARS), January 2000

FIGURE 3.16

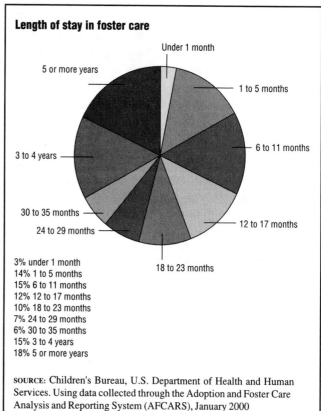

Length of stay in foster care

3% under 1 month
14% 1 to 5 months
15% 6 to 11 months
12% 12 to 17 months
10% 18 to 23 months
7% 24 to 29 months
6% 30 to 35 months
15% 3 to 4 years
18% 5 or more years

SOURCE: Children's Bureau, U.S. Department of Health and Human Services. Using data collected through the Adoption and Foster Care Analysis and Reporting System (AFCARS), January 2000

than 12 months after a child enters foster care. The federal government offers financial incentives to states to increase adoption rates; and provides technical assistance to states, courts, and communities in an effort to place children in adoptive homes within a shorter time frame.

Current or former foster youths 16 and older can obtain government assistance during their transition to independent living, through the Independent Living Program. This program provides grants to states for education and employment aid, training in daily living skills, and individual and group counseling.

As reported by the Children's Bureau, U.S. Department of Health and Human Services, in 1996 an almost equal pro-

portion of male (51 percent) and female (48 percent) foster children were adopted. Approximately 61 percent are of minority background: 46 percent are black; 13 percent, Hispanic; 1 percent, American Indian; and 1 percent, Asian/Pacific Islander. Approximately 36 percent are white.

CHILD CARE

During the 1970s, 1980s, and 1990s, one of the most dramatic changes in the structure of the American family has been the increased employment of mothers outside the home. In 1999, according to *Child Health USA 2000*, 65 percent of mothers with preschool-aged children were in the labor force (either employed or looking for work) and 61 percent were actually employed. Of those mothers, 70 percent were employed full-time and 30 percent worked part-time. Seventy-eight percent more mothers of older children (6–17 years old) worked in 1999. Of those mothers, 77 percent worked full-time and 23 percent worked part-time.

As more and more mothers hold paying jobs, the issue of child care becomes a great concern, not only for parents but also for policy-makers. The implementation of the welfare reform legislation, which requires welfare recipients to work, has further pushed the continuing problem of available child care to the forefront.

FIGURE 3.17

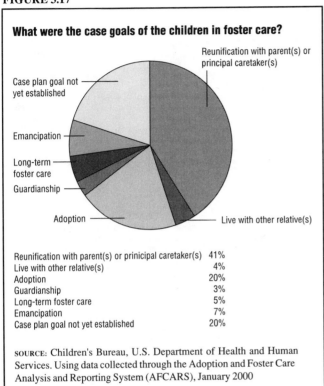

What were the case goals of the children in foster care?

Reunification with parent(s) or prinicipal caretaker(s)	41%
Live with other relative(s)	4%
Adoption	20%
Guardianship	3%
Long-term foster care	5%
Emancipation	7%
Case plan goal not yet established	20%

SOURCE: Children's Bureau, U.S. Department of Health and Human Services. Using data collected through the Adoption and Foster Care Analysis and Reporting System (AFCARS), January 2000

FIGURE 3.18

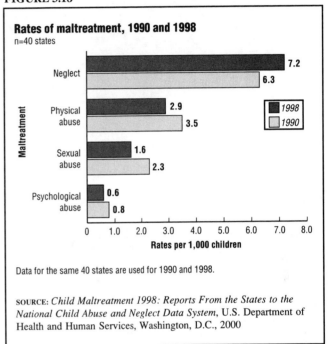

Rates of maltreatment, 1990 and 1998
n=40 states

Data for the same 40 states are used for 1990 and 1998.

SOURCE: *Child Maltreatment 1998: Reports From the States to the National Child Abuse and Neglect Data System*, U.S. Department of Health and Human Services, Washington, D.C., 2000

FIGURE 3.19

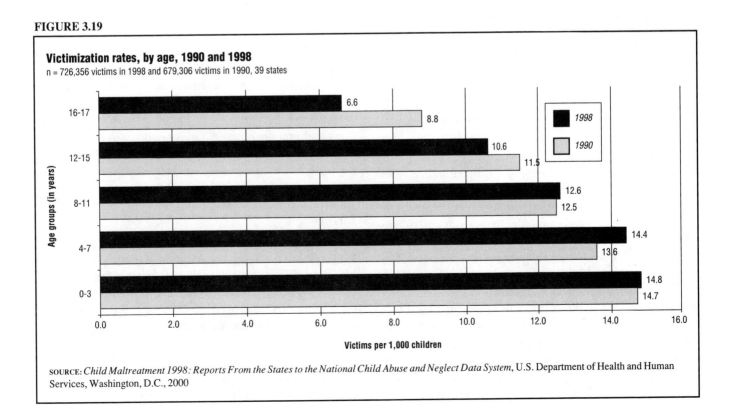

Victimization rates, by age, 1990 and 1998
n = 726,356 victims in 1998 and 679,306 victims in 1990, 39 states

SOURCE: *Child Maltreatment 1998: Reports From the States to the National Child Abuse and Neglect Data System*, U.S. Department of Health and Human Services, Washington, D.C., 2000

FIGURE 3.20

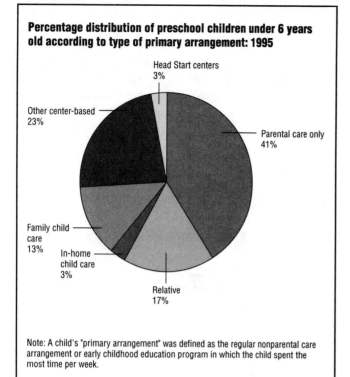

Percentage distribution of preschool children under 6 years old according to type of primary arrangement: 1995

Head Start centers
3%

Other center-based
23%

Parental care only
41%

Family child care
13%

In-home child care
3%

Relative
17%

Note: A child's "primary arrangement" was defined as the regular nonparental care arrangement or early childhood education program in which the child spent the most time per week.

SOURCE: *Characteristics of Children's Early Care and Education Programs: Data from the 1995 National Household Education Survey*, National Center for Education Statistics, Washington, D.C., 1998

FIGURE 3.21

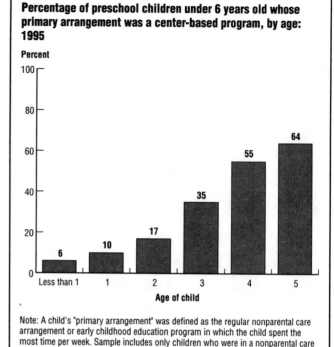

Percentage of preschool children under 6 years old whose primary arrangement was a center-based program, by age: 1995

Percent

Age of child	Percent
Less than 1	6
1	10
2	17
3	35
4	55
5	64

Note: A child's "primary arrangement" was defined as the regular nonparental care arrangement or early childhood education program in which the child spent the most time per week. Sample includes only children who were in a nonparental care arrangement or early childhood education program on a regular basis.

SOURCE: *Characteristics of Children's Early Care and Education Programs: Data from the 1995 National Household Education Survey*, National Center for Education Statistics, Washington, D.C., 1998

While previous studies found parents to be primarily concerned about the cost and convenience of child care settings, new research shows that parents are more aware of the impact that trained child care providers have on their children's cognitive and social development. The 1995 National Household Education Survey (see below) found that a child care provider's training in child development is the primary quality characteristic for which most parents are apparently willing to pay more, and which is closely linked with parents' choice of child care providers.

Preschoolers

In 1995 the National Center for Education Statistics (NCES) conducted a survey to examine the characteristics of the care and education that preschoolers (those under the age of 6) received on a regular basis from individuals and child care facilities. In *Characteristics of Children's Early Care and Education Programs: Data from the 1995 National Household Education Survey* (Sandra L. Hofferth, Kimberlee A. Shauman, Robert R. Henke, and Jerry West, U.S. Department of Education, Washington, D.C., 1998) the researchers reported that 41 percent of preschoolers were cared for by their parents only. The other 59 percent received other forms of nonparental care: 3 percent in Head Start, 23 percent in center-based care (not including Head Start), 17 percent in relative care, 13 percent in family child care, and 3 percent in in-home child care. (See Figure 3.20.)

DEFINITIONS OF NONPARENTAL CHILD CARE ARRANGEMENTS. Head Start is a government program for preschool children whose family income is below the federal poverty level and for children who have disabilities. Center-based programs refer to organized child care facilities, such as day care centers, nursery schools, or preschools. Relative care is provided by any of the child's relatives, such as siblings and grandparents. A family child care provider is a nonrelative who cares for one or more unrelated children in his or her home, and an in-home baby-sitter is a nonrelative who provides care within the child's home.

Infants

Many parents prefer to keep their infants and very young children in a home environment for as long as possible. The 1995 National Household Education Survey reported that, while fewer than 10 percent of infants were cared for in center-based programs, almost 2 in 3 (64 percent) 5-year-olds were enrolled in such facilities. (See Figure 3.21.)

Cost

The cost of child care varied with the type of care or education provided. Overall, for 68 percent of parents with children in child care, child care cost an average of $2.15 an hour. The most expensive arrangements on an hourly basis were in-home care ($3.02) and non–Head Start center-based programs ($2.39). Parents paid less for family child care ($1.84) and relative care ($1.63). (See Table 3.5.) The survey researchers noted that Head Start programs are free to eligible children. The 13 percent of parents who paid may have been ineligible families, since some Head Start centers combine both categories of children. However, the Census Bureau reported that child care costs nationwide increased 44 percent from 1985 to 1995.

Characteristics of Primary Nonparental Care

Overall, the child/staff ratio in nonparental child care was 4.2 children per care provider. For 60 percent of children, the primary care arrangement was located less than 10 minutes from home. For 47 percent, sick care was available. Fifty-eight percent were cared for by providers educated or trained in child development; and, for 94 percent, English was the primary language. (See Table 3.5.)

Latchkey Children

"Latchkey" children are children who are left alone or unsupervised during the day or who are home alone before and/or after school. The incidence of latchkey children has been a concern since World War II, a time when many mothers took over the jobs left vacant by servicemen. In the mid-1960s, when the number of mothers entering the labor force increased, the U.S. Department of Labor reported that there were approximately 1 million latchkey children in the United States. Some 18 percent of children 5–14 years old were left alone after school for an average of 6.1 hours per week ("Who's Minding the Kids? Child Care Arrangements," *Current Population Reports,* U.S. Bureau of the Census, October 2000). By the late 1900s an estimated 3.5 million children under the age of 13 spent some time at home alone each week (*Kids Count Data Book: State Profiles of Child Well-Being,* The Annie E. Casey Foundation, Baltimore, MD, 1998). This estimate does not include children who are unsupervised on a temporary or occasional basis.

Child Care for the Working Poor

Since the 1930s the federal government has subsidized child care for low-income families. The Child Care and Development Fund (CCDF), authorized by the Personal Responsibility and Work Opportunity Reconciliation Act of 1996 (PL 104-193), helps low-income families and those getting off welfare to obtain child care so they can pursue employment, job training, or education.

HEAD START. Head Start is perhaps the best known and most successful federal early-childhood program. Created in 1965 as part of President Lyndon Johnson's "War on Poverty," the program provides comprehensive early-childhood services for low-income children from

FIGURE 3.22

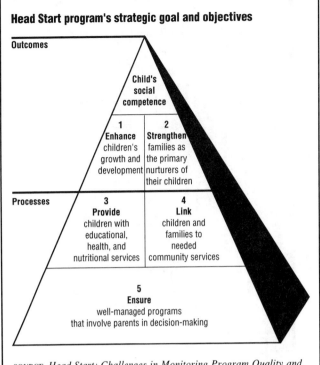

Head Start program's strategic goal and objectives

Outcomes

Child's social competence

| 1 Enhance children's growth and development | 2 Strengthen families as the primary nurturers of their children |

Processes

| 3 Provide children with educational, health, and nutritional services | 4 Link children and families to needed community services |

5 Ensure well-managed programs that involve parents in decision-making

SOURCE: *Head Start: Challenges in Monitoring Program Quality and Demonstrating Results*, U.S. General Accounting Office, 1998

birth to 5 years old. It also provides medical, nutritional, mental health, dental, and social services to these children and their families. (See Figure 3.22.)

Since the 1970s Head Start has served approximately 16 million low-income preschool children. During fiscal year 1998 approximately 822,000 preschoolers were served by Head Start programs, at a total cost of $4.3 billion to the federal government. Money for the program is expected to increase, so that an estimated 1 million children will be served by the year 2002.

When Parents Work Nonstandard Hours

Since the early 1980s many Americans have had longer work weeks. As more businesses operate during nonstandard hours—early mornings, evenings, nights, and weekends—working parents are faced with significant child care problems. A notable proportion of those working nonstandard hours are women, many of them mothers. Overall, service jobs, which include many jobs traditionally held by women, have the fastest-growing numbers of shift workers. Between 1998 and 2008, jobs for home health aides will likely increase by 58 percent; for medical assistants, by 58 percent; and for social and human service assistants, by 53 percent. Another fast-growing field is physician assistants (48 percent). (See Table 3.6.)

Some Employers Address Child Care Problems

In the United States, employer-sponsored child care benefits continue to be rare, although the trend toward on-

TABLE 3.5

Of preschool children in nonparental care, percentage whose primary arrangements[1] were paid for; average cost per hour, child/staff ratio, and number of services provided in primary arrangements; and percentage whose primary arrangements had various characteristics, by type of primary arrangement: 1995

| | | | | | | | | | | | | Percent of preschool children whose primary arrangement had characteristic | | | | | | | | |
Primary care type	Percent paying	se*	Average cost per hour[3]	se	Child/staff ratio Average	se	Number of services[2] Average	se	Less than 10-minute commute Percent	se	Provides sick child care Percent	se	Provider trained in child development Percent	se	Parent involvement encouraged[2] Percent	se	English spoken Percent	se
Total	**68**	**1.0**	**2.15**	**0.05**	**4.2**	**0.0**	**1.0**	**0.0**	**60**	**0.9**	**47**	**0.9**	**58**	**0.8**	**64**	**1.4**	**94**	**0.4**
Total center-based	75	1.3	2.37	0.08	6.5	0.1	1.0	0.0	57	1.4	12	0.8	95	0.7	64	1.4	99	0.2
Head Start center	13	2.6	1.58	0.30	6.7	0.2	2.5	0.1	46	4.3	26	3.2	97	1.2	90	2.2	96	1.2
Non-Head Start center	84	1.2	2.39	0.08	6.5	0.1	0.7	0.0	58	1.5	10	0.7	95	0.8	60	1.5	99	0.2
Family child care	95	0.7	1.84	0.04	3.5	0.1	—	—	67	1.6	63	2.1	48	1.9	—	—	94	0.9
In-home child care	86	3.1	3.02	0.32	2.0	0.1	—	—	—	—	78	3.4	33	4.4	—	—	90	2.1
Relative	33	2.0	1.63	0.10	1.6	0.0	—	—	59	2.0	85	1.1	18	1.3	—	—	87	0.8

—Too few cases for a reliable estimate.

* In all instances, "se" indicates standard error. Standard errors less than .05 were rounded to 0.0.

[1] A child's "primary arrangement" was defined as the regular nonparental care arrangement or early childhood education program in which the child spent the most time per week.
[2] Available only for children enrolled in center-based programs.
[3] Average price paid among those who paid for the primary nonparental care arrangement.

SOURCE: *Characteristics of Children's Early Care and Education Programs: Data from the 1995 National Household Education Survey*, National Center for Education Statistics, Washington, D.C., 1998

TABLE 3.6

The 10 fastest growing occupations, 1998–2008
[Numbers in thousands of jobs]

| | Employment | | Change | |
Occupation	1998	2008	Number	Percent
Computer engineers	299	622	323	108
Computer support specialists	429	869	439	102
Systems analysts	617	1,194	577	94
Database administrators	87	155	67	77
Desktop publishing specialiss	26	44	19	73
Paralegals/legal assistants	136	220	84	62
Personal care and home health aides	746	1,179	433	58
Medical assistants	252	398	146	58
Social and human service assistants	268	410	141	53
Physician assistants	66	98	32	48

SOURCE: Department of Labor, Bureau of Labor Statistics, Washington, D.C., February 2000. Available at http://stats.bls.gov/news.release/ecopro.t06.htm

TABLE 3.7

Incidence of childcare benefits in private industry, 1995–96
(in percent)

Employees with childcare benefits	All establishments	Small establishments	Medium and large establishments
All employees	4	2	7
Part-time employees	3	2	6
Full-time employees	4	2	8
Professional and technical	10	4	15
Clerical and sales	4	2	7
Blue-collar and service	2	(¹)	3
Union	2	—	3
Nonunion	5	2	9
Goods producing industries	2	(¹)	4
Service producing	5	2	10
Northeast	6	1	12
South	4	2	7
Midwest	3	2	5
West	4	2	8

¹ Less than 0.5 percent.
Dash (–) indicates zero.

SOURCE: "Employer-Sponsored Childcare Benefits," *Issues in Labor Statistics*, U.S. Bureau of Labor Statistics, Summary 98-9, August 1998

FIGURE 3.23

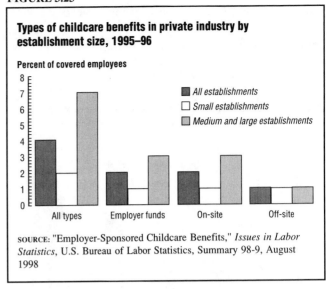

Types of childcare benefits in private industry by establishment size, 1995–96

Percent of covered employees

■ All establishments
□ Small establishments
▨ Medium and large establishments

SOURCE: "Employer-Sponsored Childcare Benefits," *Issues in Labor Statistics*, U.S. Bureau of Labor Statistics, Summary 98-9, August 1998

---

site child care is increasing. In 1995–96 private industry offered such benefits to 1 in 25 employees. These benefits included employer-managed facilities (on and off the work site) and direct payments to other child care providers. Some employers helped parents with child care expenses through reimbursement accounts that were funded with employee pretax contributions. (See Figure 3.23.) Approximately 1 in 5 employees worked for a company with such reimbursement accounts.

Employees in medium and large establishments (7 percent) were more likely than those in smaller establishments (2 percent) to receive child care benefits. Full-time employees (4 percent) were just as likely to receive these benefits as were part-time employees (3 percent). Among full-time employees, 15 percent of professional and technical employees in medium and large establishments had child care benefits, compared with less than 1 percent of blue-collar and service workers in small establishments. (See Table 3.7.)

There was a significant difference between the child care benefits offered to full-time union (2 percent) and non-union (5 percent) members, as well as between benefits provided to full-time employees in the goods-producing (2 percent) and service-producing (5 percent) sectors. Child care benefits did not differ greatly among the different geographic regions in the country. (See Table 3.7.) According to the Bureau of Labor Statistics, based on its 1994 Employee Benefits Survey, there was little difference in the incidence of child care benefits between state and local government workers and those in private industry.

FINDING CHILD CARE RESOURCES CAN BE CHALLENGING. According to a June 2000 survey conducted by the Bureau of Labor Statistics, only 13.8 percent of workers in private industry and state and local governments had access to child care resource and referral services. Most often, these services were provided to employees by outside resources rather than by their employers.

People working for large establishments (those employing 5,000 or more workers) fare best when seeking child care. Data show that 45.8 percent of these employees had access to child care resources and referral services, compared with only 4.5 percent of employees working in small businesses (those employing 100 or fewer workers). (See Figure 3.24.)

INCOME TAX CREDIT. Employees whose companies do not offer child care benefits can offset child care expenses through the child care credit provision when filing their federal income taxes. A married taxpayer filing a joint return, or a single taxpayer filing as head of household, can take a credit of up to $4,800 against his or her annual federal income taxes for children in child care.

However, those who make too little money to pay income tax are not eligible to file for income tax credit.

EXPENDITURES ON CHILDREN

The U.S. Department of Agriculture (USDA) estimates the annual expenditures on children from birth through age 17 years for husband–wife and single-parent families. These estimated expenses vary significantly according to family household income level. Expenditures include seven major budgetary components: housing, food, transportation, clothing, health care, child care and education, and miscellaneous expenses (personal care items, entertainment, and reading materials). The study demonstrates a fact of life for these families—no matter what the income bracket, it is expensive to raise a family.

In Married-Couple Families

Expenses vary considerably by household income level. Depending upon the age of the child, expenses range from $6,080 for families in the lowest income group (1999 before-tax income less than $36,800) to $8,540 for families in the middle income group (1999 before-tax income between $36,800 and $61,900) to $12,550 for families in the highest income group (1999

FIGURE 3.24

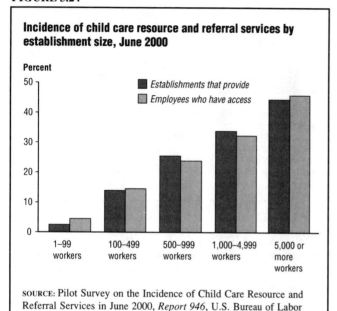

Incidence of child care resource and referral services by establishment size, June 2000

SOURCE: Pilot Survey on the Incidence of Child Care Resource and Referral Services in June 2000, *Report 946*, U.S. Bureau of Labor Statistics, November 2000

TABLE 3.8

Estimated annual expenditures* on a child by husband-wife families, 1999

Age of Child	Total	Housing	Food	Transpor-tation	Clothing	Health care	Child care and education	Miscel-laneous[†]
Before-tax income: Less than $36,800 (Average=$23,000)								
0 - 2	$6,080	$2,320	$860	$730	$380	$430	$760	$600
3 - 5	6,210	2,290	960	700	370	410	860	620
6 - 8	6,310	2,210	1,240	820	410	470	510	650
9 - 11	6,330	2,000	1,480	890	460	510	310	680
12 - 14	7,150	2,230	1,560	1,000	770	510	220	860
15 - 17	7,050	1,800	1,680	1,350	680	550	360	630
Total	$117,390	$38,550	$23,340	$16,470	$9,210	$8,640	$9,060	$12,120
Before-tax income: $36,800 to $61,900 (Average=$49,000)								
0 - 2	$8,450	$3,140	$1,030	$1,090	$450	$560	$1,250	$930
3 - 5	8,660	3,110	1,190	1,060	440	530	1,380	950
6 - 8	8,700	3,030	1,520	1,180	480	610	890	990
9 - 11	8,650	2,820	1,790	1,250	530	660	580	1,020
12 - 14	9,390	3,050	1,800	1,360	900	670	420	1,190
15 - 17	9,530	2,620	2,000	1,720	800	700	730	960
Total	$160,140	$53,310	$27,990	$22,980	$10,800	$11,190	$15,750	$18,120
Before-tax income: More than $61,900 (Average=$92,700)								
0 - 2	$12,550	$4,990	$1,370	$1,520	$590	$640	$1,880	$1,560
3 - 5	12,840	4,960	1,550	1,500	580	620	2,050	1,580
6 - 8	12,710	4,880	1,870	1,610	630	700	1,410	1,610
9 - 11	12,600	4,670	2,170	1,680	690	760	980	1,650
12 - 14	13,450	4,900	2,280	1,800	1,140	760	750	1,820
15 - 17	13,800	4,470	2,400	2,180	1,030	800	1,330	1,590
Total	$233,850	$86,610	$34,920	$30,870	$13,980	$12,840	$25,200	$29,430

*Estimates are based on 1990-92 Consumer Expenditure Survey data updated to 1999 dollars using the Consumer Price Index. For each age category, the expense estimates represent average child-rearing expenditures for each age (e.g., the expense for the 3-5 age category, on average, applies to the 3-year-old, the 4-year-old, or the 5-year-old). The figures represent estimated expenses on the younger child in a two-child family. Estimates are about the same for the older child, so to calculate expenses for two children, figures should be summed for the appropriate age categories. To estimate expenses for an only child, multiply the total expense for the appropriate age category by 1.24. To estimate expenses for each child in a family with three or more children, multiply the total expense for each appropriate age category by 0.77. For expenses on all children in a family, these totals should be summed.

[†]Miscellaneous expenses include personal care items, entertainment, and reading materials.

SOURCE: Mark Lino, *Expenditures on Children by Families, 1999 Annual Report*, U.S. Department of Agriculture, 2000

before-tax income more than $61,900). Compared with expenditures for each child in a two-child family, households with only one child spend an average of 24 percent more on the single child, while families with three or more children spend an average of 23 percent less on each child. (See Table 3.8.)

Housing accounts for the largest share of child-rearing expenses across income groups, accounting for 33–37 percent of expenses. Food is the second-largest child-rearing expense, accounting for 20–37 percent of expenses. Expenditures on children are lower in the younger age categories and higher in the older age categories. This held across all income groups.

In Single-Parent Families

The number of single-parent families continues to rise. The costs of raising a child in a single-parent household are similar to those of husband–wife families. The primary difference is that the majority of single-parent households are generally in the lower income group. However, in single-parent households with two children, approximately 7 percent less is spent on the older child than on the younger child at a specific age category. Additionally, more is spent on the child if a single-parent household has only one child, while, conversely, less is spent per child if a single-parent household has three or more children.

CHAPTER 4
SOCIAL ISSUES AFFECTING AMERICA'S CHILDREN

In 1998 George Gallup, Jr., the founder and chairman of the George H. Gallup International Institute, made several observations about American youth on the 20th anniversary of *The Gallup Youth Survey*. These observations included an enthusiasm among young people to help others, a desire to work toward world peace and health, and a positive perspective about the performance of their schools and, in particular, their teachers. Most had a happy and excited perspective about the future, a feeling of closeness with their families, a general satisfaction with their personal lives, a goal to attain the top of their chosen careers, and a belief that they would marry and have children.

Gallup also observed that, in contrast, these same youths understood they had many challenges to face. For example, Gallup's survey showed that one in five children lived below the poverty level, 10 million had no medical insurance, homicide and suicide killed approximately 7,000 of them each year, one in 4 had an unwed mother—some of these mothers being mere children themselves—and (at the time of the survey) 135 children brought guns to school each day.

CHILD POVERTY

In 1974 there were 66.1 million children under the age of 18 years. Of that number, 10.2 million (15.4 percent) lived in poverty. This was the first year that children replaced the poor elderly (3 million, or 14.6 percent of the 21.1 million elderly) as the poorest age group. In 1999 12.1 million (16.9 percent) children in all households (71.7 million), and 11.5 million (16.3 percent) related children in all families (70.5 million) were poor. These poverty rates were one-and-a-half times the rates for adults ages 18–64 years (17 million, or 10 percent, of 169 million) and for those 65 and over (3.2 million, or 9.7 percent, of 32.6 million). (See Table 4.1.)

In 1999 children under the age of 18 years represented approximately one-quarter of the total population. (See

Figure 3.2 in Chapter 3.) However, they comprised nearly 40 percent of the poor population. According to the National Center for Children in Poverty at Columbia University, New York, New York, the United States had the highest rate of child poverty among all Western industrialized nations.

Children younger than 6 years of age were particularly vulnerable. In 1999, overall, related children under the age of 6 years in all families had a poverty rate of 18 percent, although this was significantly less than the 1998 rate of 20.6 percent. Those living in families maintained by women with no spouse present had a poverty rate of 50.3 percent—more than 5 times the rate for children under the age of 6 years in married-couple families (9 percent).

In 1999 minority children continued to be poor at a much higher rate than their white peers. While the poverty rate for white children under 18 years of age was 13.5 percent of all poor children under the age of 18 years, the rate for black children in the same age group was 33.1 percent. Hispanic children had a poverty rate of 30.3 percent, and Asian/Pacific Islander children had a poverty rate of 11.8 percent. (See Table 4.1.) (Hispanics represent an ethnic group and may be of any race.)

Children living in poverty is associated with a number of serious problems that are cause for great concern. In "The High Price of Poverty for Children of the South," (*CDF Reports,* Washington, D.C., May 1998), the Children's Defense Fund, a children's advocacy group, noted some of the consequences of child poverty.

- Poverty is a greater risk to children's overall health status than is living in a single-parent family.

- Poor children are twice as likely as non-poor children to be born weighing too little or to suffer stunted growth.

- Poor children suffer more mental and physical disabilities.

TABLE 4.1

Poverty status of people by age, race, and Hispanic origin: 1959–99

[Numbers in thousands. People as of March of the following year.]

Year and characteristic	Under 18 years — All people — Total	Below poverty level Number	Below poverty level Percent	Related children in families Total	Below poverty level Number	Below poverty level Percent	18 to 64 years Total	Below poverty level Number	Below poverty level Percent	65 years and over Total	Below poverty level Number	Below poverty level Percent
All races												
1999	71,731	12,109	16.9	70,480	11,510	16.3	169,141	16,982	10.0	32,621	3,167	9.7
1998	71,338	13,467	18.9	70,253	12,845	18.3	167,326	17,623	10.5	32,394	3,386	10.5
1997	71,069	14,113	19.9	69,844	13,422	19.2	165,329	18,084	10.9	32,082	3,376	10.5
1996	70,650	14,463	20.5	69,411	13,764	19.8	163,691	18,638	11.4	31,877	3,428	10.8
1995	70,566	14,665	20.8	69,425	13,999	20.2	161,508	18,442	11.4	31,658	3,318	10.5
1994	70,020	15,289	21.8	68,819	14,610	21.2	160,329	19,107	11.9	31,267	3,663	11.7
1993	69,292	15,727	22.7	68,040	14,961	22.0	159,208	19,781	12.4	30,779	3,755	12.2
1992ʳ	68,440	15,294	22.3	67,256	14,521	21.6	157,680	18,793	11.9	30,430	3,928	12.9
1991ʳ	65,918	14,341	21.8	64,800	13,658	21.1	154,684	17,586	11.4	30,590	3,781	12.4
1990	65,049	13,431	20.6	63,908	12,715	19.9	153,502	16,496	10.7	30,093	3,658	12.2
1989	64,144	12,590	19.6	63,225	12,001	19.0	152,282	15,575	10.2	29,566	3,363	11.4
1988ʳ	63,747	12,455	19.5	62,906	11,935	19.0	150,761	15,809	10.5	29,022	3,481	12.0
1987ʳ	63,294	12,843	20.3	62,423	12,275	19.7	149,201	15,815	10.6	28,487	3,563	12.5
1986	62,948	12,876	20.5	62,009	12,257	19.8	147,631	16,017	10.8	27,975	3,477	12.4
1985	62,876	13,010	20.7	62,019	12,483	20.1	146,396	16,598	11.3	27,322	3,456	12.6
1984	62,447	13,420	21.5	61,681	12,929	21.0	144,551	16,952	11.7	26,818	3,330	12.4
1983	62,334	13,911	22.3	61,578	13,427	21.8	143,052	17,767	12.4	26,313	3,625	13.8
1982	62,345	13,647	21.9	61,565	13,139	21.3	141,328	17,000	12.0	25,738	3,751	14.6
1981	62,449	12,505	20.0	61,756	12,068	19.5	139,477	15,464	11.1	25,231	3,853	15.3
1980	62,914	11,543	18.3	62,168	11,114	17.9	137,428	13,858	10.1	24,686	3,871	15.7
1979	63,375	10,377	16.4	62,646	9,993	16.0	135,333	12,014	8.9	24,194	3,682	15.2
1978	62,311	9,931	15.9	61,987	9,722	15.7	130,169	11,332	8.7	23,175	3,233	14.0
1977	63,137	10,288	16.2	62,823	10,028	16.0	128,262	11,316	8.8	22,468	3,177	14.1
1976	64,028	10,273	16.0	63,729	10,081	15.8	126,175	11,389	9.0	22,100	3,313	15.0
1975	65,079	11,104	17.1	64,750	10,882	16.8	124,122	11,456	9.2	21,662	3,317	15.3
1974	66,134	10,156	15.4	65,802	9,967	15.1	122,101	10,132	8.3	21,127	3,085	14.6
1973	66,959	9,642	14.4	66,626	9,453	14.2	120,060	9,977	8.3	20,602	3,354	16.3
1972	67,930	10,284	15.1	67,592	10,082	14.9	117,957	10,438	8.8	20,117	3,738	18.6
1971	68,816	10,551	15.3	68,474	10,344	15.1	115,911	10,735	9.3	19,827	4,273	21.6
1970	69,159	10,440	15.1	68,815	10,235	14.9	113,554	10,187	9.0	19,470	4,793	24.6
1969	69,090	9,691	14.0	68,746	9,501	13.8	111,528	9,669	8.7	18,899	4,787	25.3
1968	70,385	10,954	15.6	70,035	10,739	15.3	108,684	9,803	9.0	18,559	4,632	25.0
1967	70,408	11,656	16.6	70,058	11,427	16.3	107,024	10,725	10.0	18,240	5,388	29.5
1966	70,218	12,389	17.6	69,869	12,146	17.4	105,241	11,007	10.5	17,929	5,114	28.5
1965	69,986	14,676	21.0	69,638	14,388	20.7	(NA)	(NA)	(NA)	(NA)	(NA)	(NA)
1964	69,711	16,051	23.0	69,364	15,736	22.7	(NA)	(NA)	(NA)	(NA)	(NA)	(NA)
1963	69,181	16,005	23.1	68,837	15,691	22.8	(NA)	(NA)	(NA)	(NA)	(NA)	(NA)
1962	67,722	16,963	25.0	67,385	16,630	24.7	(NA)	(NA)	(NA)	(NA)	(NA)	(NA)
1961	66,121	16,909	25.6	65,792	16,577	25.2	(NA)	(NA)	(NA)	(NA)	(NA)	(NA)
1960	65,601	17,634	26.9	65,275	17,288	26.5	(NA)	(NA)	(NA)	(NA)	(NA)	(NA)
1959	64,315	17,552	27.3	63,995	17,208	26.9	96,685	16,457	17.0	15,557	5,481	35.2
White												
1999	56,232	7,568	13.5	55,274	7,123	12.9	139,261	11,945	8.6	28,880	2,409	8.3
1998	56,016	8,443	15.1	55,126	7,935	14.4	138,061	12,456	9.0	28,759	2,555	8.9
1997	55,863	8,990	16.1	54,870	8,441	15.4	136,783	12,838	9.4	28,553	2,569	9.0
1996	55,606	9,044	16.3	54,599	8,488	15.5	135,586	12,940	9.5	28,464	2,667	9.4
1995	55,444	8,981	16.2	54,532	8,474	15.5	134,149	12,869	9.6	28,436	2,572	9.0

TABLE 4.1

Poverty status of people by age, race, and Hispanic origin: 1959–99 [CONTINUED]

[Numbers in thousands. People as of March of the following year.]

	Under 18 years						18 to 64 years			65 years and over		
	All people			Related children in families								
		Below poverty level			Below poverty level			Below poverty level			Below poverty level	
Year and characteristic	Total	Number	Percent	Total	Number	Percent	Total	Number	Percent	Total	Number	Percent
White-Continued												
1994	55,186	9,346	16.9	54,221	8,826	16.3	133,289	13,187	9.9	27,985	2,846	10.2
1993	54,639	9,752	17.8	53,614	9,123	17.0	132,680	13,535	10.2	27,580	2,939	10.7
1992ʳ	54,110	9,399	17.4	53,110	8,752	16.5	131,694	12,871	9.8	27,256	2,989	11.0
1991ʳ	52,523	8,848	16.8	51,627	8,316	16.1	130,312	12,097	9.3	27,297	2,802	10.3
1990	51,929	8,232	15.9	51,028	7,696	15.1	129,784	11,387	8.8	26,898	2,707	10.1
1989	51,400	7,599	14.8	50,704	7,164	14.1	128,974	10,647	8.3	26,479	2,539	9.6
1988ʳ	51,203	7,435	14.5	50,590	7,095	14.0	128,031	10,687	8.3	26,001	2,593	10.0
1987ʳ	51,012	7,788	15.3	50,360	7,398	14.7	126,991	10,703	8.4	25,602	2,704	10.6
1986	51,111	8,209	16.1	50,356	7,714	15.3	125,998	11,285	9.0	25,173	2,689	10.7
1985	51,031	8,253	16.2	50,358	7,838	15.6	125,258	11,909	9.5	24,629	2,698	11.0
1984	50,814	8,472	16.7	50,192	8,086	16.1	123,922	11,904	9.6	24,206	2,579	10.7
1983	50,726	8,862	17.5	50,183	8,534	17.0	123,014	12,347	10.0	23,754	2,776	11.7
1982	50,920	8,678	17.0	50,305	8,282	16.5	121,766	11,971	9.8	23,234	2,870	12.4
1981	51,140	7,785	15.2	50,553	7,429	14.7	120,574	10,790	8.9	22,791	2,978	13.1
1980	51,653	7,181	13.9	51,002	6,817	13.4	118,935	9,478	8.0	22,325	3,042	13.6
1979	52,262	6,193	11.8	51,687	5,909	11.4	117,583	8,110	6.9	21,898	2,911	13.3
1978	51,669	5,831	11.3	51,409	5,674	11.0	113,832	7,897	6.9	20,950	2,530	12.1
1977	52,563	6,097	11.6	52,299	5,943	11.4	112,374	7,893	7.0	20,316	2,426	11.9
1976	53,428	6,189	11.6	53,167	6,034	11.3	110,717	7,890	7.1	20,020	2,633	13.2
1975	54,405	6,927	12.7	54,126	6,748	12.5	109,105	8,210	7.5	19,654	2,634	13.4
1974	55,590	6,223	11.2	55,320	6,079	11.0	107,579	7,053	6.6	19,206	2,460	12.8
1973	(NA)	(NA)	(NA)	56,211	5,462	9.7	(NA)	(NA)	(NA)	(NA)	2,698	14.4
1972	(NA)	(NA)	(NA)	57,181	5,784	10.1	(NA)	(NA)	(NA)	(NA)	3,072	16.8
1971	(NA)	(NA)	(NA)	58,119	6,341	10.9	(NA)	(NA)	(NA)	(NA)	3,605	19.9
1970	(NA)	(NA)	(NA)	58,472	6,138	10.5	(NA)	(NA)	(NA)	(NA)	4,011	22.6
1969	(NA)	(NA)	(NA)	58,578	5,667	9.7	(NA)	(NA)	(NA)	(NA)	4,052	23.3
1968	(NA)	(NA)	(NA)	(NA)	6,373	10.7	(NA)	(NA)	(NA)	17,062	3,939	23.1
1967	(NA)	(NA)	(NA)	(NA)	6,729	11.3	(NA)	(NA)	(NA)	16,791	4,646	27.7
1966	(NA)	(NA)	(NA)	(NA)	7,204	12.1	(NA)	(NA)	(NA)	16,514	4,357	26.4
1965	(NA)	(NA)	(NA)	(NA)	8,595	14.4	(NA)	(NA)	(NA)	(NA)	(NA)	(NA)
1960	(NA)	(NA)	(NA)	(NA)	11,229	20.0	(NA)	(NA)	(NA)	(NA)	(NA)	(NA)
1959	(NA)	(NA)	(NA)	(NA)	11,386	20.6	(NA)	(NA)	(NA)	(NA)	4,744	33.1
White non-Hispanic												
1999	45,243	4,252	9.4	44,527	3,921	8.8	120,905	8,559	7.1	27,187	2,063	7.6
1998	45,355	4,822	10.6	44,670	4,458	10.0	120,283	8,761	7.3	27,118	2,217	8.2
1997	45,491	5,204	11.4	44,665	4,759	10.7	119,373	9,088	7.6	26,995	2,200	8.1
1996	45,605	5,072	11.1	44,844	4,656	10.4	118,822	9,074	7.6	27,033	2,316	8.6
1995	45,689	5,115	11.2	44,973	4,745	10.6	118,228	8,908	7.5	27,034	2,243	8.3
1994	46,668	5,823	12.5	45,874	5,404	11.8	119,192	9,732	8.2	26,684	2,556	9.6
1993	46,096	6,255	13.6	45,322	5,819	12.8	118,475	9,964	8.4	26,272	2,663	10.1
1992ʳ	45,590	6,017	13.2	44,833	5,558	12.4	117,386	9,461	8.1	26,025	2,724	10.5
1991ʳ	45,236	5,918	13.1	44,506	5,497	12.4	117,672	9,244	7.9	26,208	2,580	9.8
1990	44,797	5,532	12.3	44,045	5,106	11.6	117,477	8,619	7.3	25,854	2,471	9.6
1989	44,492	5,110	11.5	43,938	4,779	10.9	116,983	8,154	7.0	25,504	2,335	9.2
1988ʳ	44,438	4,888	11.0	43,910	4,594	10.5	116,479	8,293	7.1	25,044	2,384	9.5
1987ʳ	44,461	5,230	11.8	43,907	4,902	11.2	115,721	8,327	7.2	24,754	2,472	10.0
1986	44,664	5,789	13.0	44,041	5,388	12.2	115,157	8,963	7.8	24,298	2,492	10.3
1985	44,752	5,745	12.8	44,199	5,421	12.3	114,969	9,608	8.4	23,734	2,486	10.5

TABLE 4.1

Poverty status of people by age, race, and Hispanic origin: 1959–99 [CONTINUED]

[Numbers in thousands. People as of March of the following year.]

	Under 18 years						18 to 64 years			65 years and over		
	All people			Related children in families								
		Below poverty level			Below poverty level			Below poverty level			Below poverty level	
Year and characteristic	Total	Number	Percent	Total	Number	Percent	Total	Number	Percent	Total	Number	Percent
White non-Hispanic-Con.												
1984	44,886	6,156	13.7	44,349	5,828	13.1	114,180	9,734	8.5	23,402	2,410	10.3
1983	44,830	6,649	14.8	44,374	6,381	14.4	113,570	10,279	9.1	22,992	2,610	11.4
1982	45,531	6,566	14.4	45,001	6,229	13.8	113,717	10,082	8.9	22,655	2,714	12.0
1981	45,950	5,946	12.9	45,440	5,639	12.4	112,722	9,207	8.2	22,237	2,834	12.7
1980	46,578	5,510	11.8	45,989	5,174	11.3	111,460	7,990	7.2	21,760	2,865	13.2
1979	46,967	4,730	10.1	46,448	4,476	9.6	110,509	6,930	6.3	21,339	2,759	12.9
1978	46,819	4,506	9.6	46,606	4,383	9.4	107,481	6,837	6.4	20,431	2,412	11.8
1977	47,689	4,714	9.9	47,459	4,582	9.7	106,063	6,772	6.4	19,812	2,316	11.7
1976	48,824	4,799	9.8	48,601	4,664	9.6	104,846	6,720	6.4	19,565	2,506	12.8
1975	49,670	5,342	10.8	49,421	5,185	10.5	103,496	7,039	6.8	19,251	2,503	13.0
1974	50,759	4,820	9.5	50,520	4,697	9.3	101,894	6,051	5.9	18,810	2,346	12.5
Black												
1999	11,357	3,759	33.1	11,132	3,644	32.7	21,261	3,975	18.7	2,754	626	22.7
1998	11,317	4,151	36.7	11,176	4,073	36.4	20,836	4,223	20.3	2,723	718	26.4
1997	11,367	4,225	37.2	11,193	4,116	36.8	20,399	4,191	20.5	2,691	700	26.0
1996	11,338	4,519	39.9	11,155	4,411	39.5	20,155	4,515	22.4	2,616	661	25.3
1995	11,369	4,761	41.9	11,198	4,644	41.5	19,892	4,483	22.5	2,478	629	25.4
1994	11,211	4,906	43.8	11,044	4,787	43.3	19,585	4,590	23.4	2,557	700	27.4
1993	11,127	5,125	46.1	10,969	5,030	45.9	19,272	5,049	26.2	2,510	702	28.0
1992ʳ	10,956	5,106	46.6	10,823	5,015	46.3	18,952	4,884	25.8	2,504	838	33.5
1991ʳ	10,350	4,755	45.9	10,178	4,637	45.6	18,356	4,607	25.1	2,606	880	33.8
1990	10,162	4,550	44.8	9,980	4,412	44.2	18,097	4,427	24.5	2,547	860	33.8
1989	10,012	4,375	43.7	9,847	4,257	43.2	17,833	4,164	23.3	2,487	763	30.7
1988ʳ	9,865	4,296	43.5	9,681	4,148	42.8	17,548	4,275	24.4	2,436	785	32.2
1987ʳ	9,730	4,385	45.1	9,546	4,234	44.4	17,245	4,361	25.3	2,387	774	32.4
1986	9,629	4,148	43.1	9,467	4,037	42.7	16,911	4,113	24.3	2,331	722	31.0
1985	9,545	4,157	43.6	9,405	4,057	43.1	16,667	4,052	24.3	2,273	717	31.5
1984	9,480	4,413	46.6	9,356	4,320	46.2	16,369	4,368	26.7	2,238	710	31.7
1983	9,417	4,398	46.7	9,245	4,273	46.2	16,065	4,694	29.2	2,197	791	36.0
1982	9,400	4,472	47.6	9,269	4,388	47.3	15,692	4,415	28.1	2,124	811	38.2
1981	9,374	4,237	45.2	9,291	4,170	44.9	15,358	4,117	26.8	2,102	820	39.0
1980	9,368	3,961	42.3	9,287	3,906	42.1	14,987	3,835	25.6	2,054	783	38.1
1979	9,307	3,833	41.2	9,172	3,745	40.8	14,596	3,478	23.8	2,040	740	36.2
1978	9,229	3,830	41.5	9,168	3,781	41.2	13,774	3,133	22.7	1,954	662	33.9
1977	9,296	3,888	41.8	9,253	3,850	41.6	13,483	3,137	23.3	1,930	701	36.3
1976	9,322	3,787	40.6	9,291	3,758	40.4	13,224	3,163	23.9	1,852	644	34.8
1975	9,421	3,925	41.7	9,374	3,884	41.4	12,872	2,968	23.1	1,795	652	36.3
1974	9,439	3,755	39.8	9,384	3,713	39.6	12,539	2,836	22.6	1,721	591	34.3
1973	(NA)	(NA)	(NA)	9,405	3,822	40.6	(NA)	(NA)	(NA)	1,672	620	37.1
1972	(NA)	(NA)	(NA)	9,426	4,025	42.7	(NA)	(NA)	(NA)	1,603	640	39.9
1971	(NA)	(NA)	(NA)	9,414	3,836	40.4	(NA)	(NA)	(NA)	1,584	623	39.3
1970	(NA)	(NA)	(NA)	9,448	3,922	41.5	(NA)	(NA)	(NA)	1,422	683	48.0
1969	(NA)	(NA)	(NA)	9,290	3,677	39.6	(NA)	(NA)	(NA)	1,373	689	50.2
1968	(NA)	(NA)	(NA)	(NA)	4,188	43.1	(NA)	(NA)	(NA)	1,374	655	47.7
1967	(NA)	(NA)	(NA)	(NA)	4,558	47.4	(NA)	(NA)	(NA)	1,341	715	53.3
1966	(NA)	(NA)	(NA)	(NA)	4,774	50.6	(NA)	(NA)	(NA)	1,311	722	55.1
1959	(NA)	(NA)	(NA)	(NA)	5,022	65.6	(NA)	(NA)	(NA)	(NA)	711	62.5

TABLE 4.1

Poverty status of people by age, race, and Hispanic origin: 1959–99 [CONTINUED]

[Numbers in thousands. People as of March of the following year.]

	Under 18 years						18 to 64 years			65 years and over		
	All people			Related children in families								
		Below poverty level			Below poverty level			Below poverty level			Below poverty level	
Year and characteristic	Total	Number	Percent	Total	Number	Percent	Total	Number	Percent	Total	Number	Percent
Hispanic Origin[1]												
1999	11,560	3,506	30.3	11,300	3,382	29.9	19,356	3,575	18.5	1,752	358	20.4
1998	11,152	3,837	34.4	10,921	3,670	33.6	18,668	3,877	20.8	1,696	356	21.0
1997	10,802	3,972	36.8	10,625	3,865	36.4	18,218	3,951	21.7	1,617	384	23.8
1996	10,511	4,237	40.3	10,255	4,090	39.9	17,587	4,089	23.3	1,516	370	24.4
1995	10,213	4,080	40.0	10,011	3,938	39.3	16,673	4,153	24.9	1,458	342	23.5
1994	9,822	4,075	41.5	9,621	3,956	41.1	16,192	4,018	24.8	1,428	323	22.6
1993	9,462	3,873	40.9	9,188	3,666	39.9	15,708	3,956	25.2	1,390	297	21.4
1992[r]	9,081	3,637	40.0	8,829	3,440	39.0	15,268	3,668	24.0	1,298	287	22.1
1991[r]	7,648	3,094	40.4	7,473	2,977	39.8	13,279	3,008	22.7	1,143	237	20.8
1990	7,457	2,865	38.4	7,300	2,750	37.7	12,857	2,896	22.5	1,091	245	22.5
1989	7,186	2,603	36.2	7,040	2,496	35.5	12,536	2,616	20.9	1,024	211	20.6
1988[r]	7,003	2,631	37.6	6,908	2,576	37.3	12,056	2,501	20.7	1,005	225	22.4
1987[r]	6,792	2,670	39.3	6,692	2,606	38.9	11,718	2,509	21.4	885	243	27.5
1986	6,646	2,507	37.7	6,511	2,413	37.1	11,206	2,406	21.5	906	204	22.5
1985	6,475	2,606	40.3	6,346	2,512	39.6	10,685	2,411	22.6	915	219	23.9
1984	6,068	2,376	39.2	5,982	2,317	38.7	10,029	2,254	22.5	819	176	21.5
1983	6,066	2,312	38.1	5,977	2,251	37.7	9,697	2,148	22.5	782	173	22.1
1982	5,527	2,181	39.5	5,436	2,117	38.9	8,262	1,963	23.8	596	159	26.6
1981	5,369	1,925	35.9	5,291	1,874	35.4	8,084	1,642	20.3	568	146	25.7
1980	5,276	1,749	33.2	5,211	1,718	33.0	7,740	1,563	20.2	582	179	30.8
1979	5,483	1,535	28.0	5,426	1,505	27.7	7,314	1,232	16.8	574	154	26.8
1978	5,012	1,384	27.6	4,972	1,354	27.2	6,527	1,098	16.8	539	125	23.2
1977	5,028	1,422	28.3	5,000	1,402	28.0	6,500	1,164	17.9	518	113	21.9
1976	4,771	1,443	30.2	4,736	1,424	30.1	6,034	1,212	20.1	464	128	27.7
1975	(NA)	(NA)	(NA)	4,896	1,619	33.1	(NA)	(NA)	(NA)	(NA)	137	32.6
1974	(NA)	(NA)	(NA)	4,939	1,414	28.6	(NA)	(NA)	(NA)	(NA)	117	28.9
1973	(NA)	(NA)	(NA)	4,910	1,364	27.8	(NA)	(NA)	(NA)	(NA)	95	24.9
Asian and Pacific Islander												
1999	3,057	361	11.8	3,026	348	11.5	7,059	717	10.2	800	85	10.6
1998	3,137	564	18.0	3,099	542	17.5	6,951	698	10.0	785	97	12.4
1997	3,096	628	20.3	3,061	608	19.9	6,680	752	11.3	705	87	12.3
1996	2,924	571	19.5	2,899	553	19.1	6,484	821	12.7	647	63	9.7
1995	2,900	564	19.5	2,858	532	18.6	6,123	757	12.4	622	89	14.3
1994	1,739	318	18.3	1,719	308	17.9	4,401	589	13.4	513	67	13.0
1993	2,061	375	18.2	2,029	358	17.6	4,871	680	14.0	503	79	15.6
1992[r]	2,218	363	16.4	2,199	352	16.0	5,067	568	11.2	494	53	10.8
1991[r]	2,056	360	17.5	2,036	348	17.1	4,582	565	12.3	555	70	12.7
1990	2,126	374	17.6	2,098	356	17.0	4,375	422	9.6	514	62	12.1
1989	1,983	392	19.8	1,945	368	18.9	4,225	512	12.1	465	34	7.4
1988[r]	1,970	474	24.1	1,949	458	23.5	4,035	583	14.4	442	60	13.5
1987[r]	1,937	455	23.5	1,908	432	22.7	4,010	510	12.7	375	56	15.0

[r] For 1992, figures are based on 1990 census population controls. For 1991, figures are revised to correct for nine omitted weights from the original March 1992 CPS file. For 1988 and 1987, figures are based on new processing procedures and are also revised to reflect corrections to the files after publication of the 1988 advance report, *Money Income and Poverty Status in the United States: 1988,* P-60, No. 166.

(NA) Not available.

[1] People of Hispanic origin may be of any race.

Note: Prior to 1979, people in unrelated subfamilies were included in people in families. Beginning in 1979, people in unrelated subfamilies are included in all people but are excluded from people in families.

SOURCE: Joseph Daaker and Bernadette D. Procter, *Poverty in the United States, 1999,* U.S. Bureau of the Census, Washington, D.C., September 2000

FIGURE 4.1

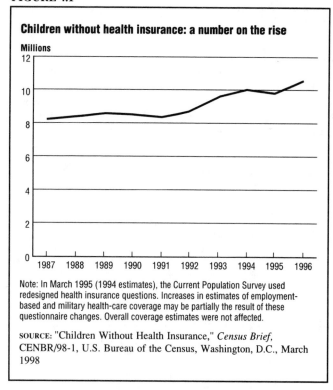

Children without health insurance: a number on the rise

Note: In March 1995 (1994 estimates), the Current Population Survey used redesigned health insurance questions. Increases in estimates of employment-based and military health-care coverage may be partially the result of these questionnaire changes. Overall coverage estimates were not affected.

SOURCE: "Children Without Health Insurance," *Census Brief,* CENBR/98-1, U.S. Bureau of the Census, Washington, D.C., March 1998

FIGURE 4.2

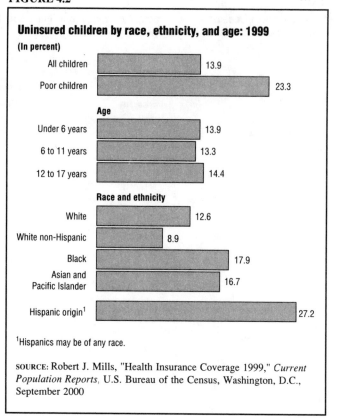

Uninsured children by race, ethnicity, and age: 1999

[1] Hispanics may be of any race.

SOURCE: Robert J. Mills, "Health Insurance Coverage 1999," *Current Population Reports,* U.S. Bureau of the Census, Washington, D.C., September 2000

- Poverty makes children hungry. Hungry children are more likely to be hyperactive and to have serious behavioral problems. They are also four times more likely to have difficulty concentrating in school.

- Poor children score lower on reading and math tests and are twice as likely to repeat a year of school as non-poor children.

- Poor children earn 25 percent lower wages when they become young adults.

LACK OF HEALTH INSURANCE

Today, for too many parents, the emergency room is the family physician for children.

— Senator Edward Kennedy (D-MA), Children's Defense Fund's 17th annual conference, March 13, 1997.

As the debate over health care delivery, managed care, and the like rages on, children are, all too often, the innocent victims. Health insurance helps children obtain adequate health care, which helps ensure their physical wellbeing and optimum development. The social and economic changes that have affected children over the last several decades of the twentieth century make access to health care even more essential. Changes in family composition and economic condition have put children in situations that often require health services—hunger, poor housing conditions, violence, neglect, and other similar situations.

Uninsured Children

From 1987 to 1996 the number of American children without health insurance climbed from 8.2 million to 10.6 million, the highest levels ever recorded by the U.S. Bureau of the Census. (See Figure 4.1.) That trend began to reverse in 1999, when the proportion of uninsured children declined to 10 million (13.9 percent), the lowest rate since 1995.

By age, children ages 12–17 years were most likely to lack health care coverage. In 1999 14.4 percent of this age group were uninsured, compared with 13.3 percent of children 6–11 years old and 13.9 percent of those under the age of 6 years. Hispanic children were far more likely to be uninsured than children of other racial and ethnic origins. More than 27.2 percent of Hispanic children, 17.9 percent of black children, 16.7 percent of Asian/Pacific Islander children, 12.6 percent of white children, and 8.9 percent of non-Hispanic white children were uninsured. (See Figure 4.2.)

According to the U.S. Census Bureau, during the 1980s the percentage of workers receiving employment-based insurance, the most common source of health coverage for Americans, declined. Since 1987 the proportion of children with private health insurance decreased, reaching the lowest level in 8 years in 1994 (65.6 percent)

By 1999, however, 86.1 percent of all children had some form of health insurance—68.9 percent had private health insurance and 20 percent were covered by Medicaid. (See Figure 4.3.) Black (36.2 percent) and Hispanic (30.8 percent) children were more likely to have Medicaid

FIGURE 4.3

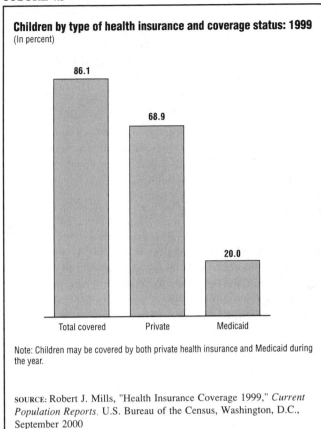

Children by type of health insurance and coverage status: 1999
(In percent)

Note: Children may be covered by both private health insurance and Medicaid during the year.

SOURCE: Robert J. Mills, "Health Insurance Coverage 1999," *Current Population Reports*, U.S. Bureau of the Census, Washington, D.C., September 2000

FIGURE 4.4

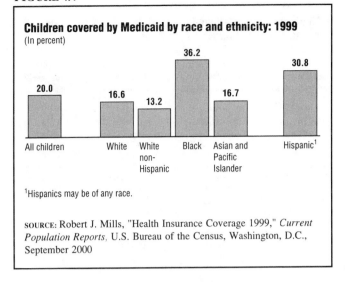

Children covered by Medicaid by race and ethnicity: 1999
(In percent)

[1]Hispanics may be of any race.

SOURCE: Robert J. Mills, "Health Insurance Coverage 1999," *Current Population Reports*, U.S. Bureau of the Census, Washington, D.C., September 2000

the Institute of Medicine, these families have a number of additional barriers to overcome—difficulty in scheduling appointments, cultural differences with medical providers, or a lack of easily accessible services. States may need to go one step further by providing culturally appropriate services and assisting with child care and transportation.

TEEN SEXUALITY

By the late twentieth century American teens were more sexually active than previous generations. While sexual activity was rare in young teens it increased as teens grew older; by the age of 17 years most teens reported at least one sexual experience. Concurrent with sexual activity are risks of sexually transmitted diseases (STDs), pregnancy, and dropping out of school.

Sexual Risk Behaviors

Unprotected sexual intercourse and multiple sex partners place young people at high risk for the human immunodeficiency virus (HIV) infection, other STDs, and pregnancy. HIV infection is the sixth leading cause of death among persons aged 15–24. By December 1999 nearly 130,000 adults aged 25–34 had died of AIDS. (See Table 4.2.) Many had contracted HIV as teens. Each year about 3 million teens contract STDs and approximately 1 million—one of every 10—females ages 15–19 get pregnant.

In "Trends in Sexual Risk Behaviors Among High School Students—United States, 1991–1997" (*Morbidity and Mortality Weekly Report*, vol. 47, no. 36, September 18, 1998), the Centers for Disease Control and Prevention (CDC) reported that, in 1997, fewer high school students were engaging in sexual behaviors that would put them at risk for HIV infection, other STDs, and pregnancy. For the first time in that decade a majority of students (51.6 percent) reported that they abstained from sexual inter-

coverage than were white (16.6 percent), non-Hispanic white (13.2 percent), and Asian/Pacific Islander (16.7 percent) children. (See Figure 4.4.)

Children in Low-Income Working Families

Most uninsured children are from low-income working families, where the children are not eligible for public assistance because their families earn too much to qualify for Medicaid, despite not earning enough to pay for their own insurance. In most cases the parents work for small companies, which are the least likely to provide health insurance. When these companies do offer insurance plans, the cost to the employees may be too much for low-income workers.

STATE CHILDREN'S HEALTH INSURANCE PROGRAM (CHIP). The State Children's Health Insurance Program (CHIP) was enacted on August 5, 1997, as part of the Balanced Budget Act of 1997 (PL 105-33) under Title XXI of the Social Security Act (PL 89-97). CHIP is intended to improve access to health care coverage for uninsured children from low-income families who are not Medicaid-eligible. States may use CHIP funding to expand their Medicaid programs or develop other initiatives.

Expanding access to health coverage, however, does not necessarily mean that children from low-income families will get appropriate health care services. According to

TABLE 4.2

AIDS deaths by race/ethnicity, age at death, and sex: cumulative totals reported through June 2000

Race/ethnicity and age at death	Males Cumulative total	Females Cumulative total	Both sexes Cumulative total
White, not Hispanic			
Under 15	566	417	983
15–24	2,525	474	2,999
25–34	54,404	4,613	59,017
35–44	79,922	5,042	84,964
45–54	36,472	1,979	38,451
55 or older	15,381	1,716	17,097
All ages	189,432	14,263	203,695
Black, not Hispanic			
Under 15	1,433	1,413	2,846
15–24	2,428	1,416	3,844
25–34	33,233	11,659	44,892
35–44	49,416	14,625	64,041
45–54	22,042	5,182	27,224
55 or older	9,405	2,289	11,694
All ages	118,079	36,616	154,695
Hispanic			
Under 15	626	574	1,200
15–24	1,329	478	1,807
25–34	20,108	4,466	24,574
35–44	25,970	4,849	30,819
45–54	10,537	1,757	12,294
55 or older	4,375	831	5,206
All ages	63,001	12,965	75,966
Asian/Pacific Islander			
Under 15	18	16	34
15–24	36	6	42
25–34	707	79	786
35–44	1,125	98	1,223
45–54	547	65	612
55 or older	247	48	295
All ages	2,682	314	2,996
American Indian/Alaska Native			
Under 15	12	8	20
15–24	24	3	27
25–34	377	72	449
35–44	392	67	459
45–54	129	26	155
55 or older	41	11	52
All ages	978	187	1,165
All racial/ethnic groups			
Under 15	2,657	2,429	5,086
15–24	6,347	2,379	8,726
25–34	108,887	20,894	129,781
35–44	156,940	24,693	181,633
45–54	69,774	9,014	78,788
55 or older	29,470	4,898	34,368
All ages	374,422	64,373	438,795

SOURCE: *HIV/AIDS Surveillance Report*, Vol. 12, No. 1, Centers for Disease Control and Prevention, National Center for HIV, STD, and TB Prevention, Divisions of HIV/AIDS Prevention, December 6, 2000

course in 1997. The proportion of students who reported having multiple partners dropped from 18.7 percent in 1991 to 16 percent in 1997. Among respondents who were sexually active at the time of the survey, condom use increased from 46.2 percent in 1991 to 56.8 percent in 1997. The proportion of students who reported current sexual activity fell from 37.4 percent in 1991 to 34.8 percent in 1997. (See Table 4.3.)

The decline in risk behaviors among high school students between 1991 and 1997 corresponded with the increase in the proportion of students who participated in HIV/AIDS education in school—from 83.3 percent in 1991 to 91.5 percent in 1997. Dr. Lloyd Kolbe, director of the CDC's Division of Adolescent and School Health, claims that the survey findings showed that teaching teenagers about safe sex does not result in more promiscuity.

Non-coital Behaviors

The growing perception among young people that non-coital behaviors are not "sex" is placing more teens at risk. A new study by the Urban Institute, a nonprofit policy research organization based in Washington, D.C. investigating social and economic problems, provided the first data on the sexual practices of 15–19-year-old boys. The study said that health educators have focused on sexual intercourse by young teens, but not on other sexual behaviors (oral sex, anal sex, and masturbation) that can also pose a danger of STDs. Most STDs—such as herpes, hepatitis B, gonorrhea, syphilis, and chlamydia—can be transmitted orally or genitally. And, although HIV is not easily transmitted through oral sex, researchers say such transmission is possible.

The study also showed that, while 55 percent of teenage males stated they had had vaginal sex, two-thirds had experienced oral or anal sex or had been masturbated by a female. More than 1 in 10 boys had engaged in oral intercourse, one-half had received oral sex from a girl, and slightly more than one-third had performed oral sex on a girl.

Researchers and public health experts found that many young people perceived these non-coital behaviors as something other than sex—and sometimes even believed they were being sexually abstinent while participating in non-coital sexual behavior.

Racial and Ethnic Differences

The survey also found significant differences among racial and ethnic groups. Black and Hispanic boys were almost twice as likely as white boys to have had anal intercourse, and white and Hispanic boys were about twice as likely as black boys to have performed oral sex on a girl. The percentage of black boys receiving oral sex more than doubled from 1988 to 1995, while that percentage stayed stable among white and Hispanic boys.

TEENAGE PREGNANCY

The pregnancy rate among teenagers 15–19 years old generally rose during the 1970s and 1980s, peaking at 116.5 pregnancies per 1,000 females in 1991. By 1996 this rate had dropped to 98.7 per 1,000 teen women in this

TABLE 4.3

Percentage of high school students who reported engaging in sexual risk behaviors, by sex, grade, race/ethnicity, and survey year— United States, Youth Risk Behavior Survey, 1991, 1993, 1995, and 1997

	Survey year	Ever had sexual intercourse		Four or more sex partners during lifetime		Currently sexually active*		Condom use during last sexual intercourse†	
		%	(95% CI§)	%	(95% CI)	%	(95% CI)	%	(95% CI)
Sex									
Male	1991	57.4	(±4.1)	23.4	(±3.0)	36.8	(±3.4)	54.5	(± 3.8)
	1993	55.6	(±3.5)	22.3	(±2.7)	37.5	(±3.0)	59.2	(± 3.8)
	1995	54.0	(±4.7)	20.9	(±2.6)	35.5	(±3.5)	60.5	(± 4.3)
	1997	48.8	(±3.4)	17.6	(±1.5)	33.4	(±2.6)	62.5	(± 2.8)
Female	1991	50.8	(±4.0)	13.8	(±1.8)	38.2	(±3.4)	38.0	(± 4.3)
	1993	50.2	(±2.5)	15.0	(±1.9)	37.5	(±1.8)	46.0	(± 2.8)
	1995	52.1	(±5.0)	14.4	(±3.5)	40.4	(±4.2)	48.6	(± 5.2)
	1997	47.7	(±3.7)	14.1	(±2.0)	36.5	(±2.7)	50.8	(± 3.0)
Grade									
9	1991	39.0	(±5.0)	12.5	(±2.9)	22.4	(±3.9)	53.3	(± 6.2)
	1993	37.7	(±4.2)	10.9	(±2.0)	24.8	(±3.2)	61.6	(± 5.7)
	1995	36.9	(±5.9)	12.9	(±3.0)	23.6	(±4.0)	62.9	(± 5.5)
	1997	38.0	(±3.8)	12.2	(±2.5)	24.2	(±3.3)	58.8	(± 5.6)
10	1991	48.2	(±5.7)	15.1	(±2.8)	33.2	(±4.6)	46.3	(± 4.7)
	1993	46.1	(±3.6)	15.9	(±2.0)	30.1	(±3.0)	54.7	(± 4.5)
	1995	48.0	(±5.1)	15.6	(±2.0)	33.7	(±3.1)	59.7	(± 4.6)
	1997	42.5	(±4.3)	13.8	(±2.7)	29.2	(±2.9)	58.9	(± 3.6)
11	1991	62.4	(±3.2)	22.1	(±3.6)	43.3	(±3.6)	48.7	(± 5.8)
	1993	57.5	(±3.5)	19.9	(±3.1)	40.0	(±3.6)	55.3	(± 3.0)
	1995	58.6	(±5.0)	19.0	(±3.7)	42.4	(±4.4)	52.3	(± 6.2)
	1997	49.7	(±5.2)	16.7	(±2.9)	37.8	(±4.8)	60.1	(± 5.2)
12	1991	66.7	(±4.4)	25.0	(±4.0)	50.6	(±4.5)	41.4	(± 3.6)
	1993	68.3	(±4.6)	27.0	(±3.6)	53.0	(±3.9)	46.5	(± 4.0)
	1995	66.4	(±4.0)	22.9	(±3.5)	49.7	(±3.9)	49.5	(± 4.4)
	1997	60.9	(±6.5)	20.6	(±3.5)	46.0	(±5.0)	52.4	(± 3.5)
Race/ethnicity¶									
Non-Hispanic white	1991	50.0	(±3.2)	14.7	(±1.8)	33.9	(±2.8)	46.5	(± 4.6)
	1993	48.4	(±2.8)	14.3	(±2.1)	34.0	(±2.1)	52.3	(± 3.9)
	1995	48.9	(±5.0)	14.2	(±2.4)	34.8	(±3.9)	52.5	(± 4.0)
	1997	43.6	(±4.2)	11.6	(±1.5)	32.0	(±3.1)	55.8	(± 2.0)
Non-Hispanic black	1991	81.4	(±3.2)	43.1	(±3.5)	59.3	(±3.8)	48.0	(± 3.8)
	1993	79.7	(±3.2)	42.7	(±3.8)	59.1	(±4.4)	56.5	(± 3.8)
	1995	73.4	(±4.5)	35.6	(±4.4)	54.2	(±4.7)	66.1	(± 4.8)
	1997	72.6	(±2.8)	38.5	(±3.6)	53.6	(±3.2)	64.0	(± 2.8)
Hispanic	1991	53.1	(±3.5)	16.8	(±2.6)	37.0	(±3.6)	37.4	(± 6.2)
	1993	56.0	(±4.1)	18.6	(±3.1)	39.4	(±3.7)	46.1	(± 4.4)
	1995	57.6	(±8.6)	17.6	(±3.7)	39.3	(±7.1)	44.4	(±11.1)
	1997	52.2	(±3.6)	15.5	(±2.4)	35.4	(±3.9)	48.3	(± 5.6)
Total	**1991**	**54.1**	**(±3.5)**	**18.7**	**(±2.1)**	**37.4**	**(±3.1)**	**46.2**	**(± 3.3)**
	1993	**53.0**	**(±2.7)**	**18.7**	**(±2.0)**	**37.5**	**(±2.1)**	**52.8**	**(± 2.7)**
	1995	**53.1**	**(±4.5)**	**17.8**	**(±2.6)**	**37.9**	**(±3.4)**	**54.4**	**(± 3.5)**
	1997	**48.4**	**(±3.1)**	**16.0**	**(±1.4)**	**34.8**	**(±2.2)**	**56.8**	**(± 1.6)**

* Sexual intercourse during the 3 months preceding the survey.
† Among currently sexually active students.
§ Confidence interval.
¶ Numbers of students in other racial/ethnic groups were too small for meaningful analysis.

SOURCE: "Trends in Sexual Risk Behaviors among High School Students—United States, 1991–1997," *Morbidity and Mortality Weekly Report,* Vol. 47, No. 36, September 18, 1998, Centers for Disease Control and Prevention, Atlanta, GA, 1998

age group, the lowest rate in 20 years. (See Figures 4.5 and 4.6.)

Some analysts ascribe the declining trend of pregnancy to the increasing use of birth control methods, especially the longer-lasting contraceptives such as Norplant and DepoProvera. The increasing use of condoms due to fear of contracting AIDS is also thought to contribute to the lower pregnancy rate. Conservative analysts, however, discount the increasing use of contraception as responsible for the lower pregnancy rates, ascribing the drop in teen pregnancy to the increasing practice of abstinence.

While there has been a decline in teen pregnancy, the United States still has the highest rate of teen pregnancy among developed countries—nearly twice as high as the next highest country, Great Britain, and nine times as high as the Netherlands or Japan. (See Figure 4.7.) An estimat-

FIGURE 4.5

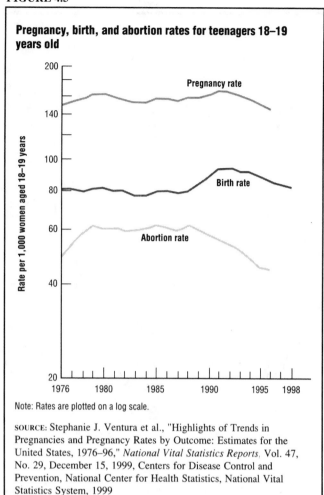

Pregnancy, birth, and abortion rates for teenagers 18–19 years old

Note: Rates are plotted on a log scale.

SOURCE: Stephanie J. Ventura et al., "Highlights of Trends in Pregnancies and Pregnancy Rates by Outcome: Estimates for the United States, 1976–96," *National Vital Statistics Reports*, Vol. 47, No. 29, December 15, 1999, Centers for Disease Control and Prevention, National Center for Health Statistics, National Vital Statistics System, 1999

FIGURE 4.6

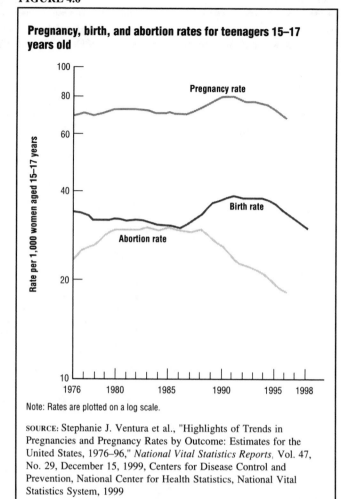

Pregnancy, birth, and abortion rates for teenagers 15–17 years old

Note: Rates are plotted on a log scale.

SOURCE: Stephanie J. Ventura et al., "Highlights of Trends in Pregnancies and Pregnancy Rates by Outcome: Estimates for the United States, 1976–96," *National Vital Statistics Reports*, Vol. 47, No. 29, December 15, 1999, Centers for Disease Control and Prevention, National Center for Health Statistics, National Vital Statistics System, 1999

ed 4 of 10 American girls become pregnant at least once before they turn 20 years old. (See Figure 4.8.) Many experts believe that the factors that predispose adolescents to drug use are the same ones that predispose them to teen pregnancy—poverty, family dysfunction, child abuse, and early education difficulties.

TEENAGE BIRTHS

According to the 1998 *National Vital Statistics Reports* entitled "Declines in Teenage Birthrates, 1991–97," the highest recorded teenage birth rate was 96.3 live births per 1,000 women ages 15–19 years in 1957. After 1965 this rate steadily decreased, as did that of the general population after the Baby Boom. In 1988 the birth rate started rising sharply, increasing from 53 live births per 1,000 women ages 15–19 years to 62.1 in 1991.

After peaking in 1991, the teenage birth rate began to decline again. By 1997 it was at 52.9 live births per 1,000 women aged 15–19, lower than it had been a decade earlier. This rate continued to decline in 1998 (51.1 per 1,000) and 1999 (49.6 per 1,000). (See Table 4.4.) This was a decline of 20.1 percent from the recent peak in 1991.

Since 1991 birth rates for teenagers 15–17 years have fallen 26 percent, and for teenagers 18–19 years 15 percent. (See Figure 4.9.)

Births, Induced Abortions, and Miscarriages

In 1996 54.4 out of every 1,000 women aged 15–19 years gave birth and 15.2 percent miscarried. Along with the decline in birth rate for teens in this age group came a decline in the rate of induced abortions, which fell 33 percent between 1988 (43.5 abortions per 1000 teenage women) and 1996 (29.2 abortions per 1000 teenage women). (See Figures 4.5 and 4.6.)

Racial and Ethnic Differences

According to the *National Vital Statistics Reports* quoted above, birth rates for women 15–19 years old of all racial and ethnic groups decreased between 1991 and 1999. Birth rates have dropped significantly for black teens in this age group, declining from a high of 115.5 per 1,000 teens 15–19 years old in 1991 to 81.1 in 1999. Statistics for Hispanic teens over the same period showed a decline from 106.7 to 93.1. Despite these declines, birth rates for black and Hispanic teens still continue to be higher than for other

FIGURE 4.7

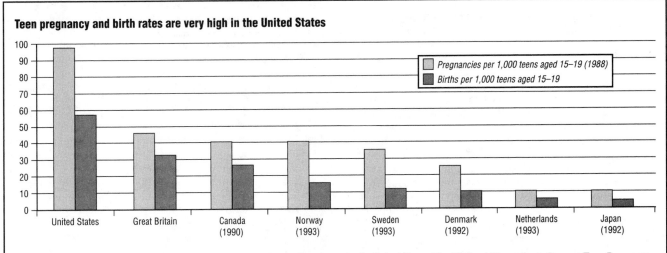

Teen pregnancy and birth rates are very high in the United States

Legend:
- Pregnancies per 1,000 teens aged 15–19 (1988)
- Births per 1,000 teens aged 15–19

Categories: United States, Great Britain, Canada (1990), Norway (1993), Sweden (1993), Denmark (1992), Netherlands (1993), Japan (1992)

SOURCE: *Whatever Happened to Childhood? The Problem of Teen Pregnancy in the United States,* The National Campaign to Prevent Teen Pregnancy, Washington, D.C., 1997

FIGURE 4.8

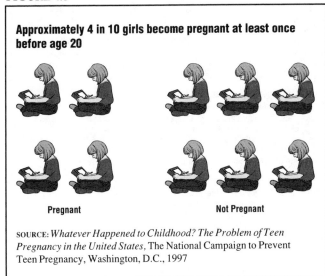

Approximately 4 in 10 girls become pregnant at least once before age 20

Pregnant   Not Pregnant

SOURCE: *Whatever Happened to Childhood? The Problem of Teen Pregnancy in the United States,* The National Campaign to Prevent Teen Pregnancy, Washington, D.C., 1997

FIGURE 4.9

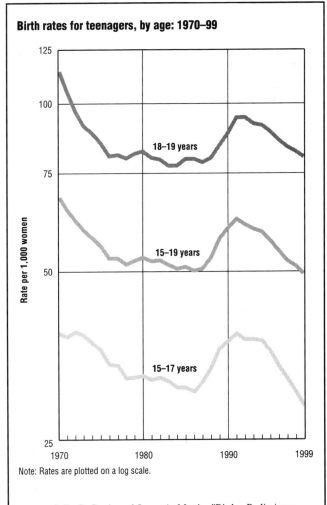

Birth rates for teenagers, by age: 1970–99

Rate per 1,000 women

18–19 years
15–19 years
15–17 years

Note: Rates are plotted on a log scale.

SOURCE: Sally C. Curtin and Joyce A. Martin, "Births: Preliminary Data for 1999," *National Vital Statistics Reports,* Vol. 48, No. 14, August 8, 2000, Centers for Disease Control and Prevention, National Center for Health Statistics, National Vital Statistics System, 2000

groups, and the rates for Hispanic teens has been higher than for black teens since 1995. Asian/Pacific Islander teens had the lowest rate in 1999 (22.8 per 1,000), followed by non-Hispanic whites (34.1), whites (44.5), and American Indians (67.7). (See Table 4.4.)

FAMILY STRUCTURE AND TEEN SEXUALITY

In *Not Just for Girls: The Roles of Boys and Men in Teen Pregnancy Prevention* (Kristin A. Moore, Anne K. Driscoll, and Theodora Ooms, National Campaign to Prevent Teen Pregnancy, Washington, D.C., 1997), the researchers analyzed the 1995 National Survey of Family Growth (NSFG) to study the impact of family structure on teen sexuality. The NSFG is a periodic survey conducted by the National Center for Health Statistics of the U.S. Department of Health and Human Services to collect

TABLE 4.4

Births and birth rates, by age, race, and Hispanic origin of mother: United States, final 1998 and preliminary 1999

[Data for 1999 are based on a continuous file of records received from the states. Figures for 1999 are based on weighted data rounded to nearest individual, so categories may not add to totals.]

Age and race/Hispanic origin	1999 Number	1999 Rate	1998 Number	1998 Rate
All races				
Total [1]	3,957,829	65.8	3,941,553	65.6
10-14 years	9,049	0.9	9,462	1.0
15-19 years	475,745	49.6	484,895	51.1
15-17 years	163,559	28.7	173,231	30.4
18-19 years	312,186	80.2	311,664	82.0
20-24 years	981,207	111.0	965,122	111.2
25-29 years	1,078,350	117.8	1,083,010	115.9
30-34 years	892,478	89.6	889,365	87.4
35-39 years	433,793	38.3	424,890	37.4
40-44 years	82,875	7.4	81,027	7.3
45-54 years [2]	4,330	0.4	3,782	0.4
White, total [3]				
Total [1]	3,130,100	65.0	3,118,727	64.6
10-14 years	4,723	0.6	4,801	0.6
15-19 years	337,323	44.5	340,694	45.4
15-17 years	111,481	24.8	116,623	25.9
18-19 years	225,842	73.4	224,071	74.6
20-24 years	747,217	106.8	736,664	107.2
25-29 years	873,586	121.1	880,688	119.1
30-34 years	739,967	93.2	737,532	90.5
35-39 years	356,546	38.7	349,799	37.8
40-44 years	67,228	7.3	65,485	7.2
45-54 years [2]	3,509	0.4	3,064	0.4
White, non-Hispanic				
Total [1]	2,349,536	57.9	2,361,462	57.7
10-14 years	2,046	0.3	2,132	0.3
15-19 years	213,223	34.1	219,169	35.2
15-17 years	63,659	17.1	68,619	18.4
18-19 years	149,564	59.0	150,550	60.6
20-24 years	515,026	90.1	511,101	90.7
25-29 years	665,018	111.3	678,227	109.7
30-34 years	601,676	90.4	603,639	88.0
35-39 years	294,585	37.3	291,202	36.4
40-44 years	55,037	6.8	53,480	6.7
45-54 years [2]	2,802	0.4	2,388	0.4
Black, total [3]				
Total [1]	606,720	70.2	609,902	71.0
10-14 years	3,981	2.6	4,289	2.9
15-19 years	121,262	81.1	126,937	85.4
15-17 years	45,979	52.1	50,103	56.8
18-19 years	75,283	122.9	76,834	126.9
20-24 years	193,483	141.9	189,088	141.9
25-29 years	139,175	102.2	139,302	101.8
30-34 years	91,596	64.5	93,785	64.7
35-39 years	47,244	30.7	46,657	30.5
40-44 years	9,562	6.5	9,496	6.7
45-54 years [2]	417	0.3	348	0.3
American Indian, total [3,4]				
Total [1]	40,015	69.4	40,272	70.7
10-14 years	203	1.7	197	1.6
15-19 years	7,905	67.7	8,201	72.1
15-17 years	2,980	41.3	3,167	44.4
18-19 years	4,925	110.4	5,034	118.4
20-24 years	13,203	136.9	13,046	139.3
25-29 years	9,549	101.4	9,529	102.2
30-34 years	5,695	64.3	5,930	66.3
35-39 years	2,822	30.5	2,795	30.2
40-44 years	613	7.0	555	6.4
45-54 years [2]	26	0.4	19	*

TABLE 4.4

Births and birth rates, by age, race, and Hispanic origin of mother: United States, final 1998 and preliminary 1999 [CONTINUED]

[Data for 1999 are based on a continuous file of records received from the states. Figures for 1999 are based on weighted data rounded to nearest individual, so categories may not add to totals.]

Age and race/Hispanic origin	1999 Number	1999 Rate	1998 Number	1998 Rate
Asian or Pacific Islander, total [3]				
Total [1]	180,993	65.7	172,652	64.0
10-14 years	142	0.4	175	0.4
15-19 years	9,255	22.8	9,063	23.1
15-17 years	3,119	12.6	3,338	13.8
18-19 years	6,135	38.8	5,725	38.3
20-24 years	27,304	70.4	26,324	68.8
25-29 years	56,040	116.3	53,491	110.4
30-34 years	55,220	109.2	52,118	105.1
35-39 years	27,182	54.6	25,639	52.8
40-44 years	5,472	11.5	5,491	12.0
45-54 years [2]	379	0.9	351	0.9
Hispanic [5]				
Total [1]	762,364	101.8	734,661	101.1
10-14 years	2,721	2.0	2,716	2.1
15-19 years	124,352	93.1	121,388	93.6
15-17 years	48,127	61.2	48,234	62.3
18-19 years	76,226	139.0	73,154	140.1
20-24 years	230,881	178.3	223,113	178.4
25-29 years	203,399	162.6	196,012	160.2
30-34 years	131,134	102.1	125,702	98.9
35-39 years	57,926	46.2	54,195	44.9
40-44 years	11,430	10.7	11,056	10.8
45-54 years [2]	519	0.6	479	0.6

* Figure does not meet standards of reliability or precision.

[1] The total number includes births to women of all ages, 10-54 years. The rate shown for all ages is the fertility rate, which is defined as the total number of births, regardless of age of mother, per 1,000 women aged 15-44 years.

[2] The number of births shown is the total for women aged 45-54 years. The birth rate is computed by relating the number of births to women aged 45-54 years to women aged 45-49 years, because most of the births in this group are to women aged 45-49.

[3] Race and Hispanic origin are reported separately on the birth certificate. Data for persons of Hispanic origin are also included in the data for each race group, according to the mother's reported race.

[4] Includes births to Aleuts and Eskimos.

[5] Includes all persons of Hispanic origin of any race.

Note: Data are subject to sampling and/or random variation.

SOURCE: Sally C. Curtin and Joyce A. Martin, "Births: Preliminary Data for 1999," *National Vital Statistics Reports,* Vol. 48, No. 14, August 8, 2000, Centers for Disease Control and Prevention, National Center for Health Statistics, National Vital Statistics System, 2000

information on the reproductive health of women in the United States.

The researchers found that girls who were raised during their entire childhood by both biological parents were less likely to have sex in their teens than were those raised in a different family structure. Slightly more than 2 of 5 (42.8 percent) female teens who grew up with both parents had had sex by the age of 20 years, compared with 3 of 5 female teens (60 percent) who grew up in a different living arrangement. (See Figure 4.10.)

The following are some of the hypotheses the authors offered to explain the possible connection between a female teen's likelihood to have sex and the family structure she grew up in:

FIGURE 4.10

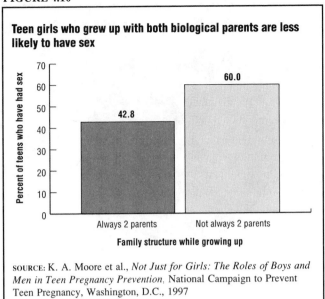

Teen girls who grew up with both biological parents are less likely to have sex

SOURCE: K. A. Moore et al., *Not Just for Girls: The Roles of Boys and Men in Teen Pregnancy Prevention*, National Campaign to Prevent Teen Pregnancy, Washington, D.C., 1997

FIGURE 4.11

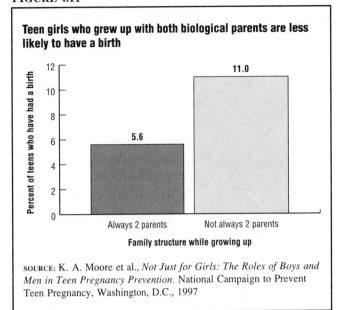

Teen girls who grew up with both biological parents are less likely to have a birth

SOURCE: K. A. Moore et al., *Not Just for Girls: The Roles of Boys and Men in Teen Pregnancy Prevention*, National Campaign to Prevent Teen Pregnancy, Washington, D.C., 1997

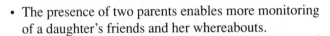

• The presence of two parents enables more monitoring of a daughter's friends and her whereabouts.

• Growing up with both parents may preclude other males, such as a stepfather or the mother's boyfriend, from having access to the adolescent.

• Married fathers, who generally earn more, are able to provide homes in safer neighborhoods and to afford activities that would remove a teen from situations where sexual activity is likely to occur.

• The parents' marriage may serve as a model for the daughter with regard to sex within marriage. The teen may also learn positive relationship skills in dealing with the opposite sex.

The National Survey of Family Growth also found that female adolescents who grew up with both parents were less likely to become teen parents. About twice as many teens who were not always raised by both parents bore a child (11 percent) as teens who were raised by two parents (5.6 percent). (See Figure 4.11.)

TEEN MOTHERS

The U.S. General Accounting Office (GAO), in *Teen Mothers—Selected Socio-Demographic Characteristics and Risk Factors* (Washington, D.C., 1998), reported on the profile of teenage mothers who gave birth in the 1990s. Nearly one-half (47 percent) were white, 3 of 5 were 18–19 years old, and three-quarters were unmarried. About two-thirds were not planning to have a child, and about one-fifth already had a child. Teen mothers graduated from high school at lower rates than all female teens: 64 percent, compared with 90 percent of all female adolescents. Nearly one-half (49 percent) received welfare within

5 years of giving birth, and more than two-thirds of births (69 percent) were paid for by Medicaid. (See Table 4.5.)

Unmarried Teen Mothers

For most observers the issue is not specifically teen births but, rather, the impact of early motherhood on unmarried young girls. Up until the 1960s it was normal for young people who were not going on to college to graduate from high school, acquire a job, and get married. Quite often, these young people were teenagers when their first, or even second, child was born.

As more young people began attending college and as more women entered the work force, before or after attending college, marriage was delayed. Far fewer marriages occurred in the late teenage years, and a growing number of marriages began taking place when couples were in their mid- to late 20s. Teenage marriages became increasingly rare and it became more socially acceptable to postpone marriage until both people had become "more mature."

This did not mean that teenage marriage had been "bad," only that times had changed and teenage marriage was no longer the accepted norm. When observers complained about the dangers of teenage marriages, it was not actually teenage marriages they were attacking (after all, it was likely their own parents were teenagers when they married). Instead, it was the growing rate of out-of-wedlock children being born. The issue was not teen marriages but unmarried teen mothers.

Since the mid-1970s the number of marriages among teenagers has declined. By the late 1990s most teenage mothers were unmarried. Between 1970 and 1997 the proportion of unmarried teenage mothers

TABLE 4.5

Profile of Teenage Mothers Who Gave Birth in the 1990s
(Numbers in percent)

	All	White	Black	Hispanic
Total number of teen mothers	492,000[a]	233,000	137,000	122,000
Age at time of birth[b]				
Under 15	2	1	4	3
15-17	38	34	42	40
18-19	60	65	53	57
Marital status at time of birth[b]				
Married	25	32	5	32
Unmarried	75	68	95	68
First or later birth[b]				
First birth	79	83	74	77
Later birth	21	17	26	23
Conception intended or unintended[c]				
Intended	35	33	25	54
Unintended	65	67	75	46
High school completion[d]				
Completed high school	64			
Did not complete high school	36			
Welfare receipt within 5 years of birth[e]				
Received	49			
Did not receive	51			
Insurance coverage for birth[f]				
Medicaid	69			
Some private	26			
Self	4			

[a] The data exclude about 21,000 births to races other than white, black, and Hispanic and those of unknown race. S.J. Ventura and others, "Report of Final Natality Statistics, 1995," *Monthly Vital Statistics Report*, Vol. 45, No. 11, Supp. 2 (Hyattsville, Md.: National Center for Health Statistics, 1997).
[b] These characteristics reflect only 1995 natality data.
[c] J.C. Abma and others, "Fertility, Family Planning, and Women's Health: New Data From the 1995 National Survey of Family Growth," *Vital and Health Statistics*, PHS 97-1995, Series 23, No. 19 (Hyattsville, Md.: HHS, 1997). The question asked about live births to teenage women in the 5 years before the survey.
[d] National Center for Education Statistics, "The Relationship Between the Parental and Marital Experiences of 1988 Eighth-Grade Girls and High School Completion as of 1994," Statistics in Brief, NCES 98-093 (Washington, D.C.: 1998). The survey upon which this study is based, NELS:88, represents U.S. eighth-graders in 1988 who should have graduated from high school in 1992.
[e] The Congressional Budget Office calculated welfare receipt (AFDC only) from NLSY data. *Sources of Support for Adolescent Mothers*, U.S. Congressional Budget Office (Sept. 1990).
[f] J.C. Abma "Fertility, Family Planning, and Women's Health." This source presents insurance coverage for the most recent live birth in the last 5 years. "Medicaid" includes Medicaid and "other government sources."

SOURCE: *Teen Mothers: Selected Socio-Demographic Characteristics and Risk Factors*, U.S. General Accounting Office, Washington, D.C., 1998

FIGURE 4.12

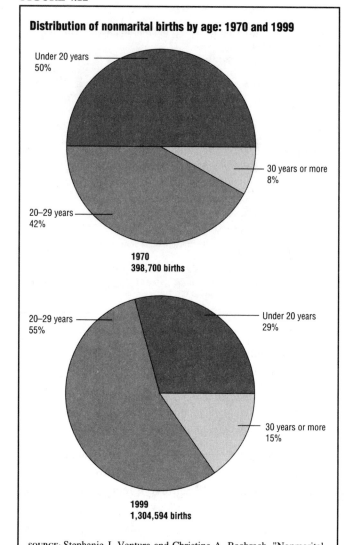

Distribution of nonmarital births by age: 1970 and 1999

Under 20 years 50%
30 years or more 8%
20–29 years 42%
**1970
398,700 births**

20–29 years 55%
Under 20 years 29%
30 years or more 15%
**1999
1,304,594 births**

SOURCE: Stephanie J. Ventura and Christine A. Bachrach, "Nonmarital Childbearing in the United States, 1940–99," *National Vital Statistics Reports*, Vol. 48, No. 16 (Revised), October 18, 2000, Centers for Disease Control and Prevention, National Center for Health Statistics, National Vital Statistics Systems, 2000

15–17 years old among all teenage mothers more than doubled (from 43 to 87 percent). Among older teenage mothers (ages 18 and 19 years), the proportion of those unmarried in 1970 (22 percent) more than tripled, reaching 72 percent in 1997.

While the percentage of unwed teens giving birth increased, the number of non-marital teen births as a percentage of non-marital births for women of all ages has declined considerably. In 1970 there were a total of 398,700 non-marital births, 50 percent of which were to women under the age of 20 years. By 1999 the number of non-marital births had increased drastically to 1.3 million; however, only 29 percent of those births were to women under the age of 20 years. (See Figure 4.12.)

Douglas Kirby, Ph.D., in *No Easy Answers: Research Findings on Programs to Reduce Teen Pregnancy* (National Campaign to Prevent Teen Pregnancy, Washington, D.C., 1997), pointed out the serious consequences that high teen pregnancy rates have on adolescents, their children, and society at large. According to Kirby the future prospects for teen women who give birth decline considerably. He says they achieve a lower standard of education, usually have larger families, and are more likely to be single parents. He also believes that the children born to teens live in a less supportive and stimulating home environment, are less healthy, do not develop as well cognitively, and do worse in school. These children seem to display higher rates of behavioral problems and of teen pregnancies themselves.

Kirby also believes that adolescent births result in a high cost to society, estimating the annual cost to taxpay-

FIGURE 4.13

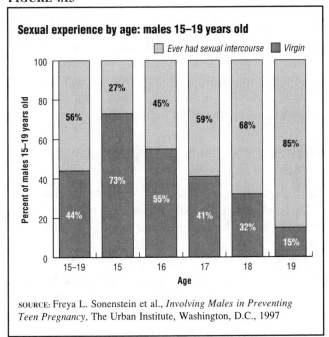

Sexual experience by age: males 15–19 years old

SOURCE: Freya L. Sonenstein et al., *Involving Males in Preventing Teen Pregnancy,* The Urban Institute, Washington, D.C., 1997

FIGURE 4.14

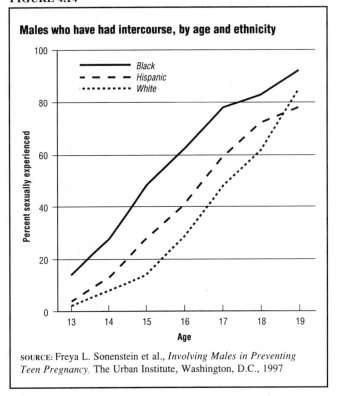

Males who have had intercourse, by age and ethnicity

SOURCE: Freya L. Sonenstein et al., *Involving Males in Preventing Teen Pregnancy,* The Urban Institute, Washington, D.C., 1997

ers is at least $6.9 billion. This includes lost tax revenues, because teen parents are usually lower income earners, as well as expenditure of tax dollars on public assistance, health care, foster care, and the criminal justice system.

TEEN FATHERS

Since the 1970s, when teenage pregnancy first became a serious social problem in the United States, research on adolescent reproductive behavior has concentrated mainly on females. As the 1990s drew to a close, however, several initiatives were undertaken to gather data on adolescent males' reproductive behavior and attitudes.

The federal government launched one such effort. As part of President Clinton's Fatherhood Initiative (June 1995), the Federal Interagency Forum on Child and Family Statistics of the U.S. Department of Health and Human Services has collected data on male fertility, family formation, and fathering.

The Urban Institute, in *Involving Males in Preventing Teen Pregnancy: A Guide for Program Planners* (Freya L. Sonenstein, Kellie Stewart, Laura D. Lindberg, Marta Pernas, and Sean Williams, Washington, D.C., 1997), reported on the reproductive attitudes and behavior of teenage males, based on data collected in the 1995 National Survey of Adolescent Males (NSAM). The NSAM is a periodic survey of 15–19-year-old males, which provides information about trends in their attitudes and behaviors.

The NSAM found that, in 1995, more than one-half (56 percent) of males ages 15–19 years had sexual intercourse. Nearly half (45 percent) had sexual intercourse by

the time they reached their 17th birthday. Not surprisingly, older male teens were more likely to have had sex than younger males (for example, 85 percent of 19-year-olds versus 27 percent of 15-year-olds). At 19 years of age, just 15 percent remained virgins. (See Figure 4.13.)

Racial and Ethnic Differences in Age at First Intercourse

The earlier an adolescent male becomes sexually active, the greater are the risks of pregnancy to his partner. Black teens were more likely to initiate sex earlier than Hispanic or white teens. While one-half of black males had sexual intercourse by the age of 15 years, it took until ages 16.5 and 17 years for half of all Hispanic and white males respectively to have had intercourse. However, by the end of their teen years, the proportion of sexually active males was generally the same across all racial and ethnic groups. (See Figure 4.14.)

Relationship Between Early Sex and Other Problem Behaviors

Since 1990 the U.S. Department of Health and Human Services (HHS) has monitored youth risk behavior. The HHS has found that problem behaviors are generally interrelated and are likely to extend into adulthood. The NSAM found that males who have early sexual experience usually have a high incidence of other problem behaviors.

Three-quarters (76 percent) of teenage males involved with illegal drugs or with past criminal history had already been sexually active, compared with 45 percent of

FIGURE 4.15

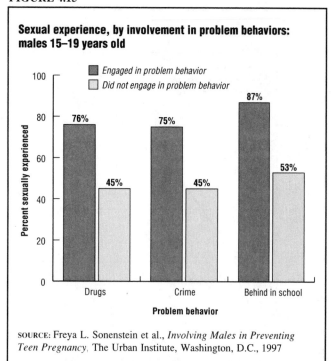

Sexual experience, by involvement in problem behaviors: males 15–19 years old

SOURCE: Freya L. Sonenstein et al., *Involving Males in Preventing Teen Pregnancy*, The Urban Institute, Washington, D.C., 1997

those who had not used drugs or committed a crime. Almost 9 of 10 (87 percent) who were 2 or more years behind in school for their age reported being sexually experienced, compared with 53 percent of those who were not behind in school. (See Figure 4.15.)

Sexual Partners

The NSAM findings show that, contrary to popular belief, while teenage men were generally sexually active they were not necessarily promiscuous. Almost one-half (44 percent) reported having just one partner in one year. Black teens (63 percent) were more likely to have multiple partners than were Hispanic (49 percent) and white teens (39 percent).

Generally, most sexually active young men had female partners close to their own age (average age difference of less than 6 months). Almost an equal percentage of 16-year-olds had sexual intercourse with females aged 16 years old or older (38 percent) and age 15 years (36 percent). However, one-quarter (26 percent) of 16-year-olds reported having had a partner 14 years old or younger. Among 19-year-old males nearly one-half (43 percent) had a partner 18 years old or older, and one-third (33 percent) had had females aged 17 years for their sexual partners. Eleven percent indicated having sexual partners who were 15 years old or younger. (See Figure 4.16.)

Pregnancy and Fatherhood

Despite the high incidence of sexual experience and the inconsistent use of contraception, relatively few adolescent males reported making a partner pregnant. Among

the 15–19-year-old males who were sexually active, 14 percent indicated that they had made someone pregnant while 6 percent had actually become a father. About 2 in 10 black and Hispanic sexually active adolescent males reported having caused a pregnancy, compared with 1 in 10 white teens. Eight to 10 percent of Hispanic and black sexually active teens fathered a child, compared with 5 percent of white teens. (See Figure 4.17.)

SUBSTANCE ABUSE AND THE CHANGING FAMILY STRUCTURE

Substance use and abuse by adolescents are risk-taking behaviors that can have serious consequences not only for the adolescents, but also for their families, communities, and society. Young people who abuse substances appear to experience varied problems ranging from difficulties in school to increased risk of injuries and diseases. They may also experience significant mental health problems, including depression, withdrawal, and suicidal tendencies.

Teen abuse of alcohol and other drugs also disrupts many aspects of family life, resulting in family dysfunction and taxing financial and emotional resources. In addition society bears the consequences of adolescent substance abuse such as gang activities, prostitution, drug trafficking, increased crimes, and even youth homicides.

Relationship Between Family Structure and Substance Use

Research suggests that adolescents in single-parent or stepfamily living arrangements are more likely than are those in two-parent families to use alcohol, tobacco, and other drugs. In 1960 nearly 9 of 10 children under 18 years of age were being raised by families with both parents present. In 1998, while 68 percent of children still lived with both parents, an increasing proportion (9 percent in 1960 and 28 percent in 1998) was living with single parents. (See Table 3.3 in Chapter 3.) Moreover, as growing numbers of parents divorce and remarry, children find themselves living with stepfamilies. Nonetheless, a percentage of children in families with long-married parents also abuse drugs.

The National Household Survey on Drug Abuse (NHSDA) was previously conducted by the National Institute on Drug Abuse. The survey, currently undertaken by the Substance Abuse and Mental Health Services Administration (SAMHSA), provides data on the prevalence, consequences, trends, and demographic patterns of substance use and abuse among the civilian, non-institutionalized American population aged 12 years and older.

Between 1991 and 1993 (the most recent survey relating to family structure) the NHSDA researchers surveyed adolescents ages 12–17 years to examine some implications of the changing family living arrangements for substance use (including alcohol and cigarettes) among

FIGURE 4.16

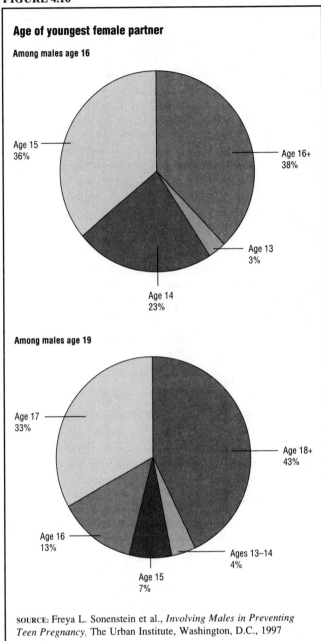

Age of youngest female partner

Among males age 16

Age 15
36%

Age 16+
38%

Age 13
3%

Age 14
23%

Among males age 19

Age 17
33%

Age 18+
43%

Age 16
13%

Ages 13–14
4%

Age 15
7%

SOURCE: Freya L. Sonenstein et al., *Involving Males in Preventing Teen Pregnancy*, The Urban Institute, Washington, D.C., 1997

FIGURE 4.17

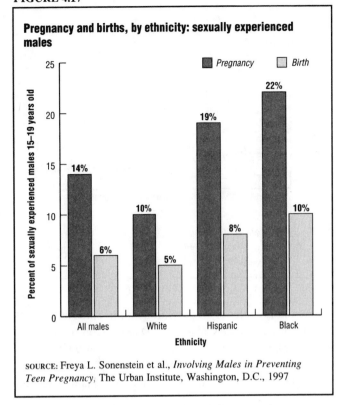

Pregnancy and births, by ethnicity: sexually experienced males

SOURCE: Freya L. Sonenstein et al., *Involving Males in Preventing Teen Pregnancy*, The Urban Institute, Washington, D.C., 1997

Alcohol Dependence

Although in most states the sale of alcohol to persons under the age of 21 years is illegal, alcohol is the most widely used drug among, and the greatest threat to, American youth. Data collected from the 1998–1999 NHSDA showed that 19.2 percent of teens aged 12–17 years used alcohol within the 30 days prior to the survey. (See Figure 4.18.)

Among the various family structures adolescents who lived in mother/father families, with their mother only, or with their mother and a non-relative, reported the lowest risks of alcohol dependence (between 1.2 and 2.5 percent). Father-only families had the highest risks of alcohol dependence (5.9 percent). Overall, male and female adolescents (2.6 and 2.7 percent respectively) showed a similar degree of alcohol dependence. However, among the different family types, male adolescents in father-only families reported the highest percentage of alcohol dependence (8.6 percent). (See Table 4.7.)

Black adolescents were less likely to be alcohol-dependent (1.6 percent) than white (3 percent) or Hispanic (2.9 percent) adolescents. This behavior was consistent in mother/father, mother only, and father only families. (See Table 4.7.)

Cigarette Use

According to the Public Health Service of the U.S. Department of Health and Human Services, approximately 80 percent of tobacco use occurs for the first time in children younger than 18 years of age. Since the early

American adolescents. This included the effects of family structure on adolescent substance use, dependence, and the need for illicit drug abuse treatment.

The NHSDA found that, regardless of the specific substance, adolescents who lived with two biological parents reported lower risks of substance use during the past year than those in other family structures. Approximately one-third (32.1 percent) of adolescents living with both their mother and father indicated using alcohol during the past year, compared with more than one-half (50.8 percent) of those living with their father and stepmother. Similarly, children living with their biological parents were less likely to abuse substances than those living in stepfamilies or with either their father or mother. (See Table 4.6.)

FIGURE 4.18

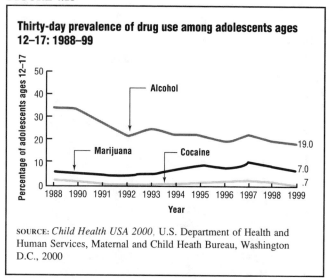

Thirty-day prevalence of drug use among adolescents ages 12–17: 1988–99

SOURCE: *Child Health USA 2000*, U.S. Department of Health and Human Services, Maternal and Child Heath Bureau, Washington D.C., 2000

1990s the prevalence of smoking among American youth has been rising. The Centers for Disease Control and Prevention (CDC) of the HHS estimates that, if the tobacco-use patterns of adolescent smokers persist, an estimated 5 million will die prematurely of smoking-related illnesses.

Cigarette dependence was highest among adolescents in father/stepmother families (7.2 percent) among both males (8.6 percent) and females (5.9 percent). Overall, white adolescents had significantly higher cigarette dependence (2.6 percent) than black (1 percent) and Hispanic (1.5 percent) adolescents. (See Table 4.8.)

Marijuana Use

According to the 1999 NHSDA, 7 percent of adolescents used marijuana in 1999. (See Figure 4.18.) The study showed that marijuana use among teens decreased during the decade of the 1990s, down from 8.3 percent in 1998, and down from 14.2 percent in 1979—the highest level ever recorded.

This is not all good news, however, since marijuana use among teens has more than doubled from the lowest recorded usage rate of 3.4 percent in 1992. A new component of the 1999 NHSDA study revealed that more than 1.5 million Americans under the age of 18 years first used marijuana in 1998. Fifty-seven percent of teens surveyed in 1999 reported that marijuana is easy to obtain, and some 16 percent of those polled said they had been approached by someone selling drugs during the month prior to the survey.

Cocaine

Despite its glamorization during the 1980s cocaine use was still perceived as extremely risky by 49.8 percent of American teens in 1999. That was a significant decrease since 1998 (54.3 percent). In 1999 only 0.7 percent of children 12–17 years old reported having used cocaine in the month prior to being surveyed. (See Figure 4.18.)

SCHOOL VIOLENCE

According to Gallup Youth Surveys as many as 4 in 10 teenagers think that, at some point in their lifetime, someone is likely to fire a gun at them. Four in 10 teens are fearful of walking alone at night in certain areas within a mile of their homes. Half believe they will at some point be mugged.

At the same time that young people held these more negative perceptions, a Gallup Youth Survey completed just before the April 1999 tragedy at Columbine High School in Littleton, Colorado, revealed that the percentage of teens that consider school a safe place was significantly higher than in earlier years. In the early part of 1999 only 15 percent of teens said they sometimes feared for their physical safety at school. In 1996, however, the percentage was nearly double this figure—28 percent. Despite this lack of concern teens said they were aware of the potential for violence at school. Seventeen percent said that "students carrying weapons to school" is a "very big" or "big" problem in their school, and 3 in 10 say they are aware of peers who have carried or regularly carry guns and knives at school.

A total of 3,523 students were expelled from school for bringing a firearm to school, according to the most recent Gun-Free Schools Act Report. (*Report on State Implementation of the Gun-Free Schools Act: School Year 1998-1999*, U.S. Department of Education, Washington, D.C., 2000.)

Other Factors Contributing to Violence

In a report entitled *Youth Gangs in Schools,* Office of Juvenile Justice and Delinquency Prevention, 2000, one-half of teens surveyed said there were guns in their homes and about half said it is at least somewhat important to know how to shoot a gun. Growing alienation from family, and attraction for the family-type environment or acceptance of a gang, is also an issue. Six percent of teens surveyed said it was very or somewhat important to belong to a gang or "posse." Thirty-seven percent of students reported there was a gang presence at their school.

Gallup's Youth Surveys shed light not only on the extent of teen violence, but also on the factors that may contribute to violence and possible strategies to deal with this situation. More than one-half of U.S. teens believed that television shows, movies, or news programs containing violence may play a role in violent behavior by teens such as gang warfare or shootings at schools. Seven in 10 teens admitted they watched too much TV, 6 in 10 believed "gangsta rap" encouraged violence, and 4 in 10 said they "liked to live dangerously."

Teens were also likely to perceive an influence by the media and Internet in terms of lifestyles. More than 6 in 10 said they had noticed changes in their friends, such as the way they talk, dress, or act, because of something they

TABLE 4.6

Percentages of adolescents aged 12–17 using specified substances in the past year, by family structure, 1991–1993

	Alcohol	Cigarettes	Marijuana	Substance Inhalants	Hallucinogens	Stimulants	Cocaine	Sedatives
Total	**36.0**	**19.1**	**9.4**	**3.7**	**2.2**	**2.0**	**1.1**	**1.0**
Both biological parents present:								
Mother/Father	32.1	15.9	6.9	2.8	1.6	1.5	0.7	0.8
Mother/Father/Other	34.8	18.0	8.4	3.1	1.6	1.5	0.9	1.4
Stepparent families:								
Mother/Stepfather	40.2	24.9	10.0	4.8	3.4	3.4	1.8	1.8
Father/Stepmother	50.8	40.7	16.8	5.2	7.5	5.5	1.6	3.4
One parent families:								
Mother only	39.1	20.4	11.5	4.0	2.0	1.5	1.5	0.9
Mother/Other relative	36.1	17.8	12.4	4.0	1.0	2.1	1.7	1.0
Mother/Nonrelative	48.2	25.4	18.3	4.2	1.7	0.7	2.4	0.4
Father only	45.0	27.6	17.1	9.1	6.6	6.0	1.7	1.9
Other family types:								
Other relative only	40.7	20.6	15.1	5.4	3.1	3.3	2.0	1.1
Spouse present	63.8	41.4	25.1	3.1	5.4	5.4	3.5	3.0

SOURCE: Robert L. Johnson et al., *The Relationship Between Family Structure and Adolescent Substance Use*, Substance Abuse and Mental Health Services Administration, Washington, D.C., 1996

TABLE 4.7

Percent of adolescents ages 12–17 reporting alcohol dependence, by family structure, gender, and race/ethnicity, 1991–93

	Group					
	Total	Male	Female	White	Black	Hispanic
Total	**2.7**	**2.6**	**2.7**	**3.0**	**1.6**	**2.9**
Both biological parents present						
Mother/father	2.5	2.3	2.8	2.7	0.8	3.0
Mother/father/other	1.2	1.7	0.7	1.3	1.3	1.3
Stepparent families						
Mother/stepfather	2.7	1.5	3.8	2.9	*	4.4
Father/stepmother	4.0	3.2	*	4.5	0.0	*
One parent families						
Mother only *	2.5	2.9	2.1	3.2	1.4	2.4
Mother/other relative	3.0	4.2	1.8	5.2	1.5	*
Mother/nonrelative	2.3	*	*	2.9	*	*
Father only	5.9	8.6	*	7.6	0.9	0.5
Other family types						
Other relative only	4.2	5.5	2.8	3.3	*	2.9
Spouse present	4.6	*	4.3	4.2	*	*

*Low precision; no estimate reported.

SOURCE: Robert A. Johnson et al., *The Relationship between Family Structure and Adolescent Substance Use,* Substance Abuse and Mental Health Services Administration, Washington, D.C., 1996

TABLE 4.8

Percent of adolescents ages 12–17 reporting cigarette dependence, by family structure, gender, and race/ethnicity, 1991–93

	Group					
	Total	Male	Female	White	Black	Hispanic
Total	**2.2**	**2.5**	**1.9**	**2.6**	**1.0**	**1.5**
Both biological parents present						
Mother/father	1.8	2.1	1.5	2.1	0.6	1.1
Mother/father/other	1.9	2.0	1.8	3.4	0.0	0.5
Stepparent families						
Mother/stepfather	2.0	2.5	1.6	2.1	0.0	3.2
Father/stepmother	7.2	8.6	5.9	7.8	*	*
One parent families						
Mother only	2.4	2.2	2.6	3.7	0.8	1.3
Mother/other relative	3.1	4.0	2.3	4.0	2.3	*
Mother/nonrelative	*	*	*	*	0.0	0.0
Father only	3.6	3.5	3.8	4.5	0.5	*
Other family types						
Other relative only	2.8	5.2	0.3	4.1	*	2.0
Spouse present	4.5	*	*	*	0.0	0.6

*Low precision; no estimate reported.

SOURCE: Robert A. Johnson et al., *The Relationship between Family Structure and Adolescent Substance Use,* Substance Abuse and Mental Health Services Administration, Washington, D.C., 1996

saw or heard in the media or on the Internet. One-third of teens (35%) said they were under a "great deal" or "some" pressure from their peers to "break rules," and many reported being teased about their appearance.

One-half said they received "too little" respect from adults, and many felt misunderstood. One teen in 8 reported that he or she had been physically abused; one-third could not talk about "life with father." When asked what

relatives lived at home with them, although 91 percent said their mother, only 67 percent said their father.

CHILDREN INVOLVED IN DIVORCE

Every year more than 1.5 million children—almost 2.5 percent of all children in the United States—experience their parents' divorce or separation. Numerous studies have been conducted to determine the effects of divorce on children's wellbeing. Two such studies are "Explaining the Higher Incidence of Adjustment Problems Among Children of Divorce Compared to Those in Intact Families," Iowa State University, Ames, IA, 1999; and Report to Congress on Out-of-Wedlock Childbearing, U.S. Department of Health and Human Services, Centers for Disease Control and Prevention, 1995. Some researchers have found that, while children involved in divorce may experience social, emotional, and psychological problems following their parents' divorce, these adverse effects usually only persist for about two or three years following the divorce.

Other studies have found long-lasting problems among some children who have undergone their parents' divorce. For instance, the teen pregnancy rates among children of divorce are estimated to be 33 percent, while high school dropout rates are 31 percent, compared with 13 percent among children raised in a two-parent family. Children experiencing the disruption of their parents' marriages tend to have poorer emotional adjustment, including being more anxious, than children not undergoing this experience. In 1987, 14 percent of children with divorced parents needed psychological help, compared with 6 percent of children in two-parent families. Generally, children in stepfamilies have also been known to exhibit similar problems. It should be noted, however, that a number of studies have found many of these problems existed before the divorce.

Impact of Divorce on Children's Wellbeing

REDUCED PARENTAL SUPPORT. In *Noncustodial Parents' Participation in Their Children's Lives: Evidence from the Survey of Income and Program Participation, Volume II* (U.S. Department of Health and Human Services, Washington, D.C., 1996), Christine Winquist Nord and Nicholas Zill discussed the impact of divorce on children's wellbeing. According to the authors divorce often results in the reduced role of the father. The father's departure from the family means reduced family income, as well as the lessening of emotional, psychological, and physical support for the children. Research shows that artificial visitations and the subsequent repeated separations are very stressful for the father, but research has not addressed the stress imposed on the children. It is assumed that children who are very close to their fathers feel the most pain at the repeated separations.

POOR PARENTAL ADJUSTMENT. The mental wellbeing of the divorcing parents generally determines how well children adjust to the new life. Some parents may be so preoccupied with their own conflicts, anger, and anxiety that they neglect their children at this vulnerable stage in their lives. In addition, when parents cannot resolve their differences even after the divorce, children find themselves constantly caught in the middle of the conflict.

STRESSFUL LIFE CHANGES. Often, due to limited finances resulting from the division of assets following divorce, one or both parents may have to move to a new home, removing the children from familiar surroundings. Children are taken away from family and friends who could have lent needed support. If one or both parents remarry the children have to adjust to yet another living arrangement. Statistics also show that up to one-half of children of divorce will witness yet another parental divorce should the parent remarry.

ECONOMIC DIFFICULTIES. Children living in single-parent families are more likely to be poor, especially if the custodial parent is the mother. Women generally earn less than men earn, even when doing the same type of work. In 1997 the poverty rate for families maintained by women with no husband present was 6 times higher than that of married-couple families. (See Chapter 5.) Children who lived in poverty prior to the divorce are more likely to be adversely affected by the marital disruption. They are more likely to live in problem neighborhoods and more likely to be deprived of the nutrition and medical care essential to their development. The University of Michigan's longitudinal study of income dynamics (ongoing since 1968) showed that, typically, the standard of living for a divorced mother and her children declined by 30 percent in the first year following the divorce.

Children of Divorce Do Survive

Sociologist Frank F. Furstenberg, Jr., of the University of Pennsylvania, believes that divorce does not have as consistent a negative effect on children as people often believe. He says researchers involved in the study of children experiencing their parent's divorce believe children fare better living with one divorced parent who is loving and attentive than growing up in a home with two fighting parents. Some experts agree with Furstenberg, adding that the shift from a two-parent family to a single-parent family does not necessarily translate to adverse effects on children. Sometimes the problem behaviors manifested by children after the divorce were present in the family long before the parental separation. The solution should be to determine what factors in the lives of children of divorce predispose them to engage in risk-taking behaviors.

However, not all the experts agree with Fustenberg. Psychologist Judith Wallerstein, widely considered one of the foremost authorities on the effects of divorce on children, studied 130 children who had gone through divorce, following them for 25 years. Wallerstein claims that only 40 percent of adult children of divorce ever marry and believes there is a long-lasting effect on children of divorce that can be overcome but not wiped out.

One Solution: Increased Paternal Involvement

Historically research on children's wellbeing has focused on mothers and children. During the 1990s fathers and their role in children's lives have received increasing

FIGURE 4.19

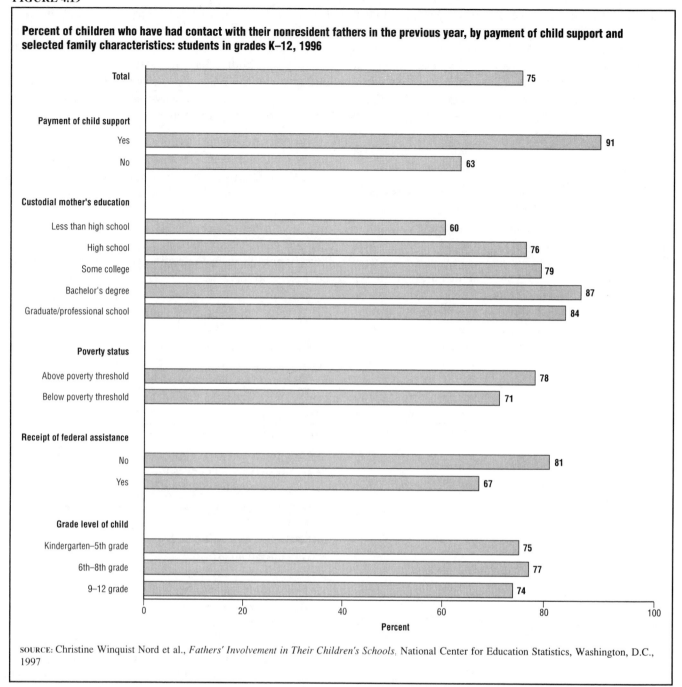

Percent of children who have had contact with their nonresident fathers in the previous year, by payment of child support and selected family characteristics: students in grades K–12, 1996

SOURCE: Christine Winquist Nord et al., *Fathers' Involvement in Their Children's Schools*, National Center for Education Statistics, Washington, D.C., 1997

attention. President Bill Clinton's Fatherhood Initiative is intended to include fathers in government research programs.

The rising divorce rates and the increasing numbers of children involved in divorce have brought the issue of the absent father and its effect on children's development to the forefront. Studies show that fatherlessness is generally a major cause of child poverty. It has also been shown to affect children's performance in school and their future job prospects.

A 1997 report by the National Center for Education Statistics provides information on nonresident fathers' involvement in their children's lives, including school (Christine

Winquist Nord, DeeAnn Brimhall, and Jerry West, Fathers' Involvement in Their Children's Schools, U. S. Department of Education, Washington, D.C., 1997). It further examines the influence nonresidential parents' school involvement had on their children's school performance.

Several factors are said to be associated with nonresident fathers' continued involvement with their children after a divorce: whether or not the fathers pay child support, the custodial mothers' education and family income levels, and the ages of the children. Children whose fathers had paid child support were more likely to have had some contact with their fathers (91 versus 63 percent). Children

FIGURE 4.20

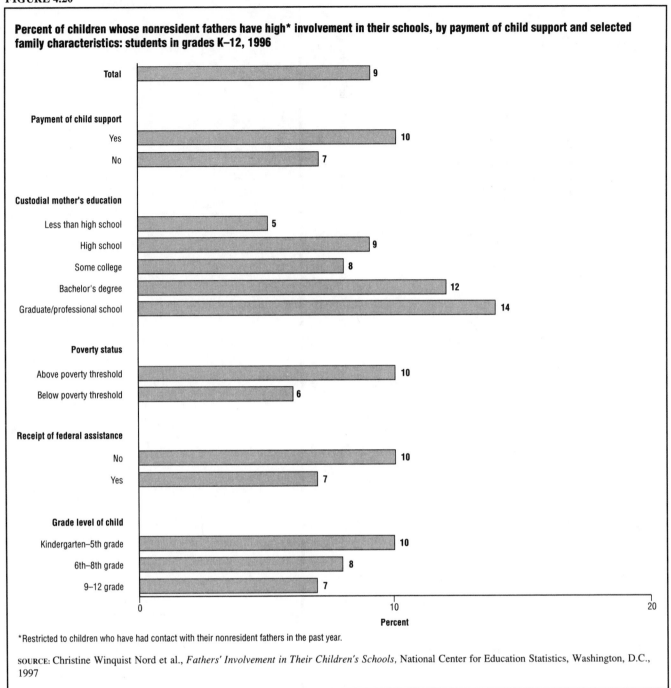

Percent of children whose nonresident fathers have high* involvement in their schools, by payment of child support and selected family characteristics: students in grades K–12, 1996

*Restricted to children who have had contact with their nonresident fathers in the past year.

SOURCE: Christine Winquist Nord et al., *Fathers' Involvement in Their Children's Schools*, National Center for Education Statistics, Washington, D.C., 1997

in families where custodial mothers were more educated and where family members were not experiencing economic hardship were also more likely to have seen their fathers regularly (78 versus 71 percent). (See Figure 4.19.)

These same factors were also related to the nonresident fathers' being highly involved in their children's schools. Fathers who had paid child support were more likely than those who had paid none (10 versus 7 percent) to be involved in their children's schools. Involvement by nonresident fathers increased as the custodial mothers' education increased and if the family was not having economic difficulties. As the children moved from kinder-

garten to the higher grades, the nonresidential fathers' involvement in their children's school activities decreased. (See Figure 4.20.)

INVOLVEMENT OF NONRESIDENTIAL PARENTS ON STUDENT OUTCOMES. The researchers also examined the effect that the nonresident parents' involvement in school had on their children's school performance. About one-third of children whose nonresidential parents were highly involved in their schools got mostly As. Children were also more likely to enjoy school (40–44 percent) if they had recent contacts with their nonresidential parents and if these parents got involved in their schools. The propor-

TABLE 4.9

Percent of children with selected student outcomes, by recency of contact with their nonresident parents, level of involvement of the nonresident parents in their schools, and type of nonresident parent: students in grades K–12, 1996

Student outcome	Nonresident fathers						Nonresident mothers				
				Contact in last year		Involvement				Contact in last year	Involvement
	Total	Never had contact	No contact in more than 1 year	Total	Low	High	Total	No contact in more than 1 year[1]	Total	Low	High
Total students (thousands)	16,752	1,549	2,588	12,614	10,496	1,093	4,138	400	3,737	2,588	740
Child gets mostly A's	29.4%	27.8%	24.5%	30.7%	29.1%	35.2%	26.5%	30.4%	26.1%	24.6%	33.0%
Child enjoys school	36.3	35.9	36.7	36.3	34.7	44.8	33.4	29.6	33.9	32.0	39.5
Child did extracurricular activities											
Kindergarten–5th grade	74.6	70.5	74.6	75.2	73.5	86.6	79.6	74.6	80.2	78.7	86.1
6th–12th grade[2]	77.1	70.0	79.5	77.4	75.5	92.0	75.2	66.3	76.1	75.0	84.2
Child has repeated a grade	17.8	19.2	23.1	16.5	18.1	7.2	17.0	11.6	17.6	19.4	11.9
Child has ever been expelled/suspended	26.6	26.4	30.3	25.8	27.8	14.4	29.7	34.8	29.2	30.9	18.5

[1] Only a small number of nonresident mothers have never had contact with their children. Therefore, this column combines mothers who have never had contact with mothers who have not had contact with their children in more than 1 year.

[2] From youth report.

SOURCE: Christine Winquist Nord et al., *Fathers' Involvement in Their Children's Schools*, National Center for Education Statistics, Washington, D.C., 1997

tion of children doing extracurricular activities (84–92 percent) increased as their parents' school involvement increased. In addition children were less likely to have repeated a grade or to have been expelled or suspended (14–18 percent) when they had seen their nonresidential parents within the last year and when the parents were involved in school. (See Table 4.9.)

The Impact of a Parent's Sexual Orientation

When one of a child's divorced parents is homosexual, it often greatly complicates the role of that parent in their lives. Some Americans consider a gay or lesbian lifestyle to be unhealthy or immoral, something to which children should not be exposed. Others disagree with these opinions on homosexuality and feel that it should not play a factor in determining custody or visitation rights.

PULLIAM V. SMITH. Like most laws concerning gay and lesbian rights, those affecting the custody and visitation of children involved in divorce are developing and often vary from state to state. Fredrick and Carol Smith were the parents of two boys, Joey and Kenny. The Smiths divorced in 1991 when Joey was six and Kenny was three. The parents agreed that they would have joint legal custody and the children would live with the father. The children lived with their father and grandmother in North Carolina. Their mother married William Pulliam and lived in Wichita, Kansas. The children visited there for two months during the summer and at Christmas.

In 1994 Tim Tipton moved in with Frederick Smith. Both men were gay. The grandmother soon moved out. Carol Pulliam sued for custody of the children claiming there was "a substantial change of circumstances affecting the welfare of [the children] which would warrant a change of custody." Two lower courts agreed, and so did a 5–1 majority of the North Carolina Supreme Court in *Pulliam v. Smith* (No. 499PA96, July 30, 1998).

The North Carolina Supreme Court claimed that it "did not rely on the mere fact that defendant is a homosexual or a 'practicing homosexual.'" Nor did the court believe that "the mere homosexual status of a parent is sufficient, taken alone, to support denying such parent custody of his or her child or children."

Rather, the court had based its decision on the finding that "the activity of the defendant will likely create emotional difficulties for the two minor children." Among the findings of fact determined by the lower court were that the two men "often kiss on the cheek and sometimes on the lips in front of the two minor children." They further engaged in sexual activity "while the minor children were present in the home." There were pictures of drag queens in the men's bedroom. The court further noted that the children "on one or more occasions observed [the two men] in bed together."

The lower court had concluded that, "the active homosexuality of the [two men] ... is detrimental to the best interest and welfare of the two minor children" and ordered that the mother "be awarded the exclusive care, custody, and control of the two minor children." The father was granted a one-month visitation during the summer and was not permitted to live with his companion when his children were present. The North Carolina Supreme Court affirmed this decision.

INSCOE V. INSCOE. Herbert Inscoe, Jr. was the son of Bonnie and Herbert Inscoe, Sr. After his parents' divorce the child went to live with his father, who raised him until he was 10 years old. Mr. Inscoe began living with a male partner and, as a result, his wife went to court to gain physical custody of the boy. An Ohio trial court ordered Herbert Jr. taken from his father's home and transferred to his mother's home because his father was "openly gay." The father appealed the decision.

On June 16, 1997, the Ohio Court of Appeals for the Fourth Appellate District overruled the lower court and ordered that the case be retried with no consideration of the father's homosexuality. "A parent's sexual orientation, standing alone," observed the court, "has no relevance to a decision concerning the allocation of parental rights and responsibilities. ... [Furthermore,] a trial court must disregard adverse impacts on the child that flow from society's disapproval of a parent's sexual orientation."

BOSWELL V. BOSWELL. Robert and Kimberly Boswell were married in 1986. Their marriage produced two children, a son Ryan born in 1988 and a daughter Amanda born in 1991. Ms. Boswell filed for divorce in 1994. The trial judge for the Circuit Court for Anne Arundel County, Maryland, limited visitation by Robert Boswell to every other Saturday, every other Sunday, and every other Wednesday. The court further prohibited any overnight visitation and any visitation in which the children would be in the presence of Boswell's male companion, or "anyone having homosexual tendencies or such persuasions, male or female, or anyone that the father may be living with in a nonmarital relationship." Neither Ms. Boswell nor the caseworker had requested such severely restricted visitations.

Mr. Boswell appealed the decision to the Court of Special Appeals which, in *Boswell v. Boswell* (701 A.2d 1153), overturned the lower court decision. The case was further appealed by Ms. Boswell who wanted the order concerning visitation in the presence of Mr. Boswell's partner reinstated. The Court of Appeals for the State of Maryland, the state's highest court, in *Boswell v. Boswell* (case 4/98T), upheld the decision of the Court of Special Appeals.

CHAPTER 5
FAMILY EMPLOYMENT, INCOME, POVERTY

EMPLOYMENT

Over the last four decades of the twentieth century the massive numbers of Baby Boomers entering the work place, as well as large numbers of women, has accounted for substantial growth in the American labor force. (For definition, the term "labor force" includes persons who hold part- or full-time jobs and those who are unemployed but looking for work.)

In 1999, of the 71.3 million American families, 83.1 percent had at least one employed member and 93 percent of those families had at least one member who worked full time (35 hours or more). (See Table 5.1.)

During an average week in 1999 (a year of record low unemployment) 6 percent (4.3 million) of all families had at least one person who was unemployed. However, 72.6 percent of families that had an unemployed person also included at least one employed person. Moreover, nearly three-quarters (65 percent) had members usually working full time. Unemployment in a family is usually easier to ride out when another family member is working. About 1 in 6 families (16.9 percent) in the United States had no family members employed, but this includes many families where both members are retired or otherwise not seeking work, which means they are not considered to be unemployed. (See Table 5.1.)

Race and Ethnicity

In 1999, 10.6 percent of all black families had an unemployed person in their household, followed by Hispanics with 9.7 percent. Whites fared better, with only 5.3 percent of families stating that a member was unemployed. White families were also the least likely, and black families the most likely, to report that they had no one in their family who was employed, or that no one in their family was employed full-time. (See Table 5.1.)

Family Types

During 1999, 84.1 percent of the 54.5 million married-couple families in the United States had some member working. Of the 4.2 million families maintained by men, 86.3 percent included some working member, compared with 77.6 percent of the 12.6 million female-headed families. (See Table 5.2.)

DUAL EARNERS. The traditional family, in which the father was the breadwinner and the mother was the homemaker, has not been the norm since some time in the 1970s. With the increasing entry of wives and mothers into the work force more and more families have dual earners. In 1999 more than one-half (53 percent) of married-couple families had both spouses working. The traditional families, in which only the husband worked, comprised just 19.3 percent of all married-couple families. (See Table 5.2.)

WORKING WIVES AND MOTHERS

Married Women and World War II

Prior to World War II (1939–45) it was common for some subgroups of women (young, single, and non-white women) to work. However, another segment of the population—middle-class wives and mothers—traditionally stayed home. During the 1920s a growing number of women entered the work force, but this growth was stopped with the Great Depression of the 1930s. During the Depression lawmakers introduced legislation to restrict females from working because they felt women took jobs from men who "needed the job more." During World War II, with more men serving in the military, an unprecedented number of women once again joined the labor force, entering traditional and nontraditional occupations. As the war escalated the government reversed its Depression-era restrictions on hiring female workers, especially married women.

TABLE 5.1

Employment and unemployment in families, by race and Hispanic origin, 1998–99 annual averages

(Numbers in thousands)

Characteristic	1998	1999
TOTAL		
Total families	70,218	71,250
With employed member(s)	57,986	59,185
As percent of total families	82.6	83.1
Some usually work full time[1]	53,945	55,123
With no employed member	12,232	12,065
As percent of total families	17.4	16.9
With unemployed member(s)	4,503	4,260
As percent of total families	6.4	6.0
Some member(s) employed	3,177	3,091
As percent of families with unemployed member(s)	70.6	72.6
Some usually work full time[1]	2,830	2,771
As percent of families with unemployed member(s)	62.8	65.0
White		
Total families	58,930	59,661
With employed member(s)	48,850	49,632
As percent of total families	82.9	83.2
Some usually work full time[1]	45,567	46,333
With no employed member	10,080	10,029
As percent of total families	17.1	16.8
With unemployed member(s)	3,299	3,134
As percent of total families	5.6	5.3
Some member(s) employed	2,463	2,374
As percent of families with unemployed member(s)	74.7	75.7
Some usually work full time[1]	2,204	2,132
As percent of families with unemployed members	66.8	68.0
Black		
Total families	8,317	8,498
With employed member(s)	6,554	6,847
As percent of total families	78.8	80.6
Some usually work full time[1]	5,953	6,249
With no employed member	1,763	1,652
As percent of total families	21.2	19.4
With unemployed member(s)	984	905
As percent of total families	11.8	10.6
Some member(s) employed	555	551
As percent of families with unemployed member(s)	56.4	60.9
Some usually work full time[1]	485	486
As percent of families with unemployed members	49.3	53.7
Hispanic origin		
Total families	7,025	7,403
With employed member(s)	5,947	6,405
As percent of total families	84.7	86.5
Some usually work full time[1]	5,545	6,017
With no employed member	1,078	998
As percent of total families	15.3	13.5
With unemployed member(s)	744	715
As percent of total families	10.6	9.7
Some member(s) employed	522	518
As percent of families with unemployed member(s)	70.2	72.4
Some usually work full time[1]	467	467
As percent of families with unemployed members	62.8	65.3

[1] Usually work 35 hours or more a week at all jobs.

Note: Detail for the above race and Hispanic-origin groups will not sum to totals because data for the "other races" group are not presented and Hispanics are included in both the white and black population groups. Data for 1999 are not strictly comparable with data for 1998 and earlier years because of the introduction of revised population controls in the household survey in January 1999. Detail may not sum to totals due to rounding.

SOURCE: "Employment Characteristics of Families in 1999," *Bureau of Labor Statistics News,* U.S. Department of Labor, Washington, D.C., June 2000

TABLE 5.2

Families by presence and relationship of employed members and by family type, 1998–99 annual averages

(Numbers in thousands)

Characteristic	Number 1998	Number 1999	Percent distribution 1998	Percent distribution 1999
MARRIED-COUPLE FAMILIES				
Total	53,689	54,468	100.0	100.0
Member(s) employed, total	45,061	45,800	83.9	84.1
Husband only	10,285	10,533	19.2	19.3
Wife only	2,843	2,980	5.3	5.5
Husband and wife	28,531	28,882	53.1	53.0
Other employment combinations	3,402	3,404	6.3	6.2
No member(s) employed	8,628	8,669	16.1	15.9
FAMILIES MAINTAINED BY WOMEN[1]				
Total	12,447	12,625	100.0	100.0
Members(s) employed, total	9,417	9,797	75.7	77.6
Householder only	5,322	5,566	42.8	44.1
Householder and other member(s)	2,582	2,663	20.7	21.1
Other member(s), not householder	1,513	1,568	12.2	12.4
No member(s) employed	3,029	2,827	24.3	22.4
FAMILIES MAINTAINED BY MEN[1]				
Total	4,083	4,158	100.0	100.0
Members(s) employed, total	3,509	3,588	85.9	86.3
Householder only	1,746	1,718	42.8	41.3
Householder and other member(s)	1,283	1,353	31.4	32.5
Other member(s), not householder	480	517	11.8	12.4
No member(s) employed	574	569	14.1	13.7

[1] No spouse present.

Note: Data for 1999 are not strictly comparable with data for 1998 and earlier years because of the introduction of revised population controls in the household survey in January 1999. Detail may not sum to totals due to rounding.

SOURCE: "Employment Characteristics of Families in 1999," *Bureau of Labor Statistics News,* U.S. Department of Labor, Washington, D.C., June 2000

In 1940, before America's involvement in World War II, 28 percent of American women worked (about 11 million); by 1944, 36 percent were working outside the home. Throughout the war years more than 19 million women filled the vacancies left by 16 million servicemen, as well as the new jobs created by the war industry. The Women's Bureau of the Department of Labor, established by the federal government in June 1920 to specifically promote the welfare of wage-earning women, reported that about 26 percent of wives had paying jobs, and that a majority did volunteer work.

Increased Labor Force Participation

According to the U.S. Department of Labor, after the war, women were encouraged to stay home to make room for returning servicemen. The economic boom, however, was able to accommodate women interested in working outside the home, and educated, middle-class married women re-entered the labor force. In 1946, the year the

TABLE 5.3

Women in the labor force, 1960–97

(Numbers in thousands)

Year	Civilian labor force
1960	23,268
1965	26,200
1970	31,543
1975	37,475
1980	45,487
1985	51,050
1990	56,289
1995	60,944
1997	63,036

SOURCE: *Equal Pay: A Thirty-Five Year Perspective,* Women's Bureau, U.S. Department of Labor, Washington, D.C., 1998

FIGURE 5.1

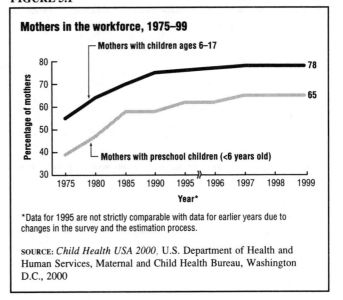

Mothers in the workforce, 1975–99

*Data for 1995 are not strictly comparable with data for earlier years due to changes in the survey and the estimation process.

SOURCE: *Child Health USA 2000*, U.S. Department of Health and Human Services, Maternal and Child Health Bureau, Washington D.C., 2000

war ended, 31 percent of women were in the labor force; 7 percent of this group were middle-class wives.

In 1950, 18 million women (29 percent of all women) were in the work force—about one-half of them married women. By 1960, 23.3 million women workers (37.7 percent of all women) were in the nation's labor force. Among married women 30.5 percent worked, contributing about 26 percent of total family income. In 1997, 63 million women (59.8 percent of all women) comprised 46.2 percent of the total labor force. Nearly two-thirds (62.1 percent) were married women. (See Tables 5.3 and 5.4.)

Married and Unmarried Mothers

WITH OWN CHILDREN UNDER 18 YEARS. Mothers continue to account for the increase in women's overall labor force participation. In 1960 only a little more than one-quarter (27.6 percent) of married women with children worked outside the home or were looking for work. By 1975 almost one-half (44.9 percent) of married women with children were in the labor force. (See Table 5.4.)

From 1975 to 1996 the proportion of working mothers with school-age children (6–17 years old) rose 41 percent, from 54.8 to 77.2 percent. Meanwhile, the labor force participation rate for mothers of preschoolers rose 61 percent, from 38.8 to 62.3 percent. By 1999, 78 percent of mothers with school-age children and 65 percent with preschoolers were in the labor force. (See Table 5.5 and Figure 5.1.) These are huge changes in a short period of time, indicating significant changes in American society.

In 1999, according to the Bureau of Labor Statistics of the U.S. Department of Labor, there were 34.3 million married-couple families with their own children under the age of 18 years. More than two-thirds (68.2 percent) of these families had working mothers, and 64.1 percent had fathers who were employed as well. Of the 14.9 million married-couple families with children under the age of 6 years old, 60.7 percent had mothers in the labor force and 57.4 percent had both mother and father working. (See Table 5.6.)

Unmarried mothers are also very active in the labor force. Their earnings usually comprise about three-quarters of the total family income. In 1999, of the 7.7 million female-headed families with children under the age of 18 years, mothers had a labor force participation of 74.7 percent. Among the 2.9 million female-headed families with children younger than 6 years of age, 67.4 percent of mothers were employed. (See Table 5.6.)

MOTHERS OF VERY YOUNG CHILDREN. The number of working, married women with children continues to rise. In 1999, of the 7 million married-couple families with children under the age of 3 years old, 59.6 percent of mothers were in the labor force. (This includes mothers holding part-time or full-time jobs and unemployed mothers looking for work.) Of the 2.2 million families maintained by women the labor force participation rate of mothers was 67.5 percent. (See Table 5.7.)

During the 1990s the labor force participation among working mothers of very young children—children less than 1 year old—has been increasing overall. (See Table 5.8.) Many of these women held a job before the birth of their newest child. Most had been in the labor force some time, often taking a brief maternity leave before going back to work. Others who left their job to spend an indefinite time with their newborn were usually able to return to the labor force because of their past work experience. In 1999 an average of 56.6 percent of all working mothers were back on the job by their infant's first birthday (55.9 percent for married-couple families and 58.9 percent for female-headed families). (See Table 5.7.)

INCOME

In 1999 the Census Bureau reported that, after 10 years, the median income (the level at which half earned more and half earned less) for all U.S. households (family

TABLE 5.4

Labor force participation rate of women, 1960–97

	1960	1965	1970	1975	1980	1985	1990	1995	1997
Labor force participation rate of women, 16 years and over	37.7	39.3	43.3	46.3	51.5	54.5	57.5	58.9	59.8
Percentage of married women in the labor force	30.5*	34.7	40.8	44.4	50.1	54.2	58.2	61.1	62.1
Percentage of married women with children in the labor force	27.6*	32.2	39.7	44.9	54.1	60.8	66.3	70.2	71.1

*For 1960, civilian non-institutional persons 14 years and over. Thereafter, 16 years and over.

SOURCE: *Equal Pay: A Thirty-Five Year Perspective,* Women's Bureau, U.S. Department of Labor, Washington, D.C., 1998

TABLE 5.5

Population, labor force, and labor force participation rates of women ages 16 and older, by presence and age of own children: selected years, March 1975–96

[Numbers in thousands]

Presence and age of own children and labor force status	March of:									
	1975	1980	1985	1990	1991	1992	1993	1994	1995	1996
Total women:										
Population	79,453	87,939	93,455	98,152	98,970	99,783	100,654	102,181	103,128	104,058
Labor force	36,496	44,934	50,891	56,138	56,373	57,244	57,558	59,646	60,538	61,229
Labor force participation rate	45.9	51.1	54.5	57.2	57.0	57.4	57.2	58.4	58.7	58.8
With no children under 18:										
Population	48,856	56,483	61,160	64,890	65,424	65,925	66,207	66,808	67,714	68,864
Labor force	22,028	27,144	30,850	33,942	34,047	34,487	34,495	35,455	35,843	36,509
Labor force participation rate	45.1	48.1	50.4	52.3	52.0	52.3	52.1	53.1	52.9	53.0
With children under 18:										
Population	30,597	31,456	32,295	33,262	33,546	33,859	34,448	35,373	35,413	35,194
Labor force	14,467	17,790	20,041	22,196	22,327	22,756	23,063	24,191	24,695	24,720
Labor force participation rate	47.3	56.6	62.1	66.7	66.6	67.2	67.0	68.4	69.7	70.2
With children 6 to 17, none younger:										
Population	16,182	17,489	16,929	17,123	17,058	17,368	17,827	18,248	18,721	18,679
Labor force	8,875	11,252	11,826	12,799	12,691	13,183	13,441	13,863	14,300	14,427
Labor force participation rate	54.8	64.3	69.9	74.7	74.4	75.9	75.4	76.0	76.4	77.2
With children under 6:										
Population	14,415	13,966	15,366	16,139	16,488	16,491	16,620	17,125	16,692	16,515
Labor force	5,592	6,538	8,215	9,397	9,636	9,573	9,621	10,328	10,395	10,293
Labor force participation rate	38.8	46.8	53.5	58.2	58.4	58.0	57.9	60.3	62.3	62.3

Note: Data beginning in 1994 are not strictly comparable with data for prior years because they incorporate the results of a major redesign of the Current Population Survey (CPS) and 1990 census-based population controls adjusted for the estimated undercount.

"Own children" are defined as sons, daughters, adopted, or step-children. Excluded are grandchildren, nieces, nephews, other related children, and unrelated children.

SOURCE: Howard V. Hayghe, "Developments in Women's Labor Force Participation," *Monthly Labor Review,* Vol. 120, No. 9, September 1997, U.S. Department of Labor, Bureau of Labor Statistics, Washington, D.C., 1997

and nonfamily) had increased for all groups, with highs set or equaled for all. The year 1989 was the peak year before the most recent recessionary period (a period in which there is a decline in business activity). This recession lasted from July 1990 to March 1991. The 1999 average median income for all households (family and nonfamily) was $40,816, higher than the 1989 median income of $38,721 (in 1999 dollars). (See Table 5.9.)

Families

In 1999 married-couple families earned a median income of $56,827. (See Table 5.9 and Figure 5.2.) Work-

ing wives contributed substantially to this income. For example in 1997, working wives contributed an average of 36.5 percent of total family earnings. White wives contributed 35.8 percent, black wives 43.7 percent, and Hispanic wives 37.5 percent. (See Figure 5.3.)

Families maintained by women with no husband present traditionally earn the lowest median income of all families. In 1989 female householders with no husband present earned 45 percent of the income of married-couple households and 57 percent of male-headed households with no wife present. In 1999 the comparable proportions were 46 and 62.5 percent respectively. Also in 1999 female-headed

TABLE 5.6

Families with own children: employment status of parents, by age of youngest child and family type, 1998–99 annual averages
(Numbers in thousands)

Characteristic	Number		Percent distribution	
	1998	1999	1998	1999
WITH OWN CHILDREN UNDER 18 YEARS OF AGE				
Total	**34,232**	**34,340**	**100.0**	**100.0**
Parent(s) employed	31,100	31,493	90.9	91.7
No parent employed	3,130	2,847	9.1	8.3
Married-couple families	24,820	24,904	100.0	100.0
Parent(s) employed	24,088	24,243	97.1	97.3
Mother employed	16,911	16,995	68.1	68.2
Both parents employed	15,906	15,958	64.1	64.1
Mother employed, not father	1,005	1,037	4.0	4.2
Father employed, not mother	7,178	7,249	28.9	29.1
Neither parent employed	731	662	2.9	2.7
Families maintained by women[1]	7,573	7,653	100.0	100.0
Mother employed	5,440	5,713	71.8	74.7
Mother not employed	2,133	1,940	28.2	25.3
Families maintained by men[1]	1,839	1,782	100.0	100.0
Father employed	1,572	1,537	85.5	86.3
Father not employed	266	245	14.5	13.7
WITH OWN CHILDREN 6 TO 17 YEARS OF AGE NONE YOUNGER				
Total	**19,209**	**19,364**	**100.0**	**100.0**
Parent(s) employed	17,551	17,825	91.4	92.1
No parent employed	1,658	1.539	8.6	7.9
Married-couple families	13,496	13,565	100.0	100.0
Parent(s) employed	13,065	13,175	96.8	97.1
Mother employed	9,991	10,113	74.0	74.6
Both parents employed	9,338	9,446	69.2	69.6
Mother employed, not father	653	668	4.8	4.9
Father employed, not mother	3,074	3,061	22.8	22.6
Neither parent employed	431	390	3.2	2.9
Families maintained by women[1]	4,638	4,722	100.0	100.0
Mother employed	3,573	3.737	77.0	79.1
Mother not employed	1,065	985	23.0	20.9
Families maintained by men[1]	1,075	1,077	100.0	100.0
Father employed	913	913	84.9	84.8
Father not employed	162	164	15.1	15.2
WITH OWN CHILDREN UNDER 6 YEARS OF AGE				
Total	**15,023**	**14,976**	**100.0**	**100.0**
Parent(s) employed	13,550	13,670	90.2	91.3
No parent employed	1,473	1,307	9.8	8.7
Married-couple families	11,324	11,340	100.0	100.0
Parent(s) employed	11,023	11,070	97.3	97.6
Mother employed	6,920	6,882	61.1	60.7
Both parents employed	6,567	6,512	58.0	57.4
Mother employed, not father	352	370	3.1	3.3
Father employed, not mother	4,103	4,188	36.2	36.9
Neither parent employed	301	270	2.7	2.4
Families maintained by women[1]	2,936	2,931	100.0	100.0
Mother employed	1,867	1,976	63.6	67.4
Mother not employed	1,068	956	36.4	32.6
Families maintained by men[1]	763	705	100.0	100.0
Father employed	660	624	86.5	88.5
Father not employed	104	81	13.6	11.5

[1] No spouse present.

NOTE: "Own children" include sons, daughters, step-children, and adopted children. Not included are nieces, nephews, grandchildren, and other related and unrelated children. Data for 1999 are not strictly comparable with data for 1998 and earlier years because of the introduction of revised population controls in the household survey in January 1999. Detail may not sum to totals due to rounding.

SOURCE: "Employment Characteristics of Families in 1999," *Bureau of Labor Statistics News*, U.S. Department of Labor, Washington, D.C., June 2000

families with no husband present earned a median income of $26,164 while male householders with no wife present earned $41,838. (See Table 5.9 and Figure 5.2.)

Racial and Ethnic Differences

In 1999 the typical white family earned considerably more ($42,504) than the typical black ($27,910) or Hispanic ($30,735) family. Asian/Pacific Islander families were the highest income earners ($51,205). (See Table 5.9 and Figure 5.4.) According to *Income 1999, Comparison of Summary Measures of Income by Selected Characteristics 1989, 1998 and 1999*, U.S. Census Bureau, December 2000, the large proportion of minority families maintained by females without a husband present accounted for this great disparity. Female-headed families of all racial and ethnic groups with no husband present earned well below their male counterparts. However, black ($18,244) and Hispanic ($18,701) female householders earned much less than white female householders ($26,529).

In married couple families incomes were much higher ($57,089 for whites, $50,656 for blacks, and $37,132 for Hispanics).

Unequal Pay for Women

[Equal pay] is a family issue. Today, nearly three out of four women with children work. In many cases, women are the sole breadwinners. When women aren't paid equally, the whole family suffers . . .. [T]his is a kitchen table economic issue and an issue about simple right and wrong. Working women pay the same as men for goods and services—and should be paid the same for their work in producing goods and services.

— Alexis M. Herman, U.S. Secretary of Labor, on the 35th anniversary of the Equal Pay Act and 78th anniversary of the founding of the Women's Bureau of the US. Department of Labor, June 1998.

Despite women's significant contributions to the war effort, the traditional notion that a woman's place was in the home persisted well into the 1950s and 1960s. Having experienced the self-fulfillment and the economic advantages of earning a paycheck, many women were frustrated with society's slow acceptance of their desire to work. Many women worked to support their families and those who were able to obtain the same jobs held by men were frustrated by not receiving equal pay.

During the 1960s the civil rights movement motivated many American women to fight for their economic rights. In 1961, upon recommendation by the Women's Bureau of the Department of Labor, President John F. Kennedy appointed the first President's Commission on the Status of Women under the chairmanship of Eleanor Roosevelt, widow of former President Franklin D. Roosevelt and a leading political figure in her own right. The Commission's report included the impact of married women's increasing presence in the labor force.

TABLE 5.7

Employment status of mothers with own children under 3 years of age, by age of youngest child and marital status, 1998–99 annual averages

(Numbers in thousands)

| Characteristic | Civilian noninsti-tutional population | Civilian labor force | | Employed | | | | Unemployed | |
		Total	Percent of popula-tion	Total	Percent of popula-tion	Full-time workers[1]	Part-time workers[2]	Number	Percent of labor force
1998									
TOTAL MOTHERS									
With own children under 3 years old	9,333	5,779	61.9	5,384	57.7	3,626	1,758	395	6.8
2 years	2,772	1,786	64.4	1,673	60.4	1,149	524	113	6.3
1 year	3,213	2,055	64.0	1,917	59.7	1,281	636	138	6.7
Under 1 year	3,348	1,938	57.9	1,794	53.6	1,196	598	144	7.4
Married, spouse present									
With own children under 3 years old	7,110	4,316	60.7	4,145	58.3	2,765	1,380	171	4.0
2 years	2,073	1,291	62.3	1,244	60.0	831	413	47	3.6
1 year	2,493	1,560	62.6	1,497	60.0	989	508	63	4.0
Under 1 year	2,544	1,465	57.6	1,404	55.2	945	459	61	4.2
Other marital status[3]									
With own children under 3 years old	2,225	1,463	65.8	1,238	55.6	860	379	223	15.2
2 years	700	495	70.7	429	61.3	318	111	65	13.1
1 year	721	495	68.7	420	58.3	292	129	75	15.2
Under 1 year	804	473	58.8	389	48.4	250	139	83	17.5
1999									
TOTAL MOTHERS									
With own children under 3 years old	9,339	5,742	61.5	5,390	57.7	3,692	1,696	353	6.1
2 years	2,890	1,888	65.3	1,788	61.9	1,257	530	101	5.3
1 year	3,283	2,062	62.8	1,934	58.9	1,298	635	128	6.2
Under 1 year	3,166	1,792	56.6	1,668	52.7	1,137	531	124	6.9
Married, spouse present									
With own children under 3 years old	7,089	4,224	59.6	4,078	57.5	2,744	1,335	147	3.5
2 years	2,175	1,356	62.3	1,316	60.5	898	419	40	2.9
1 year	2,522	1,532	60.7	1,477	58.6	964	513	56	3.7
Under 1 year	2,392	1,336	55.9	1,285	53.7	882	403	51	3.8
Other marital status[3]									
With own children under 3 years old	2,249	1,519	67.5	1,310	58.2	950	363	207	13.6
2 years	714	533	74.6	471	66.0	360	112	62	11.6
1 year	761	530	69.6	457	60.1	335	123	72	13.6
Under 1 year	774	456	58.9	382	49.4	255	128	73	16.0

[1] Usually work 35 hours or more a week at all jobs.
[2] Usually work less than 35 hours a week at all jobs.
[3] Includes never-married, divorced, separated, and widowed persons.

SOURCE: "Employment Characteristics of Families in 1999," *Bureau of Labor Statistics News,* U.S. Department of Labor, Washington, D.C., June 2000

The President's Commission's findings of sex discrimination in the workplace facilitated the passage of the Equal Pay Act (PL 88-38) in 1963. The law required that companies pay equal wages regardless of sex for the same job. In 1963 the average full-time, year-round female worker earned 58.9 percent of the wages of the average men. (See Table 5.10 and Figure 5.5.) According to the Bureau of Labor Statistics the wage gap between men and women tends to widen during most of women's working years. (See Figure 5.6.)

A report entitled "Highlights of Women's Earnings in 1999," U.S. Department of Labor, Bureau of Labor Statistics, May 2000, showed that, in 1999, the average weekly earnings of full-time working women remained significant-

TABLE 5.8

Working mothers with children under 1 year of age

March of:	Participation rate
1990	49.5
1991	51.9
1992	52.2
1993	52.6
1994	54.6
1995	56.9
1996	55.4

SOURCE: Howard V. Hayghe, "Developments in Women's Labor Force Participation," *Monthly Labor Review,* Vol. 120, No. 9, September 1997, U.S. Department of Labor, Bureau of Labor Statistics, Washington, D.C., 1997

FIGURE 5.2

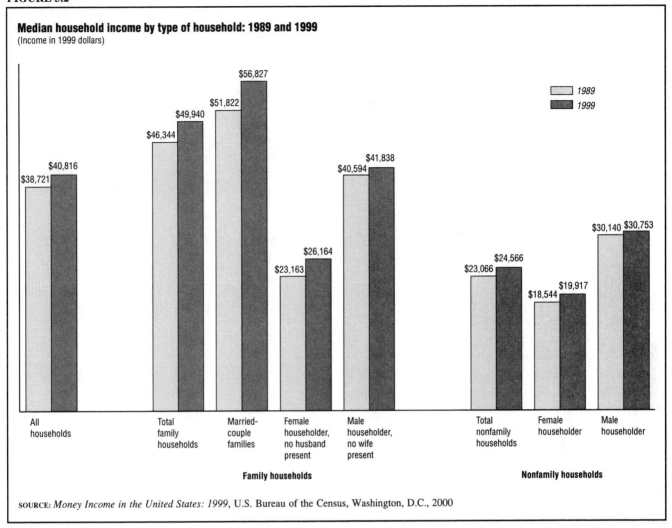

Median household income by type of household: 1989 and 1999
(Income in 1999 dollars)

1989
1999

Family households

Nonfamily households

SOURCE: *Money Income in the United States: 1999*, U.S. Bureau of the Census, Washington, D.C., 2000

ly lower than men's (77 percent of the wages of men). That was just a slight improvement over the 1997 discrepancy of 74.4 percent. (See Table 5.11.) The Women's Bureau points out that, although federal, state, and local laws mandate equal pay for equal work, "traditional" women's jobs, such as librarian, nurse, teacher, and food service worker, have been undervalued. "Traditional" women's jobs are considered to be an extension of women's traditional family and household duties and, on the surface, do not seem to call for special skills. Consequently, employers often feel these jobs do not warrant higher wages, even though many of these professions, like other better-paid occupations, require many years of schooling.

THE EFFECT OF UNEQUAL PAY ON FAMILIES. The gap between men's and women's earnings affects not only women but also families. In the 1950s and 1960s many women entered the work force for economic motives. As the 1900s became the 2000s most women continued to work for the same reasons. For many families the wife's earnings determine whether or not that family would live in poverty. The U.S. Department of Labor reported that, in 1997, 7.7 percent of white families, 11.4 percent of black

FIGURE 5.3

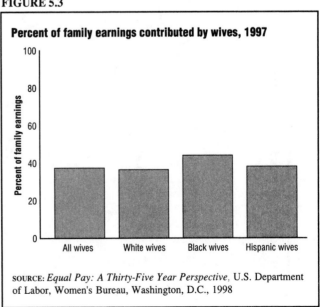

Percent of family earnings contributed by wives, 1997

SOURCE: *Equal Pay: A Thirty-Five Year Perspective*, U.S. Department of Labor, Women's Bureau, Washington, D.C., 1998

TABLE 5.9

Comparison of summary measures of income, by selected characteristics: 1989, 1998, and 1999
(Households and people as of March of the following year.)

Characteristics	Number (thousands)	1999 Median income		Median income in 1998 (in 1999 dollars)		Median income in 1989[r] (in 1999 dollars)		Percent change in real income 1998 to 1999		Percent change in real income 1989[r] to 1999	
		Value (dollars)	90% confidence interval (+/-) (dollars)	Value (dollars)	90% confidence interval (+/-) (dollars)	Value (dollars)	90% confidence interval (+/-) (dollars)	Percent change	90% confidence interval (+/-)	Percent change	90% confidence interval (+/-)
HOUSEHOLDS											
All households	104,705	40,816	314	39,744	387	38,721	351	2.7 *	1.0	5.4 *	1.3
Type of household											
Family households	72,025	49,940	449	48,517	419	46,344	422	2.9 *	1.0	7.8 *	1.4
Married-couple families	55,311	56,827	502	55,475	541	51,822	469	2.4 *	1.1	9.7 *	1.4
Female householder, no husband present	12,687	26,164	594	24,932	669	23,163	617	4.9 *	3.0	13.0 *	4.0
Male householder, no wife present	4,028	41,838	1,311	40,284	1,670	40,594	1,642	3.9	4.4	3.1	5.3
Non-family households	32,680	24,566	444	23,959	477	23,066	371	2.5 *	2.2	6.5 *	2.6
Female householder	18,039	19,917	454	19,026	472	18,544	484	4.7 *	2.8	7.4 *	3.7
Male householder	14,641	30,753	568	31,086	572	30,140	674	-1.1	2.1	2.0	3.0
Race and Hispanic origin of householder											
All races [1]	104,705	40,816	314	39,744	387	38,721	351	2.7 *	1.0	5.4 *	1.3
White	87,671	42,504	393	41,816	343	40,732	327	1.6 *	1.0	4.3 *	1.3
Non-Hispanic	78,819	44,366	459	43,376	410	41,693	338	2.3 *	1.2	6.4 *	1.4
Black	12,849	27,910	854	25,911	667	24,479	807	7.7 *	3.5	14.0 *	5.1
Asian and Pacific Islander	3,337	51,205	3,088	47,667	2,182	48,383	2,051	7.4 *	6.6	5.8	7.8
Hispanic [2]	9,319	30,735	747	28,956	916	29,264	902	6.1 *	2.9	5.0 *	4.1
Age of householder											
15 to 24 years	5,860	25,171	689	24,084	748	24,940	771	4.5 *	3.5	0.9	4.2
25 to 34 years	18,627	42,174	661	40,954	711	39,903	617	3.0 *	1.9	5.7 *	2.3
35 to 44 years	23,955	50,873	653	49,521	747	50,399	690	2.7 *	1.6	0.9	1.9
45 to 54 years	20,927	56,917	875	55,344	898	55,780	913	2.8 *	1.9	2.0	2.3
55 to 64 years	13,592	44,597	1,063	44,120	1,010	41,465	897	1.1	2.7	7.6 *	3.5
65 years and over	21,745	22,812	375	22,209	404	21,177	389	2.7 *	2.0	7.7 *	2.7
Nativity of householder											
Native born	93,062	41,383	336	40,553	398	(NA)	(NA)	2.0 *	1.1	X	X
Foreign born	11,643	36,048	949	33,691	1,258	(NA)	(NA)	7.0 *	4.0	X	X
Naturalized citizen	5,383	43,947	2,418	41,934	1,848	(NA)	(NA)	4.8	6.0	X	X
Not a citizen	6,260	31,199	1,031	28,903	1,226	(NA)	(NA)	7.9 *	4.7	X	X

TABLE 5.9

Comparison of summary measures of income, by selected characteristics: 1989, 1998, and 1999 [CONTINUED]

(Households and people as of March of the following year.)

Characteristics	1999 Median income			Median income in 1998 (in 1999 dollars)		Median income in 1989[r] (in 1999 dollars)		Percent change in real income 1998 to 1999		Percent change in real income 1989[r] to 1999	
	Number (thousands)	Value (dollars)	90% confidence interval (+/-) (dollars)	Value (dollars)	90% confidence interval (+/-) (dollars)	Value (dollars)	90% confidence interval (+/-) (dollars)	Percent change	90% confidence interval (+/-)	Percent change	90% confidence interval (+/-)
Region											
Northeast	20,087	41,984	699	41,531	789	43,724	725	1.1	2.5	-4.0 *	2.3
Midwest	24,508	42,679	832	41,506	614	38,517	656	2.8 *	1.8	10.8 *	2.9
South	37,303	37,442	548	36,588	511	34,682	482	2.3 *	2.1	8.0 *	2.2
West	22,808	42,720	783	41,888	678	41,604	712	2.0	2.8	2.7 *	2.6
Residence											
Inside metropolitan areas	84,259	42,785	456	41,888	361	41,677	354	2.1 *	1.1	2.7 *	1.4
Inside central cities	31,825	35,573	505	33,883	652	(NA)	(NA)	5.0 *	2.0	X	X
Outside central cities	52,433	47,708	625	47,427	523	(NA)	(NA)	0.6	1.4	X	X
Outside metropolitan areas	20,447	33,021	931	32,729	644	30,042	650	0.9	2.8	9.9 *	3.7
EARNINGS OF FULL-TIME, YEAR-ROUND WORKERS											
Male	57,511	36,476	224	36,126	224	36,516	248	1.0 *	0.7	-0.1	0.9
Female	40,404	26,324	186	26,433	198	25,158	276	-0.4	0.8	4.6 *	1.4
PER CAPITA INCOME											
All races [1]	274,087	21,181	206	20,564	206	18,683	132	3.0 *	1.2	13.4 *	1.3
White	224,806	22,375	243	21,867	243	19,813	150	2.3 *	1.3	12.9 *	1.3
Non-Hispanic	193,633	24,109	288	23,459	285	(NA)	(NA)	2.8 *	1.5	X	X
Black	35,509	14,397	383	13,243	334	11,658	247	8.7 *	3.3	23.5 *	3.8
Asian and Pacific Islander	10,925	21,134	1,179	19,122	1,124	(NA)	(NA)	10.5 *	7.5	X	X
Hispanic [2]	32,804	11,621	373	11,687	424	11,008	283	-0.6	3.6	5.6 *	4.1

* Statistically significant change at the 90% confidence level.
[r] Revised to reflect the population distribution reported in the 1990 census.
[1] Data for American Indians and Alaska Natives are not shown separately in this table.
[2] Hispanics may be of any race.

SOURCE: U.S. Census Bureau, Current Population Survey, March 1990, 1999, and 2000

FIGURE 5.4

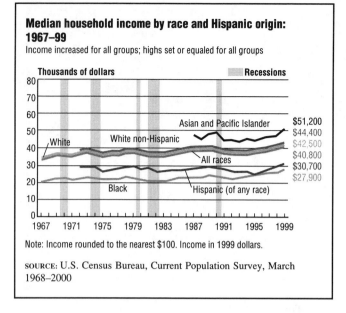

Median household income by race and Hispanic origin: 1967–99

Income increased for all groups; highs set or equaled for all groups

Note: Income rounded to the nearest $100. Income in 1999 dollars.

SOURCE: U.S. Census Bureau, Current Population Survey, March 1968–2000

families, and up to 25 percent of Hispanic families, had avoided poverty because both spouses were employed.

LONG-TERM AFFECT OF UNEQUAL PAY. The consequences of unequal pay affect a woman over her entire lifetime. Unequal pay determines how much—or, in most cases, how little—her pension and Social Security benefits will be. As women generally living longer than men, earning less means having less money to live on after retirement. Older women are twice as likely to be poor as older men. A 1998 report entitled *Equal Pay: A Thirty-Five Year Perspective* by the Women's Bureau noted that, in 1999, 11.8 percent (2.2 million) of women 65 years and older lived below the poverty level, compared with only 6.9 percent (960,000) of men in the same age group. According to the Pension and Welfare Benefits Administration of the Department of Labor (*Retirement Benefits of American Workers: New Findings from the September 1994 Current Population Survey,* September 1995), the median pension for women in 1994 was only $3,000, compared with $7,800 for men. Only 38 percent of female retirees obtained pension benefits, and just 21 percent received health insurance that would last their lifetime.

POVERTY

The economic growth following World War II spilled into the next two decades, but not every American reaped the economic benefits. In 1965 newly elected President Lyndon B. Johnson declared a "War on Poverty," calling for sweeping legislative changes to help the disadvantaged. From a high of 22.4 percent in 1959, when data on poverty were first tabulated, the overall poverty rate declined to about 11–12 percent for most of the 1970s. It began rising in the 1980s, reaching 15.2 percent in 1983,

TABLE 5.10

Median annual earnings for year-round, full-time workers by sex, 1951–96

| | Earnings (real dollars) | | Women/men |
Year	Women	Men	(percent)
1951	8,865	13,865	63.9
1952	9,238	14,449	63.9
1953	9,682	15,142	63.9
1954	9,658	15,108	63.9
1955	10,146	15,866	63.9
1956	10,393	16,419	63.3
1957	10,705	16,772	63.8
1958	10,734	17,048	63.0
1959	10,973	17,900	61.3
1960	11,003	18,135	60.7
1961	11,087	18,712	59.2
1962	11,298	19,053	59.3
1963	11,520	19,542	58.9
1964	11,835	20,010	59.1
1965	12,152	20,279	59.9
1966	12,179	21,160	57.6
1967	12,425	21,503	57.8
1968	12,807	22,023	58.2
1969	13,561	23,038	58.9
1970	13,719	23,108	59.4
1971	13,810	23,207	59.5
1972	14,122	24,407	57.9
1973	14,268	25,194	56.6
1974	14,138	24,063	58.8
1975	13,948	23,714	58.8
1976	14,234	23,647	60.2
1977	14,221	24,135	58.9
1978	14,340	24,126	59.4
1979	13,982	23,435	59.7
1980	13,589	22,587	60.2
1981	13,202	22,288	59.2
1982	13,486	21,841	61.7
1983	13,971	21,969	63.6
1984	14,225	22,346	63.7
1985	14,520	22,486	64.6
1986	14,810	23,044	64.3
1987	14,886	22,840	65.2
1988	14,883	22,533	66.0
1989	15,136	22,041	68.7
1990	15,166	21,177	71.6
1991	15,090	21,601	69.9
1992	15,235	21,523	70.8
1993	15,050	21,043	71.5
1994	14,983	20,819	72.0
1995	14,762	20,667	71.4
1996	15,112	20,487	73.8

SOURCE: *Equal Pay: A Thirty-Five Year Perspective,* U.S. Department of Labor, Women's Bureau, Washington, D.C., 1998

fluctuating over the next decade, and reaching 15.1 percent in 1993. Since then it has been on a downward trend; however, in 1999, an estimated 11.8 percent of all Americans (32.3 million) were still living in poverty. (See Table 5.12 and Figure 5.7.)

Poor Families

In 1999 the poverty rate for all families was 9.3 percent, accounting for 6.6 million families, down from 7.1 million families (10 percent) in 1998. (See Table 5.13.) The poverty rates for blacks dropped to a record low of 23.6 percent in 1999 from a previous low of 26.1 percent in 1998. However, this rate is still about two and a half

FIGURE 5.5

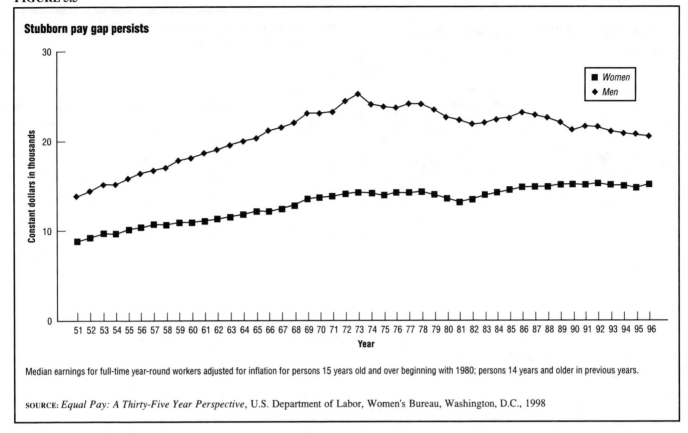

Stubborn pay gap persists

Median earnings for full-time year-round workers adjusted for inflation for persons 15 years old and over beginning with 1980; persons 14 years and older in previous years.

SOURCE: *Equal Pay: A Thirty-Five Year Perspective*, U.S. Department of Labor, Women's Bureau, Washington, D.C., 1998

times that of whites (9.8 percent). The poverty rate for Hispanics declined from 25.6 percent in 1998 to 22.8 in 1999. The 1999 average poverty rate for American Indians and Alaska Natives (not shown in the table) was 25.9 percent, higher than for white non-Hispanics and Asians/Pacific Islanders. It was not, however, statistically different from blacks and Hispanics. Poverty rates for Asians/Pacific Islanders also declined, from 12.5 percent in 1998 to 10.7 percent in 1999, equaling the record low in 1987 when data for this ethnic group first became available. (See Table 5.14.)

Married-Couple Families

In 1999 married-couple families had a poverty rate of 4.8 percent, down from 5.3 percent in 1998. The Census Bureau pointed out that, although married-couple families had the lowest poverty rate, they still account for a large proportion of poor families (40 percent) because they are the most common family type. Hispanic married-couple families have a much higher poverty rate (14.2 percent) than black (7.1 percent) or white (4.4 percent) married-couple families. (See Table 5.14.)

Families Maintained by Women

Historically, the incidence of poverty among families headed by women has been very high. The total number of female-headed families below the poverty level increased from almost 2 million in 1960 to nearly 3 million in 1980. In 1999, of the 6.6 million poor families, 3.5 million (52.8 percent) were maintained by women.

Nonetheless, the proportion of female-headed families living in poverty actually dropped over the past several decades. In 1960, 42.4 percent of all female-headed families were living in poverty. In 1970 the poverty rate for these families declined almost 10 percentage points to 32.5 percent, but rose again to hover around 35 percent for much of the 1980s and 1990s. In 1999 it was down to 27.8 percent. (See Table 5.13.) In 1999, across all racial and ethnic groups, families maintained by women with no husband present were much more likely to be poor than married-couple families. (See Tables 5.13 and 5.14.)

Poor Families with Children

Families with children are more likely to be at risk of poverty than families without children. Children add to expenses, stretching the family income to accommodate their needs.

Between 1959 and 1969 the poverty rate for families with children under 18 years of age declined nearly 10 percentage points, from 20.3 to 10.8 percent. It rose again during the 1970s and 1980s, peaking at 18.5 percent in 1993. Since then it has dropped again, reaching 13.8 percent in 1999. (See Table 5.13.) However, children are still the most likely group in the United States to live in poverty. (See Chapter 4.)

FIGURE 5.6

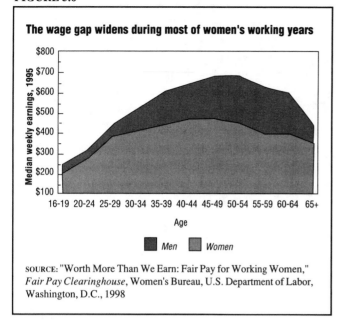

The wage gap widens during most of women's working years

SOURCE: "Worth More Than We Earn: Fair Pay for Working Women," *Fair Pay Clearinghouse*, Women's Bureau, U.S. Department of Labor, Washington, D.C., 1998

RACIAL AND ETHNIC DIFFERENCES. In 1999 white families with children had a far lower poverty rate (10.8 percent) than black (28.9 percent) and Hispanic (25 percent) families with children. The poverty rate for Hispanic married-couple families with children (16.8 percent) was nearly three times that of whites (5.9 percent) and more than twice that of blacks (8.6 percent). (See Table 5.13.)

Hispanic families headed by males (no wife present) with children under the age of 18 years had a slightly higher poverty rate (26 percent) than similar black (21.4 percent) and white (14.7 percent) families. Among female-headed families (no husband present) with children under 18 years of age, the poverty rate for blacks was (46.1 percent), Hispanics (46.6 percent) and whites (30.1 percent). (See Table 5.13.)

HOMELESS FAMILIES

Since the 1980s the incidence of homelessness has increased and, at the beginning of the twenty-first century, homeless people could be found on the streets of virtually every American city. While the number of homeless people is based largely on estimates, families with children have reportedly become the fastest growing segment of the homeless population, making up 37 percent of all homeless people. Children (27 percent), including unaccompanied youth (7 percent), comprised more than one-quarter of homeless persons in 1999. (See Table 5.15.)

Increasing numbers of studies show that battered women who leave their homes may end up in the streets. In its latest survey of hunger and homelessness in 26 American cities, the U.S. Conference of Mayors reported that domestic violence was cited as the main cause of homelessness by 58 percent of responding cities.

TABLE 5.11

Median weekly earnings of full-time wage and salary workers by state, 1997 annual averages

	Women	Men	Women's earnings as a percent of men's
Total, U.S.	**$431**	**$579**	**74.4**
Alabama	$362	$493	73.4
Alaska	$557	$762	73.1
Arizona	$399	$487	81.9
Arkansas	$329	$439	74.9
California	$497	$589	84.4
Colorado	$460	$617	74.6
Connecticut	$513	$692	74.1
Delaware	$443	$598	74.1
District of Columbia	$567	$584	97.1
Florida	$407	$492	82.7
Georgia	$427	$567	75.3
Hawaii	$463	$562	82.4
Idaho	$382	$509	75.0
Illinois	$460	$639	72.0
Indiana	$389	$590	65.9
Iowa	$398	$538	74.0
Kansas	$410	$553	74.1
Kentucky	$386	$539	71.6
Louisiana	$339	$509	66.6
Maine	$397	$521	76.2
Maryland	$503	$676	74.4
Massachusetts	$512	$640	80.0
Michigan	$457	$654	69.9
Minnesota	$477	$634	75.2
Mississippi	$343	$464	73.9
Missouri	$419	$568	73.8
Montana	$344	$497	69.2
Nebraska	$386	$533	72.4
Nevada	$410	$555	73.9
New Hampshire	$459	$603	76.1
New Jersey	$503	$667	75.4
New Mexico	$391	$508	77.0
New York	$485	$603	80.4
North Carolina	$394	$507	77.7
North Dakota	$347	$509	68.2
Ohio	$427	$595	71.8
Oklahoma	$362	$493	73.4
Oregon	$416	$553	75.2
Pennsylvania	$437	$609	71.8
Rhode Island	$465	$575	80.9
South Carolina	$379	$499	76.0
South Dakota	$358	$479	74.7
Tennessee	$374	$512	73.0
Texas	$402	$512	78.5
Utah	$408	$552	73.9
Vermont	$419	$531	78.9
Virginia	$461	$586	78.7
Washington	$491	$643	76.4
West Virginia	$370	$516	71.7
Wisconsin	$420	$613	68.5
Wyoming	$364	$579	62.9

Note: Data exclude the incorporated self-employed.

SOURCE: *Equal Pay: A Thirty-Five Year Perspective,* U.S. Department of Labor, Women's Bureau, Washington, D.C., 1998

Many of the mayors who participated in the survey also reported that the strong economy has not benefited the homeless in their city. They cited the increasing housing costs, for example, which made it more difficult for the poor to afford housing. In 1999 every participating city reported a lack of affordable housing. Low-skill jobs, generally the only type of work for which many homeless people would qualify, were also difficult to find. Welfare

TABLE 5.12

Poverty status of people by family relationship: 1959–1999

[Numbers in thousands; people as of March of the following year]

	All people			People in families — All families			Families with female householder, no husband present			Unrelated individuals		
		Below poverty level			Below poverty level			Below poverty level			Below poverty level	
Year and characteristic	Total	Number	Percent	Total	Number	Percent	Total	Number	Percent	Total	Number	Percent
All races												
1999	273,493	32,258	11.8	228,633	23,396	10.2	38,223	11,607	30.4	43,432	8,305	19.1
1998	271,059	34,476	12.7	227,229	25,370	11.2	39,000	12,907	33.1	42,539	8,478	19.9
1997	268,480	35,574	13.3	225,369	26,217	11.6	38,412	13,494	35.1	41,672	8,687	20.8
1996	266,218	36,529	13.7	223,955	27,376	12.2	38,584	13,796	35.8	40,727	8,452	20.8
1995	263,733	36,425	13.8	222,792	27,501	12.3	38,908	14,205	36.5	39,484	8,247	20.9
1994	261,616	38,059	14.5	221,430	28,985	13.1	37,253	14,380	38.6	38,538	8,287	21.5
1993	259,278	39,265	15.1	219,489	29,927	13.6	37,861	14,636	38.7	38,038	8,388	22.1
1992r	256,549	38,014	14.8	217,936	28,961	13.3	36,446	14,205	39.0	36,842	8,075	21.9
1991r	251,192	35,708	14.2	212,723	27,143	12.8	34,795	13,824	39.7	36,845	7,773	21.1
1990	248,644	33,585	13.5	210,967	25,232	12.0	33,795	12,578	37.2	36,056	7,446	20.7
1989	245,992	31,528	12.8	209,515	24,066	11.5	32,525	11,668	35.9	35,185	6,760	19.2
1988r	243,530	31,745	13.0	208,056	24,048	11.6	32,164	11,972	37.2	34,340	7,070	20.6
1987r	240,982	32,221	13.4	206,877	24,725	12.0	31,893	12,148	38.1	32,992	6,857	20.8
1986	238,554	32,370	13.6	205,459	24,754	12.0	31,152	11,944	38.3	31,679	6,846	21.6
1985	236,594	33,064	14.0	203,963	25,729	12.6	30,878	11,600	37.6	31,351	6,725	21.5
1984	233,816	33,700	14.4	202,288	26,458	13.1	30,844	11,831	38.4	30,268	6,609	21.8
1983	231,700	35,303	15.2	201,338	27,933	13.9	30,049	12,072	40.2	29,158	6,740	23.1
1982	229,412	34,398	15.0	200,385	27,349	13.6	28,834	11,701	40.6	27,908	6,458	23.1
1981	227,157	31,822	14.0	198,541	24,850	12.5	28,587	11,051	38.7	27,714	6,490	23.4
1980	225,027	29,272	13.0	196,963	22,601	11.5	27,565	10,120	36.7	27,133	6,227	22.9
1979	222,903	26,072	11.7	195,860	19,964	10.2	26,927	9,400	34.9	26,170	5,743	21.9
1978	215,656	24,497	11.4	191,071	19,062	10.0	26,032	9,269	35.6	24,585	5,435	22.1
1977	213,867	24,720	11.6	190,757	19,505	10.2	25,404	9,205	36.2	23,110	5,216	22.6
1976	212,303	24,975	11.8	190,844	19,632	10.3	24,204	9,029	37.3	21,459	5,344	24.9
1975	210,864	25,877	12.3	190,630	20,789	10.9	23,580	8,846	37.5	20,234	5,088	25.1
1974	209,362	23,370	11.2	190,436	18,817	9.9	23,165	8,462	36.5	18,926	4,553	24.1
1973	207,621	22,973	11.1	189,361	18,299	9.7	21,823	8,178	37.5	18,260	4,674	25.6
1972	206,004	24,460	11.9	189,193	19,577	10.3	21,264	8,114	38.2	16,811	4,883	29.0
1971	204,554	25,559	12.5	188,242	20,405	10.8	20,153	7,797	38.7	16,311	5,154	31.6
1970	202,183	25,420	12.6	186,692	20,330	10.9	19,673	7,503	38.1	15,491	5,090	32.9
1969	199,517	24,147	12.1	184,891	19,175	10.4	17,995	6,879	38.2	14,626	4,972	34.0
1968	197,628	25,389	12.8	183,825	20,695	11.3	18,048	6,990	38.7	13,803	4,694	34.0
1967	195,672	27,769	14.2	182,558	22,771	12.5	17,788	6,898	38.8	13,114	4,998	38.1
1966	193,388	28,510	14.7	181,117	23,809	13.1	17,240	6,861	39.8	12,271	4,701	38.3
1965	191,413	33,185	17.3	179,281	28,358	15.8	16,371	7,524	46.0	12,132	4,827	39.8
1964	189,710	36,055	19.0	177,653	30,912	17.4	(NA)	7,297	44.4	12,057	5,143	42.7
1963	187,258	36,436	19.5	176,076	31,498	17.9	(NA)	7,646	47.7	11,182	4,938	44.2
1962	184,276	38,625	21.0	173,263	33,623	19.4	(NA)	7,781	50.3	11,013	5,002	45.4
1961	181,277	39,628	21.9	170,131	34,509	20.3	(NA)	7,252	48.1	11,146	5,119	45.9
1960	179,503	39,851	22.2	168,615	34,925	20.7	(NA)	7,247	48.9	10,888	4,926	45.2
1959	176,557	39,490	22.4	165,858	34,562	20.8	(NA)	7,014	49.4	10,699	4,928	46.1

r For 1992, figures are based on 1990 census population controls. For 1991, figures are revised to correct for nine omitted weights from the original March 1992 CPS file. For 1988 and 1987, figures are based on new processing procedures and are also revised to reflect corrections to the files after publication of the 1988 advance report, Money Income and Poverty Status in the United States: 1988, P-60, No. 166.

(NA) Not available.

Note: Prior to 1979, people in unrelated subfamilies were included in "People in families." Beginning in 1979, people in unrelated subfamilies are included in "All people" but are excluded from "People in families."

SOURCE: Joseph Daaker and Bernadette D. Procter, *Poverty in the United States, 1999*, U.S. Bureau of the Census, Washington, D.C., September 2000

reform has also sparked an increase in the number of requests for emergency food assistance (18 percent). (See Table 5.15.)

FIGURE 5.7

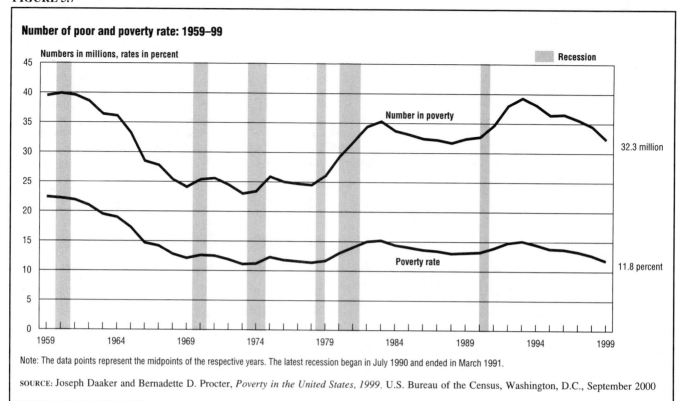

Number of poor and poverty rate: 1959–99

Note: The data points represent the midpoints of the respective years. The latest recession began in July 1990 and ended in March 1991.

SOURCE: Joseph Daaker and Bernadette D. Procter, *Poverty in the United States, 1999*, U.S. Bureau of the Census, Washington, D.C., September 2000

TABLE 5.13

Poverty status of families, by type of family, presence of related children, race, and Hispanic origin: 1959–1999

[Numbers in thousands; families as of March of the following year]

Year and characteristic	All families Total	All families Below poverty level Number	All families Below poverty level Percent	Married-couple families Total	Married-couple families Below poverty level Number	Married-couple families Below poverty level Percent	Male householder, no wife present Total	Male householder, no wife present Below poverty level Number	Male householder, no wife present Below poverty level Percent	Female householder, no husband present Total	Female householder, no husband present Below poverty level Number	Female householder, no husband present Below poverty level Percent
All races												
With and without children under 18 years												
1999	72,031	6,676	9.3	55,315	2,673	4.8	4,028	472	11.7	12,687	3,531	27.8
1998	71,551	7,186	10.0	54,778	2,879	5.3	3,977	476	12.0	12,796	3,831	29.9
1997	70,884	7,324	10.3	54,321	2,821	5.2	3,911	508	13.0	12,652	3,995	31.6
1996	70,241	7,708	11.0	53,604	3,010	5.6	3,847	531	13.8	12,790	4,167	32.6
1995	69,597	7,532	10.8	53,570	2,982	5.6	3,513	493	14.0	12,514	4,057	32.4
1994	69,313	8,053	11.6	53,865	3,272	6.1	3,228	549	17.0	12,220	4,232	34.6
1993	68,506	8,393	12.3	53,181	3,481	6.5	2,914	488	16.8	12,411	4,424	35.6
1992ʳ	68,216	8,144	11.9	53,090	3,385	6.4	3,065	484	15.8	12,061	4,275	35.4
1991ʳ	67,175	7,712	11.5	52,457	3,158	6.0	3,025	392	13.0	11,693	4,161	35.6
1990	66,322	7,098	10.7	52,147	2,981	5.7	2,907	349	12.0	11,268	3,768	33.4
1989	66,090	6,784	10.3	52,137	2,931	5.6	2,884	348	12.1	10,890	3,504	32.2
1988ʳ	65,837	6,874	10.4	52,100	2,897	5.6	2,847	336	11.8	10,890	3,642	33.4
1987ʳ	65,204	7,005	10.7	51,675	3,011	5.8	2,833	340	12.0	10,696	3,654	34.2
1986	64,491	7,023	10.9	51,537	3,123	6.1	2,510	287	11.4	10,445	3,613	34.6
1985	63,558	7,223	11.4	50,933	3,438	6.7	2,414	311	12.9	10,211	3,474	34.0
1984	62,706	7,277	11.6	50,350	3,488	6.9	2,228	292	13.1	10,129	3,498	34.5
1983	62,015	7,647	12.3	50,081	3,815	7.6	2,038	268	13.2	9,896	3,564	36.0
1982	61,393	7,512	12.2	49,908	3,789	7.6	2,016	290	14.4	9,469	3,434	36.3
1981	61,019	6,851	11.2	49,630	3,394	6.8	1,986	205	10.3	9,403	3,252	34.6
1980	60,309	6,217	10.3	49,294	3,032	6.2	1,933	213	11.0	9,082	2,972	32.7
1979	59,550	5,461	9.2	49,112	2,640	5.4	1,733	176	10.2	8,705	2,645	30.4
1978	57,804	5,280	9.1	47,692	2,474	5.2	1,654	152	9.2	8,458	2,654	31.4
1977	57,215	5,311	9.3	47,385	2,524	5.3	1,594	177	11.1	8,236	2,610	31.7
1976	56,710	5,311	9.4	47,497	2,606	5.5	1,500	162	10.8	7,713	2,543	33.0
1975	56,245	5,450	9.7	47,318	2,904	6.1	1,445	116	8.0	7,482	2,430	32.5
1974	55,698	4,922	8.8	47,069	2,474	5.3	1,399	125	8.9	7,230	2,324	32.1
1973	55,053	4,828	8.8	46,812	2,482	5.3	1,438	154	10.7	6,804	2,193	32.2
1972	54,373	5,075	9.3	46,314	(NA)	(NA)	1,452	(NA)	(NA)	6,607	2,158	32.7
1971	53,296	5,303	10.0	45,752	(NA)	(NA)	1,353	(NA)	(NA)	6,191	2,100	33.9
1970	52,227	5,260	10.1	44,739	(NA)	(NA)	1,487	(NA)	(NA)	6,001	1,952	32.5
1969	51,586	5,008	9.7	44,436	(NA)	(NA)	1,559	(NA)	(NA)	5,591	1,827	32.7
1968	50,511	5,047	10.0	43,842	(NA)	(NA)	1,228	(NA)	(NA)	5,441	1,755	32.3
1967	49,835	5,667	11.4	43,292	(NA)	(NA)	1,210	(NA)	(NA)	5,333	1,774	33.3
1966	48,921	5,784	11.8	42,553	(NA)	(NA)	1,197	(NA)	(NA)	5,171	1,721	33.1
1965	48,278	6,721	13.9	42,107	(NA)	(NA)	1,179	(NA)	(NA)	4,992	1,916	38.4
1964	47,836	7,160	15.0	41,648	(NA)	(NA)	1,182	(NA)	(NA)	5,006	1,822	36.4
1963	47,436	7,554	15.9	41,311	(NA)	(NA)	1,243	(NA)	(NA)	4,882	1,972	40.4
1962	46,998	8,077	17.2	40,923	(NA)	(NA)	1,334	(NA)	(NA)	4,741	2,034	42.9
1961	46,341	8,391	18.1	40,405	(NA)	(NA)	1,293	(NA)	(NA)	4,643	1,954	42.1
1960	45,435	8,243	18.1	39,624	(NA)	(NA)	1,202	(NA)	(NA)	4,609	1,955	42.4
1959	45,054	8,320	18.5	39,335	(NA)	(NA)	1,226	(NA)	(NA)	4,493	1,916	42.6

TABLE 5.13

Poverty status of families, by type of family, presence of related children, race, and Hispanic origin: 1959–1999 [CONTINUED]

[Numbers in thousands; families as of March of the following year]

Year and characteristic	All families			Married-couple families			Male householder, no wife present			Female householder, no husband present		
		Below poverty level			Below poverty level			Below poverty level			Below poverty level	
	Total	Number	Percent	Total	Number	Percent	Total	Number	Percent	Total	Number	Percent
All races												
With children under 18 years												
1999	37,277	5,129	13.8	26,373	1,662	6.3	2,169	350	16.2	8,736	3,116	35.7
1998	37,268	5,628	15.1	26,226	1,822	6.9	2,108	350	16.6	8,934	3,456	38.7
1997	37,427	5,884	15.7	26,430	1,863	7.1	2,175	407	18.7	8,822	3,614	41.0
1996	37,204	6,131	16.5	26,184	1,964	7.5	2,063	412	20.0	8,957	3,755	41.9
1995	36,719	5,976	16.3	26,034	1,961	7.5	1,934	381	19.7	8,751	3,634	41.5
1994	36,782	6,408	17.4	26,367	2,197	8.3	1,750	395	22.6	8,665	3,816	44.0
1993	36,456	6,751	18.5	26,121	2,363	9.0	1,577	354	22.5	8,758	4,034	46.1
1992ʳ	35,851	6,457	18.0	25,907	2,237	8.6	1,569	353	22.5	8,375	3,867	46.2
1991ʳ	34,862	6,170	17.7	25,357	2,106	8.3	1,513	297	19.6	7,991	3,767	47.1
1990	34,503	5,676	16.4	25,410	1,990	7.8	1,386	260	18.8	7,707	3,426	44.5
1989	34,279	5,308	15.5	25,476	1,872	7.3	1,358	246	18.1	7,445	3,190	42.8
1988ʳ	34,251	5,373	15.7	25,598	1,847	7.2	1,292	232	18.0	7,361	3,294	44.7
1987ʳ	33,996	5,465	16.1	25,464	1,963	7.7	1,316	221	16.8	7,216	3,281	45.5
1986	33,801	5,516	16.3	25,571	2,050	8.0	1,136	202	17.8	7,094	3,264	46.0
1985	33,536	5,586	16.7	25,496	2,258	8.9	1,147	197	17.1	6,892	3,131	45.4
1984	32,942	5,662	17.2	25,038	2,344	9.4	1,072	194	18.1	6,832	3,124	45.7
1983	32,787	5,871	17.9	25,216	2,557	10.1	949	192	20.2	6,622	3,122	47.1
1982	32,565	5,712	17.5	25,276	2,470	9.8	892	184	20.6	6,397	3,059	47.8
1981	32,587	5,191	15.9	25,278	2,199	8.7	822	115	14.0	6,488	2,877	44.3
1980	32,773	4,822	14.7	25,671	1,974	7.7	802	144	18.0	6,299	2,703	42.9
1979	32,397	4,081	12.6	25,615	1,573	6.1	747	116	15.5	6,035	2,392	39.6
1978	31,735	4,060	12.8	25,199	1,495	5.9	699	103	14.7	5,837	2,462	42.2
1977	31,637	4,081	12.9	25,284	1,602	6.3	644	95	14.8	5,709	2,384	41.8
1976	31,434	4,060	12.9	25,515	1,623	6.4	609	94	15.4	5,310	2,343	44.1
1975	31,377	4,172	13.3	25,704	1,855	7.2	554	65	11.7	5,119	2,252	44.0
1974	31,319	3,789	12.1	25,857	1,558	6.0	545	84	15.4	4,917	2,147	43.7
1973	30,977	3,520	11.4	25,983	(NA)	(NA)	397	(NA)	(NA)	4,597	1,987	43.2
1972	30,807	3,621	11.8	26,085	(NA)	(NA)	401	(NA)	(NA)	4,321	1,925	44.5
1971	30,725	3,683	12.0	26,201	(NA)	(NA)	447	(NA)	(NA)	4,077	1,830	44.9
1970	30,070	3,491	11.6	25,789	(NA)	(NA)	444	(NA)	(NA)	3,837	1,680	43.8
1969	29,827	3,226	10.8	26,083	(NA)	(NA)	360	(NA)	(NA)	3,384	1,519	44.9
1968	29,325	3,347	11.4	25,684	(NA)	(NA)	372	(NA)	(NA)	3,269	1,459	44.6
1967	29,032	3,586	12.4	25,482	(NA)	(NA)	360	(NA)	(NA)	3,190	1,418	44.5
1966	28,592	3,734	13.4	25,197	(NA)	(NA)	436	(NA)	(NA)	2,959	1,410	47.1
1965	28,100	4,379	15.6	24,829	(NA)	(NA)	398	(NA)	(NA)	2,873	1,499	52.2
1964	28,277	4,771	16.9	25,017	(NA)	(NA)	367	(NA)	(NA)	2,893	1,439	49.7
1963	28,317	4,991	17.6	25,084	(NA)	(NA)	400	(NA)	(NA)	2,833	1,578	55.7
1962	28,174	5,460	19.4	24,990	(NA)	(NA)	483	(NA)	(NA)	2,701	1,613	59.7
1961	27,600	5,500	19.9	24,509	(NA)	(NA)	404	(NA)	(NA)	2,687	1,505	56.0
1960	27,102	5,328	19.7	24,164	(NA)	(NA)	319	(NA)	(NA)	2,619	1,476	56.3
1959	26,992	5,443	20.3	24,099	(NA)	(NA)	349	(NA)	(NA)	2,544	1,525	59.9

TABLE 5.13

Poverty status of families, by type of family, presence of related children, race, and Hispanic origin: 1959–1999 [CONTINUED]

[Numbers in thousands; families as of March of the following year]

Year and characteristic	All families			Married-couple families			Male householder, no wife present			Female householder, no husband present		
		Below poverty level			Below poverty level			Below poverty level			Below poverty level	
	Total	Number	Percent	Total	Number	Percent	Total	Number	Percent	Total	Number	Percent
White												
With children under 18 years												
1999	29,841	3,236	10.8	22,660	1,333	5.9	1,681	247	14.7	5,500	1,656	30.1
Black												
With children under 18 years												
1999	5,585	1,615	28.9	2,307	199	8.6	385	83	21.4	2,892	1,333	46.1
Hispanic origin[1]												
With children under 18 years												
1999	5,320	1,330	25.0	3,609	607	16.8	358	93	26.0	1,353	630	46.6

[r] For 1992, figures are based on 1990 census population controls. For 1991, figures are revised to correct for nine omitted weights from original March 1992 CPS file. For 1988 and 1987, figures are based on new processing procedures and are also revised to reflect corrections to the files after publication of the 1988 advance report, *Money Income and Poverty Status in the United States: 1988,* P-60, No. 166.

(NA) Not available.

[1] People of Hispanic origin may be of any race.

Note: Prior to 1979, unrelated subfamilies were included in "All families." Beginning in 1979, unrelated subfamilies are excluded from "All families."

SOURCE: Joseph Daaker and Bernadette D. Procter, *Poverty in the United States, 1999,* U.S. Bureau of the Census, Washington, D.C., September 2000

TABLE 5.14

People and families in poverty, by selected characteristics: 1998 and 1999

[Numbers in thousands.]

Characteristic	1999 below poverty				1998 below poverty				Change[1] 1998 to 1999			
	Number	90% C.I. (±)	Percent	90% C.I.(±)	Number	90% C.I. (±)	Percent	90% C.I. (±)	Number	90% C.I. (±)	Percent	90% C.I.(±)
PEOPLE												
Total	**32,258**	**893**	**11.8**	**0.3**	**34,476**	**920**	**12.7**	**0.3**	* **-2,218**	**951**	* **-0.9**	**0.3**
Family status												
In families	23,396	775	10.2	0.3	25,370	804	11.2	0.3	* -1,974	829	* -0.9	0.3
Householder	6,676	237	9.3	0.3	7,186	248	10.0	0.3	* -510	255	* -0.8	0.3
Related children under 18	11,510	457	16.3	0.7	12,845	479	18.3	0.7	* -1,335	490	* -2.0	0.7
Related children under 6	4,170	290	18.0	1.3	4,775	309	20.6	1.5	* -604	314	* -2.6	1.5
In unrelated subfamilies	558	61	39.1	4.9	628	66	48.8	5.9	* -70	66	* -9.7	5.8
Reference person	216	38	37.9	7.6	247	41	47.4	9.2	-31	41	* -9.4	8.9
Children under 18	336	86	41.0	11.7	361	89	50.5	14.1	-25	90	-9.5	13.8
Unrelated individual	8,305	271	19.1	0.7	8,478	275	19.9	0.7	-173	286	* -0.8	0.7
Male	3,398	160	16.3	0.8	3,465	161	17.0	0.8	-68	169	-0.7	0.8
Female	4,907	197	21.7	1.0	5,013	201	22.6	1.0	-106	209	-0.9	1.0
Race[2] and Hispanic origin												
White	21,922	752	9.8	0.3	23,454	776	10.5	0.3	* -1,532	872	* -0.8	0.3
Non-Hispanic	14,875	628	7.7	0.3	15,799	646	8.2	0.3	* -925	727	* -0.5	0.3
Black	8,360	423	23.6	1.2	9,091	434	26.1	1.3	* -731	451	* -2.4	1.3
Asian and Pacific Islander	1,163	173	10.7	1.6	1,360	181	12.5	1.6	* -197	186	* -1.9	1.6
Hispanic[3]	7,439	401	22.8	1.2	8,070	411	25.6	1.3	* -631	341	* -2.8	1.0
Age												
Under 18 years	12,109	467	16.9	0.7	13,467	487	18.9	0.7	* -1,358	500	* -2.0	0.7
18 to 64 years	16,982	663	10.0	0.3	17,623	674	10.5	0.3	-641	701	* -0.5	0.5
18 to 24 years	4,603	207	17.3	0.8	4,312	201	16.6	0.8	* 291	214	0.7	0.8
25 to 34 years	3,968	201	10.5	0.5	4,582	214	11.9	0.5	* -614	217	* -1.4	0.5
35 to 44 years	3,733	194	8.3	0.5	4,082	202	9.1	0.5	* -349	209	* -0.8	0.5
45 to 54 years	2,466	158	6.7	0.5	2,444	158	6.9	0.5	23	166	-0.2	0.5
55 to 59 years	1,179	110	9.2	0.8	1,165	110	9.2	0.8	15	115	-0.1	1.0
60 to 64 years	1,033	104	9.8	1.0	1,039	104	10.1	1.0	-6	109	-0.3	1.0
65 years and over	3,167	174	9.7	0.5	3,386	179	10.5	0.5	* -219	186	* -0.7	0.5
Nativity												
Native	27,507	831	11.2	0.3	29,707	860	12.1	0.3	* -2,200	887	* -0.9	0.3
Foreign born	4,751	413	16.8	1.5	4,769	413	18.0	1.6	-18	433	-1.3	1.6
Naturalized citizen	968	188	9.1	1.8	1,087	199	11.0	2.0	-119	202	-1.9	2.0
Not a citizen	3,783	368	21.3	2.1	3,682	364	22.2	2.1	101	385	-0.9	2.3
Region												
Northeast	5,678	364	10.9	0.7	6,357	385	12.3	0.8	* -680	393	* -1.4	0.8
Midwest	6,210	419	9.8	0.7	6,501	428	10.3	0.7	-292	444	-0.5	0.7
South	12,538	602	13.1	0.7	12,992	612	13.7	0.7	-454	637	-0.6	0.7
West	7,833	482	12.6	0.8	8,625	505	14.0	0.8	* -792	518	* -1.5	0.8
Residence												
Inside metropolitan areas	24,816	796	11.2	0.3	26,997	827	12.3	0.3	* -2,181	852	* -1.1	0.3
Inside central cities	13,123	592	16.4	0.8	14,921	630	18.5	0.8	* -1,798	642	* -2.1	0.8
Outside central cities	11,693	561	8.3	0.3	12,076	569	8.7	0.5	-382	592	* -0.5	0.5
Outside metropolitan areas	7,442	553	14.3	1.2	7,479	554	14.4	1.2	-37	581	-0.1	1.2
FAMILIES												
Total	**6,676**	**237**	**9.3**	**0.3**	**7,186**	**248**	**10.0**	**0.3**	* **-510**	**278**	* **-0.8**	**0.3**
White	4,377	184	7.3	0.3	4,829	196	8.0	0.3	* -452	225	* -0.8	0.3
Non-Hispanic	2,942	148	5.5	0.3	3,264	156	6.1	0.3	* -322	181	* -0.6	0.3
Black	1,898	117	21.9	1.5	1,981	118	23.4	1.5	-84	135	-1.5	1.6
Asian and Pacific Islander	258	41	10.3	1.6	270	43	11.0	1.8	-11	48	-0.7	2.0
Hispanic[3]	1,525	104	20.2	1.5	1,648	109	22.7	1.5	* -123	100	* -2.5	1.5
Type of family												
Married-couple	2,673	140	4.8	0.3	2,879	146	5.3	0.3	* -206	163	* -0.4	0.3
White	2,161	125	4.4	0.3	2,400	132	5.0	0.3	* -239	151	* -0.5	0.3
Non-Hispanic	1,457	100	3.3	0.2	1,639	107	3.8	0.3	* -182	123	* -0.4	0.3
Black	294	44	7.1	1.2	290	44	7.3	1.2	5	51	-0.2	1.3
Asian and Pacific Islander	162	33	8.1	1.6	156	33	7.9	1.6	6	38	0.2	2.0
Hispanic[3]	728	71	14.2	1.5	775	72	15.7	1.5	-48	67	* -1.5	1.5
Female householder, no husband present	3,531	163	27.8	1.5	3,831	171	29.9	1.5	* -300	191	* -2.1	1.6

TABLE 5.14

People and families in poverty, by selected characteristics: 1998 and 1999 [CONTINUED]

[Numbers in thousands.]

Characteristic	1999 below poverty				1998 below poverty				Change[1] 1998 to 1999			
	Number	90% C.I. (±)	Percent	90% C.I.(±)	Number	90% C.I. (±)	Percent	90% C.I. (±)	Number	90% C.I. (±)	Percent	90% C.I. (±)
White	1,883	115	22.5	1.5	2,123	123	24.9	1.6	*–240	141	* –2.4	1.8
Non-Hispanic	1,255	94	18.6	1.5	1,428	100	20.7	1.5	*173	115	* –2.0	1.8
Black	1,499	102	39.3	3.0	1,557	105	40.8	3.1	-58	118	-1.5	3.5
Asian and Pacific Islander	76	23	23.1	7.4	93	25	29.2	8.9	-16	26	-6.2	9.4
Hispanic[3]	686	69	38.8	4.3	756	72	43.7	4.8	* –69	66	* –4.9	4.3

* Statistically significant at the 90% confidence level (C.I.).

[1] As a result of rounding, some differences may appear to be slightly higher or lower than the difference of the reported rates.

[2] Data for American Indians and Alaska Natives are not shown separately.

[3] Hispanics may be of any race.

SOURCE: Joseph Daaker and Bernadette D. Procter, *Poverty in the United States, 1999,* U.S. Bureau of the Census, Washington, D.C., September 2000

TABLE 5.15

Hunger and homelessness in America's cities: a 15-year comparison of data

Indicator	1985	1986	1987	1988	1989	1990	1991	1992	1993	1994	1995	1996	1997	1998	1999
HUNGER															
Increase in demand for emergency food	28%	25%	18%	19%	19%	22%	26%	18%	13%	12%	9%	11%	16%	14%	18%
Cities in which demand for food increased	96%	88%	92%	88%	96%	90%	93%	96%	83%	83%	72%	83%	86%	78%	85%
Increase in demand by families for food assistance	30%	24%	18%	17%	14%	20%	26%	14%	13%	14%	10%	10%	13%	14%	15%
Portion of those requesting food assistance who are families with children	NA	NA	67%	62%	61%	75%	68%	68%	67%	64%	63%	62%	58%	61%	58%
Demand for emergency food unmet	17%	23%	18%	15%	17%	14%	17%	21%	16%	15%	18%	18%	19%	21%	21%
Cities in which food assistance facilities must turn people away	67%	55%	67%	62%	73%	86%	79%	68%	68%	73%	59%	50%	71%	47%	54%
Cities which expect demand for emergency food to increase next year	88%	84%	84%	85%	89%	100%	100%	89%	100%	81%	96%	96%	92%	96%	84%
HOMELESSNESS															
Increase in demand for emergency shelter	25%	20%	21%	13%	25%	24%	13%	14%	10%	13%	11%	5%	3%	11%	12%
Cities in which demand increased	88%	96%	96%	93%	89%	80%	89%	88%	81%	80%	63%	71%	59%	72%	69%
Demand for emergency shelter unmet	NA	24%	23%	19%	22%	19%	15%	23%	25%	21%	19%	20%	27%	26%	25%
Cities in which shelters must turn people away	60%	72%	65%	67%	59%	70%	74%	75%	77%	72%	82%	81%	88%	67%	73%
Cities which expect demand for shelter to increase next year	88%	84%	92%	89%	93%	97%	100%	93%	88%	71%	100%	100%	100%	93%	92%
Composition of homeless population															
Single men	60%	56%	49%	49%	46%	51%	50%	55%	43%	48%	46%	45%	47%	45%	43%
Families with children	27%	28%	33%	34%	36%	34%	35%	32%	34%	39%	36%	38%	36%	38%	37%
Single women	12%	15%	14%	13%	14%	12%	12%	11%	11%	11%	14%	14%	14%	14%	13%
Unaccompanied youth	NA	NA	4%	5%	4%	3%	3%	2%	4%	3%	4%	3%	4%	3%	7%
Children	NA	NA	NA	25%	25%	23%	24%	22%	30%	26%	25%	27%	25%	25%	27%
Severely mentally ill	33%	29%	23%	25%	25%	28%	29%	28%	27%	26%	23%	24%	27%	24%	19%
Substance abusers	37%	29%	35%	34%	44%	38%	40%	41%	48%	43%	46%	43%	43%	38%	31%
Employed	NA	19%	22%	23%	24%	24%	18%	17%	18%	19%	20%	18%	17%	22%	21%
Veterans	NA	NA	NA	26%	26%	26%	23%	18%	21%	23%	23%	19%	22%	22%	14%

SOURCE: *A Status Report on Hunger and Homelessness in America's Cities, 1999: A 26-City Survey, December 1999*, The United States Conference of Mayors, Washington, D.C., 1999

CHAPTER 6
CHANGING FAMILY PATTERNS

THE FAMILY'S FLIGHT TO THE SUBURBS

The economic prosperity following World War II enabled many American families to pursue what was perceived to be a better life in the wide-open spaces of the outlying, newly developing suburbs. The ties that bound the nuclear family, the extended family, and the ethnic neighborhood—all of which existed before the war—were loosened. With government aid, most notably Veterans' Administration (VA) mortgages, newlyweds and young couples with children bought homes in the suburbs. Leaving their parents and relatives, these young families soon became self-sufficient entities tending to their own needs.

The G.I. Bill also helped returning veterans to pursue a postsecondary education. Many men from lower-income families, aided by a college education, soon joined the growing middle class. Government loans also allowed new families to acquire homes. By 1960 suburban residents, for the first time, outnumbered those living in the city.

Additionally, in 1956, the federal government enacted the National Defense Highway Act, which provided for the construction of more than 40,000 miles of interstate highway. The expansion of the nation's highway system, coupled with low gas prices, also facilitated the suburbanization of America. By 1960, 75 percent of families in the United States owned a car, compared with about 50 percent in the late 1940s. Many businesses also left the cities to move to the suburbs. It did not take long for shopping and entertainment centers to follow.

Decades of Decline

During the 1970s and 1980s more middle-class and affluent families migrated to the suburbs. With the loss of many businesses and jobs to the suburbs, city dwellers began to see their quality of life diminish. Cities struggled with fewer jobs, poverty, high crime rates, and drug-related problems.

Migration to Suburbs Continues

The migration of families from cities to suburbs continued through the 1990s. According to the U.S. Department of Housing and Urban Development (HUD), in 1996 alone, 2.7 million people moved from the city to the suburbs, while only 800,000 people moved from the suburbs to the city. Between 1990 and 1997 suburban population grew 9.6 percent, twice the rate of city population (4.2 percent). Similarly, the number of suburban families (9.5 percent) increased at a faster rate than the number of families who lived in the city (6 percent). (See Figure 6.1.)

HUD Secretary Andrew Cuomo, in *The State of the Cities 1998* (Washington, D.C., 1998), noted that "the long-run trend is more stark—a 60 percent jump in the number of suburban families between 1970 and 1997 versus the modest 12-percent increase for cities over that period." In *The State of the Cities 2000* (Washington,

FIGURE 6.1

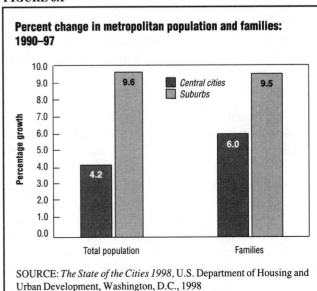

Percent change in metropolitan population and families: 1990–97

SOURCE: *The State of the Cities 1998*, U.S. Department of Housing and Urban Development, Washington, D.C., 1998

FIGURE 6.2

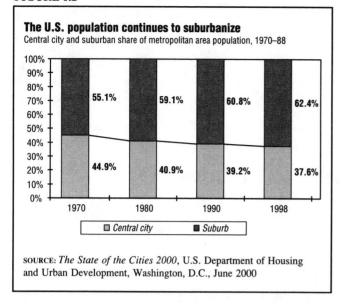

The U.S. population continues to suburbanize
Central city and suburban share of metropolitan area population, 1970–88

SOURCE: *The State of the Cities 2000*, U.S. Department of Housing and Urban Development, Washington, D.C., June 2000

D.C., 2000) Cuomo noted that "compared with the suburbs, city population growth was quite modest." Suburban population in 331 metro areas jumped by 11.9 percent between 1990 and 1998. Cities continue to lose population share in their metro areas. For example in 1970 nearly 45 percent of metropolitan population lived in the urban core; by 1998 that proportion had declined to 37.6 percent. (See Figure 6.2.)

Labor Force Participation of City Dwellers and Suburbanites

Regardless of age, sex, race, or ethnicity, city dwellers are less likely than suburbanites to participate in the labor force. (The labor force includes persons who hold part-time or full-time jobs and those who are unemployed but looking for work.) Those who live in the central cities are also more likely to be unemployed.

Among the different racial and ethnic groups, the differences in labor participation and unemployment rates were markedly disparate among blacks. In 1997, 60.2 percent of blacks living in the 25 largest central cities were in the labor force, compared with 73.3 percent of blacks living in the suburbs of those cities. (See Table 6.1.)

EDUCATIONAL ATTAINMENT. Education greatly affects employment outcomes. In 1997, across all racial and ethnic groups, labor force participation increased with the level of education. (See Table 6.1.) However, there were some urban/suburban differences. Among black city dwellers 16 and older, those who did not finish high school had a lower labor force participation (35.4 percent) than those who graduated from college (82.2 percent). On the other hand, there were somewhat more suburbanite blacks in the labor force (43.1 percent with less than a high school diploma, and 87.1 percent of college graduates). (See Table 6.2.)

TABLE 6.1

Labor force participation and unemployment rates of persons living in the 25 largest cities and their suburbs, 1997 annual averages

Characteristic	Labor force participation rates[1]		Unemployment rates[2]	
	Central cities	Suburbs	Central cities	Suburbs
Age and sex				
Total, 16 years and over	**64.6**	**69.9**	**7.3**	**4.0**
16 to 24 years	58.4	65.4	15.5	9.8
25 t o 54 years	80.6	85.3	5.9	3.1
55 years and over	29.3	34.4	4.5	2.8
Men	73.3	78.2	7.2	3.9
Women	56.9	61.9	7.3	4.1
Race and Hispanic origin				
White	66.2	69.8	5.5	3.7
Black	60.2	73.3	12.5	7.6
Hispanic orgin	64.3	71.3	8.1	6.1
Educational attainment [3]				
Less than a high school diploma	44.0	47.3	14.7	9.8
High school graduates, no college	64.0	65.8	8.0	4.3
Some college, no degree	74.6	74.9	5.8	3.6
College graduates	81.7	81.5	3.1	2.0

[1] Percent of population that is in the labor force.
[2] Percent of labor force that is unemployed.
[3] Data refer to persons 25 years and older.

SOURCE: "Labor Market Outcomes for City Dwellers and Suburbanites," *Issue in Labor Statistics*, Summary 98-12, December 1998

In 1997 the unemployment rates for workers who lived in the city were higher across the board than for suburbanites. In both cities and suburbs, those with more education were less likely to be unemployed. Among college graduates, city dwellers (3.1 percent) and suburbanites (2 percent) had similar unemployment rates. (See Table 6.1.)

The New Demography

While an increasing share of residents in both cities and suburbs are getting older, a disproportionate number of the elderly poor live in cities. At the same time, cities and suburbs are becoming more racially and ethnically diverse. Groups that usually have poorer employment outcomes continue to be overrepresented in the cities. In 1997 blacks and Hispanics comprised 27.2 and 23 percent, respectively, of the 16-and-older population in the central cities, compared with just 7.6 and 11.3 percent, respectively, of the suburban population. More than one-quarter (27.3 percent) of city dwellers did not have a high school diploma, compared with 16.9 percent of suburbanites. There were also fewer college graduates among the city population. (See Figure 6.3.)

According to HUD, growth in metropolitan areas is continuing at a faster pace in suburbs than in central cities. The 2000 estimated total U.S. population of 275 million is projected to rise to 350 million by 2030, with

TABLE 6.2

Labor force participation rates for blacks

	Central cities	Suburbs
Less than a high school diploma	35.4	43.1
High school diploma, no college	65.7	73.9
Some college, no degree	71.0	81.3
College graduates	82.2	87.1

SOURCE: "Labor Market Outcomes for City Dwellers and Suburbanites," *Issue in Labor Statistics*, Summary 98-12, December 1998

TABLE 6.3

Affordability status of a modestly priced home for families and unrelated individuals, using conventional, fixed-rate, 30-year financing: 1984, 1988, 1991, and 1993

	Percentage of families that can afford to buy			
	All families	Unrelated individuals	Renter families	Renter unrelated individuals
1984	60.4	33.5	12.6	13.4
1988	59.7	33.9	14.0	12.8
1991	57.6	33.4	13.1	12.2
1993	57.7	33.5	11.7	11.2

SOURCE: Howard A. Savage, "Who Can Afford to Buy a House in 1993?," *Current Housing Reports,* H121/97, July 1997

FIGURE 6.3

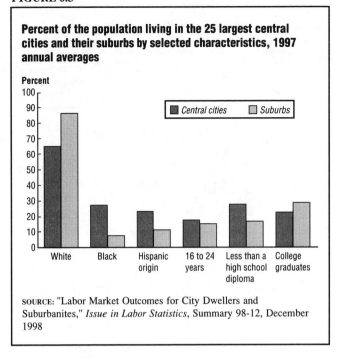

Percent of the population living in the 25 largest central cities and their suburbs by selected characteristics, 1997 annual averages

SOURCE: "Labor Market Outcomes for City Dwellers and Suburbanites," *Issue in Labor Statistics*, Summary 98-12, December 1998

75 million being new immigrants, and many immigrants are already moving to the suburbs.

Both city and suburb populations are also aging. In 2030 the elderly population will reach 70 million, doubling the current number of elderly Americans and accounting for 20 percent of the overall U.S. population. Cities will continue to house disproportionate numbers of the nation's seniors who live below or near the poverty line.

HUD also noted that the traditional divide between blacks and whites is blurring into a multiracial, multiethnic society. Cities—historically home to the nation's newcomers, as well as to most of its minorities—remain the most diverse, but suburbs are becoming much more heterogeneous. Between 1980 and 1998 the minority share of the population in central cities rose from 34.8 to 47 percent. In suburbs during the same period, the proportion of minorities nearly doubled, from 13.4 to 21.7 percent. The proportion of Hispanics rose from 5.3 percent to 9.6 percent in suburbs, and the percentage of black suburbanites expanded as well, from 6.1 to 7.6 percent.

HOMEOWNERSHIP

Who Can Afford to Buy a Home?

For most people, part of the American dream is to own a home. In *Who Can Afford to Buy a House in 1993?* (Washington, D.C., 1997) the U.S. Bureau of the Census

reported that 57.7 percent of families could afford a modestly priced house. (See Table 6.3.) This means that they could qualify for conventional, fixed-rate, 30-year financing with a 5 percent down payment. A modestly priced house is one that is priced so that 25 percent of all owner-occupied houses in the neighborhood are below this value and 75 percent are above it.

AFFORDABILITY DIFFERS BETWEEN HOMEOWNERS AND RENTERS. The ability to buy a modestly priced house differs markedly by whether a family currently owns or rents its present residence. In 1993, 73 percent (not shown) of homeowners and just 11.7 percent of renter families could afford a modestly priced house. (See Table 6.3.)

FAMILY TYPE AND MARITAL STATUS AFFECT AFFORDABILITY. Whether a person or family can afford a home varies greatly by type of family and marital status. In 1993 two-thirds of married couples, about 2 in 5 families maintained by men with no spouse present, and one-quarter of female-maintained families with no spouse present could afford a modestly priced house. The presence of children under the age of 18 also influenced a family's ability to buy a house. About 3 in 5 married couples with children under 18 could afford a house, while over three-quarters of those without children could afford a house.

AFFORDABILITY STATUS BY RACE AND ETHNICITY. In 1993, among current homeowners, about four-fifths of white (79 percent) and non-Hispanic (78 percent) families, and more than half of black (56 percent) and Hispanic (57 percent) families, could afford a modestly priced house. Among renter families, only 3 percent of black families and 4 percent of Hispanic families could afford a

FIGURE 6.4

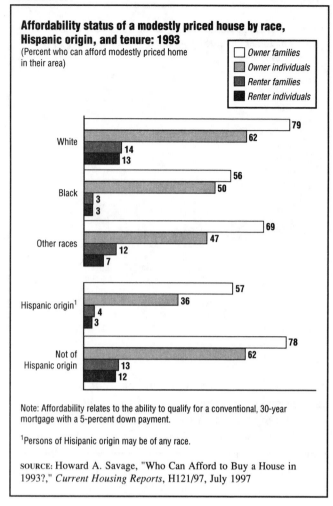

Affordability status of a modestly priced house by race, Hispanic origin, and tenure: 1993
(Percent who can afford modestly priced home in their area)

Legend:
- Owner families
- Owner individuals
- Renter families
- Renter individuals

White
- 79
- 62
- 14
- 13

Black
- 56
- 50
- 3
- 3

Other races
- 69
- 47
- 12
- 7

Hispanic origin[1]
- 57
- 36
- 4
- 3

Not of Hispanic origin
- 78
- 62
- 13
- 12

Note: Affordability relates to the ability to qualify for a conventional, 30-year mortgage with a 5-percent down payment.

[1]Persons of Hisipanic origin may be of any race.

SOURCE: Howard A. Savage, "Who Can Afford to Buy a House in 1993?," *Current Housing Reports*, H121/97, July 1997

house, compared with more than 10 percent of other racial and ethnic groups. (See Figure 6.4.)

According to the Census Bureau's 1997 report quoted above, in 1993 an equal proportion (83 percent) of white and non-Hispanic married-couple homeowners could afford to buy another modestly priced house, while 63 percent of Hispanic and 70 percent of black married-couple homeowners could do so. About 1 of 5 white (19 percent) and non-Hispanic (20 percent) married-couple renters could afford a house, compared with 8 percent of black and 7 percent of Hispanic married-couple renters.

Homeownership Rates in 1999

Between 1992 and 1999 more than 8.7 million households became homeowners. The national homeownership rate reached 66.8 percent in 1999, and rose even higher in the first quarter of 2000 to an all-time high of 67.1 percent. (See Figure 6.5.)

According to the U.S. Census Bureau and HUD, all racial and ethnic groups have shared in this trend. As of 1999, 45.5 percent of Hispanics, 46.7 percent of non-Hispanic blacks, and 54.1 percent of other non-Hispanics minorities owned their own homes. These were record

rates for all three groups. Minorities comprise 30 percent of first-time homebuyers and 40 percent of the increase in homeownership.

Home ownership in central city areas was a record 51.2 percent during the first quarter of 2000. Minority homeownership rates for this period were: Hispanics, 45.7 percent; blacks, 47.8 percent; and other minorities, 54.2 percent.

Despite this significant progress there remained a great disparity between family homeownership in the suburbs and in the cities. While 72.1 percent of suburban families owned their own homes, only 49.8 percent of families in the cities were homeowners.

Immigrant Families Who Own Homes

Many immigrants who have attained U.S. citizenship consider homeownership an indicator that they have established roots in the United States. According to the U.S. Bureau of the Census, regardless of citizenship status, married-couple families are more likely to own a home. In 1996, 83 percent of native-born married-couple families owned their homes as did 78.3 percent of foreign-born married-couple families and 41.9 percent of noncitizen married-couple families. In comparison, for other families with no spouse present, the homeownership rate was 50.3 percent for native-born citizens, 50.8 percent for foreign-born citizens, and just 23.5 percent for noncitizens.

SHORTAGE OF AFFORDABLE HOUSING

Many experts agree that the United States is suffering from an ongoing—and increasing—shortage of quality affordable housing. According to HUD, between 1997 and 1999, house prices rose at more than twice the rate of general inflation, and rent increases exceeded inflation in all 3 years, with rents going up 3 percent and housing prices by 16 percent.

Jennifer Daskal, in *In Search of Shelter: the Growing Shortage of Affordable Rental Housing* (Center on Budget and Policy Priorities, Washington, D.C., 1998), says that, in 1970, there were about 6.5 million low-cost rental units costing less than $300 per month (in 1995 dollars). At the time, there was enough housing to accommodate the approximately 6.2 million low-income renters (renters with yearly incomes of less than $12,000 in 1995 dollars). By 1995 the number of low-income renters (10.5 million) had far outstripped the number of low-cost rental units, resulting in a shortage of 4.4 million affordable units—by far the biggest housing shortage on record. (See Figure 6.6.)

Federal Housing Subsidies

Since the Housing Act of 1937 was passed, the federal government has subsidized housing for low-income renters. Families receiving subsidies pay the equivalent of 30 percent of their net income in rent and the federal government pays the balance of the rent. In 1998 housing

FIGURE 6.5

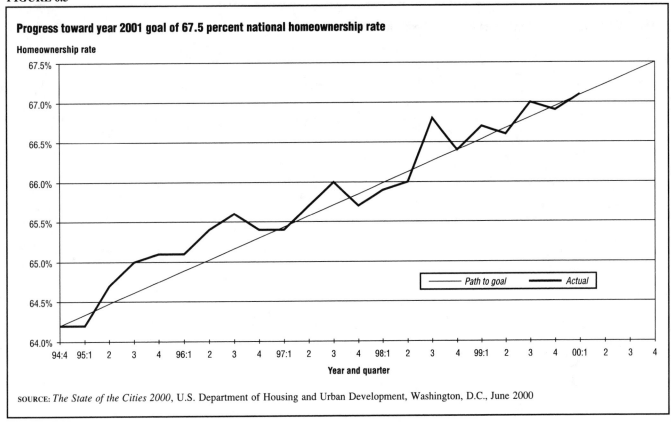

Progress toward year 2001 goal of 67.5 percent national homeownership rate

SOURCE: *The State of the Cities 2000*, U.S. Department of Housing and Urban Development, Washington, D.C., June 2000

assistance helped more than 2 million low-income families and households in central cities. Nonetheless, another 2.75 million urban renters needed help.

In *A Picture of Subsidized Households in 1998* (U.S. Department of Housing and Urban Development, Washington, D.C., 1998) the Office of Policy Development and Research reported that 40 percent of families and households receiving housing subsidies consisted of a single adult with children. One-third of households and families were elderly and more than one-half were minorities. A quarter of the overall families and households were employed, with an annual average income of $9,500. About 17 percent earned below $5,000. On average, families receiving a subsidy had been in the program for 6 years; newer residents usually had to wait 21 months before they received subsidized housing.

Typically, the average subsidized housing unit is located in an area where one-eighth of the neighborhood residents are subsidized, one-fourth are poor, and one-half are members of a minority.

It should be noted that the federal government subsidizes virtually all housing in America by permitting tax deductions for interest paid on home mortgages.

Rental Housing Affordability

Each year the National Low Income Housing Coalition (NLIHC) updates *Out of Reach,* a report quantifying

FIGURE 6.6

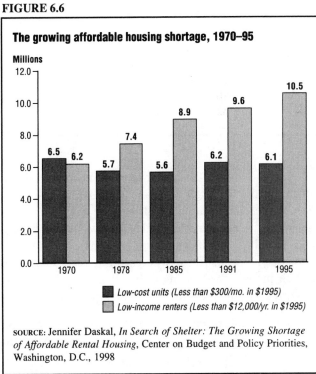

The growing affordable housing shortage, 1970–95

SOURCE: Jennifer Daskal, *In Search of Shelter: The Growing Shortage of Affordable Rental Housing*, Center on Budget and Policy Priorities, Washington, D.C., 1998

the increasing problem of affordable housing. In the 1997 edition, *Out of Reach: Rental Housing at What Cost?* (Tracy L. Kaufman, Washington, D.C., 1997), the Coalition reported that approximately one-third of all people eligible by law to receive federal housing assistance do, in

FIGURE 6.7

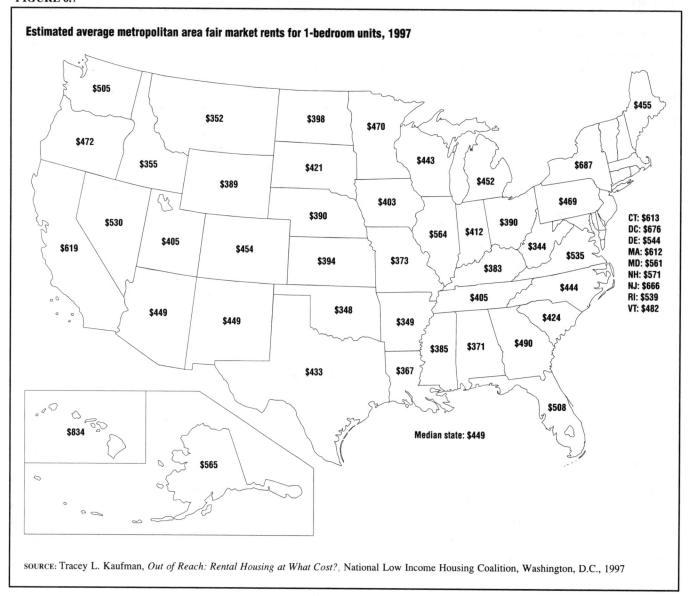

Estimated average metropolitan area fair market rents for 1-bedroom units, 1997

$505
$352
$398
$470
$455
$472
$355
$421
$443
$687
$389
$452
$403
$469
$530
$390
$390
$405
$564 $412
$344
$619
$454
$373
$535
$394
$383
$444
$449
$449
$348
$405
$424
$349
$385 $371 $490
$433
$367
$508
$834
$565

CT: $613
DC: $676
DE: $544
MA: $612
MD: $561
NH: $571
NJ: $666
RI: $539
VT: $482

Median state: $449

SOURCE: Tracey L. Kaufman, *Out of Reach: Rental Housing at What Cost?*, National Low Income Housing Coalition, Washington, D.C., 1997

fact, receive it. With changes occurring in congressional policy, the numbers receiving assistance is decreasing for two reasons: fewer households receive assistance, and there is an increase in the number of low-income households. Yet, in 1999, the number of households with worst-case housing needs (those who pay more than 50 percent of their income for housing or live in substandard housing) has grown to a record 5.4 million households.

HUD establishes Fair Market Rents (FMRs) for all 50 states. (See Figures 6.7 and 6.8.) In 1999 the FMRs for each state and their metropolitan areas were compared with the estimated median renter incomes. The NLIHC found that nearly one-half (40 percent) of renter families and households in 46 percent of the states could not afford the FMR without paying more than 30 percent of their income. (The federal standard for affordable housing established in 1981 under the Reagan administration is 30 percent of income.) (See Figure 6.9.) This means that fam-

ilies had to allot less money for basic necessities, such as food, clothing, and health care, in order to cover the rent.

Some states are more expensive to live in than others. *Out of Reach* reports that New Jersey, the District of Columbia, Hawaii, Massachusetts, New York, Connecticut, California, Alaska, and New Hampshire have the most expensive FMRs. A worker in these states would have to earn between $14 to $17 per hour simply to afford a two-bedroom apartment.

TANF Grants and Housing Costs

The Personal Responsibility and Work Opportunity Reconciliation Act of 1996 (PL 104-193) eliminated the 60-year-old Aid to Families with Dependent Children (AFDC) program. In its place, the law (commonly referred to as Welfare Reform) created a single, cash welfare block grant called Temporary Assistance for Needy Families (TANF), providing eligible families with short-term assistance.

FIGURE 6.8

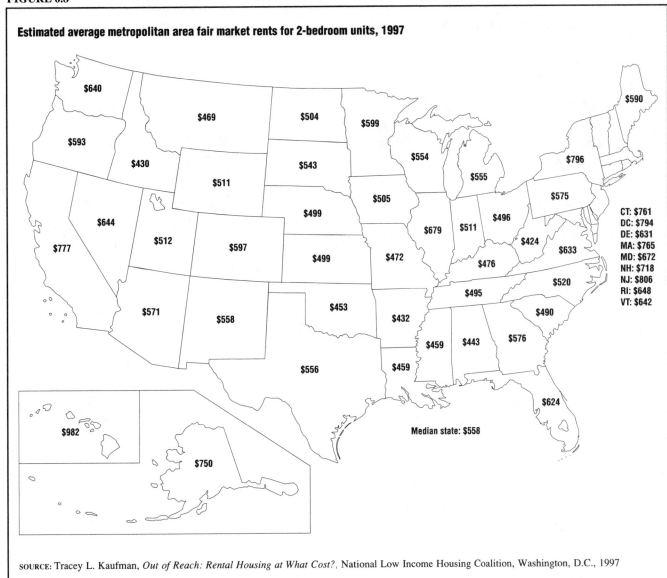

Estimated average metropolitan area fair market rents for 2-bedroom units, 1997

$640
$469
$504
$599
$590
$593
$430
$543
$554
$796
$511
$505
$555
$575
$644
$499
$679 $511 $496
CT: $761
$777 $512 $597
$499 $472 $424 $633
DC: $794
DE: $631
$476
MA: $765
$571 $558
$453 $495 $520
MD: $672
$432 $490
NH: $718
NJ: $806
$459 $443 $576
RI: $648
$459
VT: $642
$556
$624
$982
Median state: $558
$750

SOURCE: Tracey L. Kaufman, *Out of Reach: Rental Housing at What Cost?*, National Low Income Housing Coalition, Washington, D.C., 1997

In 1997 the NLIHC found that, in all states except Alaska and in more than 350 metropolitan areas, the maximum TANF grant for a family of three was not enough to cover the rent. (See Figure 6.10.) TANF recipients in Mississippi and Texas were the hardest hit; their grants covered just one-fourth and one-third, respectively, of the FMRs in their areas. However, the NLIHC reported that a study conducted by the National Campaign for Jobs and Income in early 2000 revealed that 45 states and the District of Columbia had accumulated $7 billion in unspent federal anti-poverty funds. This was at a time when poverty rates remained high and some poor families were falling deeper into poverty. Moreover, at least six states were diverting funds from the TANF block grants to pay for tax cuts and other state programs. The Campaign for Jobs and Income called on the governors to use these funds as they were intended: to provide support and opportunities for low-income people in their states.

Most former TANF recipients who find work are still poor, earning between $5.50 and $7.00 per hour. Their median monthly earnings amount to $1,149, which is below the official poverty line for a family of three. One-quarter of these former welfare recipients moved because they couldn't pay their rent. In most states the median monthly fair market cost of housing for a family of three is considerably higher than the entire TANF grant.

SUBFAMILIES

It is becoming increasingly common for adults from two or more generations to share one household. The U.S. Census Bureau refers to such groups as "subfamilies." In 1998 there were approximately 2.8 million subfamilies with children under the age of 18 years in the United States. Between 1970 and 1997 the number of these subfamilies tripled. (See Table 6.4.)

FIGURE 6.9

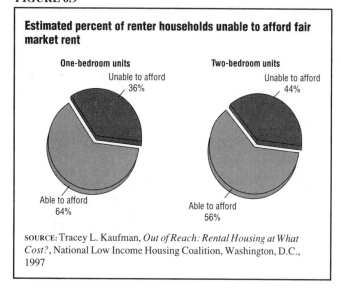

Estimated percent of renter households unable to afford fair market rent

SOURCE: Tracey L. Kaufman, *Out of Reach: Rental Housing at What Cost?*, National Low Income Housing Coalition, Washington, D.C., 1997

FIGURE 6.10

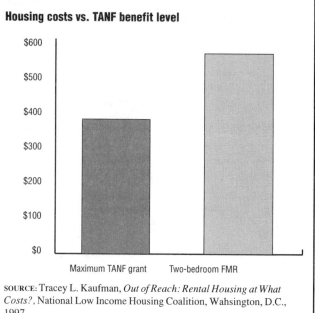

Housing costs vs. TANF benefit level

SOURCE: Tracey L. Kaufman, *Out of Reach: Rental Housing at What Costs?*, National Low Income Housing Coalition, Wahsington, D.C., 1997

Subfamilies are further categorized into related and unrelated subfamilies. Related subfamilies may consist of a young couple living with their parents while saving for a house, an unmarried mother who moves back in with her parents after the birth of a child, or a woman or man with children who may return home after a divorce. In 1998 there were nearly 2.3 million related subfamilies with children under the age of 18. (See Table 6.4.)

Unrelated subfamilies may consist of a couple or a parent and child living with a person to whom they are not related. The most common pattern of unrelated subfamilies consists of a mother and her children living with a householder (the person who owns or rents the home). In 1998 there were 549,000 unrelated subfamilies with their own children under the age of 18. (See Table 6.4.)

LIVING ARRANGEMENTS OF YOUNG ADULTS

Young adults are not only delaying marriage but more and more are living at home with their parents. The most significant increase in this living arrangement for those 18–24 years old occurred during the 1980s. In 1980, 48.4 percent of 18- to 24-year-olds lived with their parents. By 1990 this proportion had risen to 53 percent. In 1998 the percentage had stayed the same (53 percent), with 59 percent of males and 48 percent of females living at home with their parents. (See Table 6.5.)

A similar pattern of living arrangement also exists among young adults 25–34 years old. In 1980 just 8.7 percent lived with their parents. By 1990 the rate had risen to 11.5 percent. In 1998 a similar proportion (11.5 percent) of adults in this age group (15 percent of males and 8 percent of females) lived with their parents. (See Table 6.5.)

ADOPTION IN AMERICA

Historically, adoption in the United States involved homeless, orphaned, abandoned, and older children. Dur-

ing the mid-1800s, adoption laws were enacted to regulate the adoption of children born out of wedlock. State laws further protected the privacy of unmarried mothers and their children, who were often stigmatized by society. The adoption of newborns did not occur until the early 1900s when the introduction of infant formula gave pregnant women the option of giving up their babies for adoption immediately after birth.

After World War II (1939–45) and the Korean War (1950–53) the international adoption of "war orphans" provided an option for the parentless children who had survived. During the 1950s, America's child welfare system considered adoption as an alternative for "hard-to-place" children who had spent many years in foster care. These toddlers and older children are now known as children with "special needs." They are generally children with physical, mental, or emotional disabilities; minority children; and sibling groups.

Legal and Societal Changes Affect Adoption

In 1973 the historic U.S. Supreme Court decision *Roe v. Wade* (410 U.S. 113), which legalized abortion, gave women with unwanted pregnancies another legal option besides adoption. During the 1970s unmarried fathers' legal rights were upheld by the High Court. *Stanley v. Illinois* (405 U.S. 645, 1972) required paternal notification, and *Caban v. Mohammed* (441 U.S. 380, 1979) required paternal consent in adoption cases, regardless of the fathers' responsibility before the adoption.

During the last few decades of the 20th century, the rise in nonmarital childbearing and divorce led to a reduc-

TABLE 6.4

Family groups by selected characteristics: 1970–98

		Related subfamilies		One parent Maintained by	
Years	Total with own children under 18	Two-parent	Total	Mother	Father
All races					
1998	2,348	425	1,923	1,673	250
1997	2,360	465	1,895	1,651	244
1996	2,316	421	1,895	1,706	189
1995	2,241	377	1,864	1,668	195
1994	2,305	505	1,800	1,636	164
1993	2,136	410	1,726	1,556	170
1992	2,011	415	1,596	1,462	134
1991	1,984	424	1,560	1,418	142
1990	1,893	361	1,531	1,378	153
1989	1,844	342	1,503	1,398	104
1988	1,998	366	1,632	1,480	152
1987	1,916	342	1,574	1,451	123
1986	1,883	353	1,530	1,399	131
1985	1,857	348	1,508	1392	116
1984	1,820	344	1,476	1,363	113
1983	1,869	368	1,501	1,355	146
1982	1,568	316	1,252	1,139	113
1981	939	283	656	578	78
1980	825	257	568	512	56
1970	819	282	537	489	48
Unrelated subfamilies					
All races					
1998	549	14	535	463	72
1997	594	29	564	487	77
1996	558	21	538	493	45
1995	631	22	609	550	59
1994	684	34	650	571	78
1993	666	40	625	557	68
1992	622	44	577	523	55
1991	587	42	545	504	41
1990	488	23	466	421	45
1989	443	19	424	398	26
1988	427	11	416	393	23
1987	428	18	409	380	29
1986	386	27	360	338	22
1985	384	15	369	339	30
1984	380	18	362	329	33
1983	340	8	332	322	10
1982	307	15	292	279	13
1981	335	8	327	301	26
1980	303	13	291	273	18
1970	81	9	72	68	4

SOURCE: *Household and Family Characteristics: March 1998*, U.S. Bureau of the Census, Washington, D.C., 1999

FIGURE 6.11

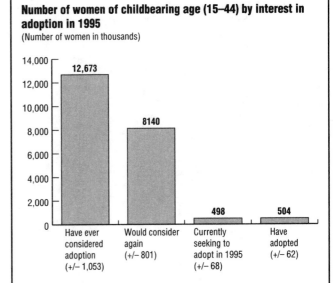

Number of women of childbearing age (15–44) by interest in adoption in 1995
(Number of women in thousands)

The numbers in parentheses represent the possible variation in estimation due to sampling error.

SOURCE: Christine Devere et al., *Adoption: Characteristics of Women Interested in Adopting a Child*, Congressional Research Service, Washington, D.C., 1998

tion in the stigma attached to single motherhood. Consequently, many unwed mothers chose to raise their children instead of giving them up for adoption. Moreover, welfare benefits provided economic support for many single-parent families. These factors have contributed to a decline in the number of infants available for adoption.

Women Interested in Adoption

Since 1973 the National Survey of Family Growth (NSFG), conducted by the National Center for Health Statistics, has periodically collected information about adoption. According to the CRS Report for Congress (Christine Devere, Gene Falk, and Karen Spar, "Adoption: Characteristics of Women Interested in Adopting a Child," The Library of Congress, Washington, D.C., 1998) adoption remains a relatively rare occurrence in the United States. Despite the large number (about 100,000) of foster children awaiting adoption, just a small proportion leave foster care for an adoptive home. (For more on foster care, see Chapter 3.)

Projections based on the 1995 NSFG estimated that nearly 12.7 million (23 percent) women of childbearing age (women 15–44 years old) had ever considered adoption. About 8 million (13.5 percent) said they would consider adoption again, and about 500,000 (0.9 percent) were currently seeking to adopt. However, just 504,000 (0.8 percent) women actually adopted a child. (See Figure 6.11 and Table 6.6.)

Characteristics of Women Interested in Adoption

While women across all income groups were interested in adoption, those who earned more money were more likely to adopt. The likelihood of having actually adopted a child, or of currently seeking to adopt, increased with a woman's age. Marital status also affected a woman's decision to adopt, with married women most likely to have adopted a child. (See Table 6.6.) Still, a significant proportion of never-married women had either considered, or were seeking, adoption. (The "never-married women" category includes the growing number of lesbian couples seeking to adopt.)

A woman's education also had a bearing on her interest in adoption. Women with more education were more likely to consider adoption and to have actually adopted a

TABLE 6.5

Young adults living at home: 1960–98

(Numbers in thousands. Data based on Current Population Survey (CPS) unless otherwise specified)

Age	Male			Female		
	Total	Child of householder	Percent	Total	Child of householder	Percent
18 to 24 years						
1998	12,633	7,399	59	12,568	5,974	48
1997	12,534	7,501	60	12,452	6,006	48
1996	12,402	7,327	59	12,441	5,955	48
1995	12,545	7,328	58	12,613	5,896	47
1994	12,683	7,547	60	12,792	5,924	46
1993	12,049	7,145	59	12,260	5,746	47
1992	12,083	7,296	60	12,351	5,929	48
1991	12,275	7,385	60	12,627	6,163	49
1990	12,450	7,232	58	12,860	6,135	48
1989	12,574	7,308	58	13,055	6,141	47
1988	12,835	7,792	61	13,226	6,398	48
1987	13,029	7,981	61	13,433	6,375	47
1986	13,324	7,831	59	13,787	6,433	47
1985	13,695	8,172	60	14,149	6,758	48
1984	14,196	8,764	62	14,482	6,779	47
1983	14,344	8,803	61	14,702	7,001	48
1982	14,368	(NA)	(NA)	14,815	(NA)	(NA)
1981	14,367	(NA)	(NA)	14,848	(NA)	(NA)
1980 Census	14,278	7,755	54	14,844	6,336	43
1970 Census	10,398	5,641	54	11,959	4,941	41
1960 Census	6,842	3,583	52	7,876	2,750	35
25 to 34 years						
1998	19,526	2,845	15	19,828	1,680	8
1997	20,039	2,909	15	20,217	1,745	9
1996	20,390	3,213	16	20,528	1,810	9
1995	20,589	3,166	15	20,800	1,759	8
1994	20,873	3,261	16	21,073	1,859	9
1993	20,856	3,300	16	21,007	1,844	9
1992	21,125	3,225	15	21,368	1,874	9
1991	21,319	3,172	15	21,586	1,887	9
1990	21,462	3,213	15	21,779	1,774	8
1989	21,461	3,130	15	21,777	1,728	8
1988	21,320	3,207	15	21,649	1,791	8
1987	21,142	3,071	15	21,494	1,655	8
1986	20,956	2,981	14	21,097	1,686	8
1985	20,184	2,685	13	20,673	1,661	8
1984	19,876	2,626	13	20,297	1,548	8
1983	19,438	2,664	14	19,903	1,520	8
1982	19,090	(NA)	(NA)	19,614	(NA)	(NA)
1981	18,625	(NA)	(NA)	19,203	(NA)	(NA)
1980 Census	18,107	1,894	10	18,689	1,300	7
1970 Census	11,929	1,129	9	12,637	829	7
1960 Census	10,896	1,185	11	11,587	853	7

Note: Unmarried college students living in dormitories are counted as living in their parent(s) home.

NA Not available.

SOURCE: *Marital Status and Living Arrangements: March 1998*, U.S. Bureau of the Census, Washington, D.C., 1999

child. A woman's ability to bear her own child also affects her interest in adopting and her decision to actually adopt. Nonsurgically sterile women were the most likely to have considered adoption, to be currently seeking to adopt, and to have adopted a child. (See Table 6.6.)

Child Preferences among Women Seeking to Adopt

The 1995 NSFG asked women what types of children they wanted to adopt. One-third (33.3 percent) preferred to adopt a girl while one-fifth (21.2 percent) preferred a boy. Generally, women expressed indifference to the child's religion (76.2 percent). (See Table 6.7.)

Although more than one-quarter (28.8 percent) of women were interested in adopting white children, most (42.3 percent) were indifferent to the child's race. (See Table 6.7 and Figure 6.12.) However, one-half (52 percent) of black women preferred black children, and an equal number (51 percent) of white women preferred white children (not shown).

TABLE 6.6

Percent of women of childbearing age (15–44) interested in adoption or who adopted a child, by selected characteristics in 1995

	Ever adopted	Currently seeking to adopt	Considered adoption and would consider again
Total Population[a]	**0.84%**	**0.90%**	**13.52%**
Income (As a Percent of the Poverty Level)			
Less than 151% of the poverty level	0.27%	0.82%	11.69%
15I-300% of the poverty level	0.69%	0.74%	13.20%
301-450% of the poverty level	1.21%	0.62%	13.61%
45I-600% of the poverty level	1.03%	0.91%	15.96%
Greater than 600% of the poverty level	1.50%	1.80%	14.72%
Age			
15 to 25 years of age	0.04%	0.36%	11.01%
26 to 34 years of age	0.41%	0.72%	18.16%
35 to 44 years of age	1.96%	1.44%	11.75%
Formal Marital Status[b]			
Married	1.33%	1.07%	13.92%
Divorced/separated	1.05%	1.08%	13.52%
Never married	0.07%	0.55%	13.05%
Education			
No degree	0.28%	1.67%	6.83%
High school or equivalent	0.80%	0.70%	14.67%
Associate's degree	1.64%	0.97%	16.93%
Bachelor's degree	1.05%	1.12%	16.70%
Beyond bachelor's degree (Master's degree or Ph.D.)	1.76%	0.51%	16.22%
Some other academic degree	3.28%	0.00%	10.06%
Race			
Hispanic	0.54%	1.13%	15.34%
White (non-Hispanic)	0.90%	0.66%	12.77%
Black (non-Hispanic)	0.89%	1.73%	15.13%
Other (non-Hispanic)	0.42%	1.74%	15.82%
Ability to bear own child			
Surgically sterile for Contraceptive reasons	0.95%	1.08%	10.90%
Surgically sterile for Noncontraceptive reasons	3.91%	1.70%	13.33%
Nonsurgically sterile	8.30%	5.34%	24.90%
Difficulty conceiving or delivering a child/Long interval with no pregnancy	2.08%	1.53%	24.23%
Able to conceive	0.27%	0.55%	12.78%

[a] The samples for women who had adopted a child or who were currently seeking to adopt a child are relatively small, so some of the differences shown may reflect the imprecision of the estimates due to these small sample sizes, rather than actual differences among the categories of women.

[b] Results for the population of widowed women are not presented because of their small subgroup.

SOURCE: Christine Devere et al., *Adoption: Characteristics of Women Interested in Adopting a Child,* Congressional Research Service, Washington, D.C., 1998

Most adoptive women (57.5 percent) were interested in getting a child younger than 2 years of age, and more than one-quarter (28.1 percent) preferred a child between 2 and 5. Very few wanted to adopt a child 6 or older. (See Table 6.7 and Figure 6.13.)

TABLE 6.7

Preferences for children of women currently seeking to adopt a child in 1995

	Percent	Standard error
If you could choose exactly the child you wanted, would you prefer to adopt		
Sex		
a girl?	33.27%	6.63
a boy?	21.16%	5.99
indifferent?	45.57%	6.38
Race		
a black child?	13.75%	4.78
a white child?	28.80%	6.15
a child of some other race?	15.10%	3.92
indifferent?	42.35%	5.88
Age		
a child younger than 2 years?	57.52%	5.49
a 2–5 year old child?	28.12%	5.30
a 6–12 year old child?	6.84%	2.69
a child 13 years or older?	0.53%	0.53
indifferent?	6.99%	2.77
Disability		
a child with no disability?	54.20%	6.53
a child with a mild disability?	24.79%	5.44
a child with a severe disability?	5.47%	4.30
indifferent?	15.55%	3.75
Number of children		
a single child?	64.72%	6.47
2 or more brothers and sisters at once?	26.32%	5.87
indifferent?	8.97%	3.02
Religion		
same religious background?	17.06%	4.10
different religious background?	6.75%	3.39
indifferent?	76.19%	5.48

Detail may not sum to 100 due to rounding.

SOURCE: Christine Devere et al., *Adoption: Characteristics of Women Interested in Adopting a Child,* Congressional Research Service, Washington, D.C., 1998

Most women (54.2 percent) preferred to adopt a child with no disability; nearly one-quarter (24.8 percent) were interested in adopting a child with a mild disability; but few (5.5 percent) wanted a child with severe disabilities. However, about 15.5 percent were indifferent to a child's level of disability. (See Table 6.7 and Figure 6.14.)

Almost two-thirds (64.7 percent) wanted to adopt just one child, although more than one-fourth (26.3 percent) indicated they would adopt two or more siblings at the same time. (See Table 6.7 and Figure 6.15.)

Implications of NSFG Data

In 1999, 500,000 children were being cared for in the foster care system. According to the U.S. Department of Health and Human Services, nearly three-quarters (63 percent) of foster children were 6 or older. (See Figure 3.13 in Chapter 3.) In addition, some were "special needs" children, while others were siblings who wanted to be adopted together.

FIGURE 6.12

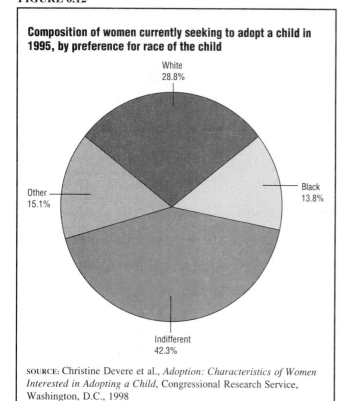

Composition of women currently seeking to adopt a child in 1995, by preference for race of the child

White
28.8%

Other
15.1%

Black
13.8%

Indifferent
42.3%

SOURCE: Christine Devere et al., *Adoption: Characteristics of Women Interested in Adopting a Child*, Congressional Research Service, Washington, D.C., 1998

FIGURE 6.14

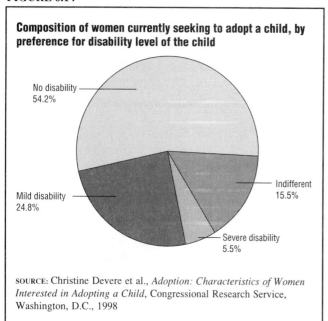

Composition of women currently seeking to adopt a child, by preference for disability level of the child

No disability
54.2%

Mild disability
24.8%

Indifferent
15.5%

Severe disability
5.5%

SOURCE: Christine Devere et al., *Adoption: Characteristics of Women Interested in Adopting a Child*, Congressional Research Service, Washington, D.C., 1998

FIGURE 6.13

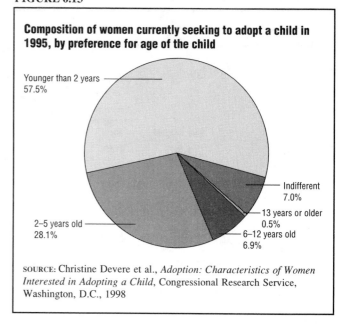

Composition of women currently seeking to adopt a child in 1995, by preference for age of the child

Younger than 2 years
57.5%

Indifferent
7.0%

13 years or older
0.5%

6–12 years old
6.9%

2–5 years old
28.1%

SOURCE: Christine Devere et al., *Adoption: Characteristics of Women Interested in Adopting a Child*, Congressional Research Service, Washington, D.C., 1998

FIGURE 6.15

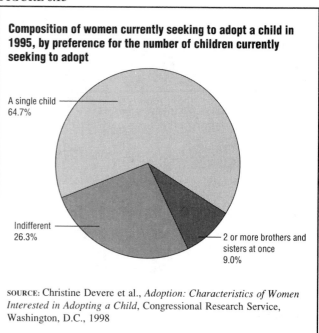

Composition of women currently seeking to adopt a child in 1995, by preference for the number of children currently seeking to adopt

A single child
64.7%

Indifferent
26.3%

2 or more brothers and sisters at once
9.0%

SOURCE: Christine Devere et al., *Adoption: Characteristics of Women Interested in Adopting a Child*, Congressional Research Service, Washington, D.C., 1998

Because of the very small number of infants available for adoption in the United States, many individuals seek adoption in foreign countries. (See Chapter 3 for more on intercountry adoption.) Some seek foreign adoption because they fear that a birth mother here in the United States may change her mind and want her child back.

Sibling Rights in Adoption

Some foster children who have difficulty being adopted are members of sibling groups (brothers and sisters). As seen in the 1995 NSFG, most women interested in adoption want just one child. Every year about 35,000 siblings end up being placed in separate adoptive homes.

In December 1998, in Boston, Massachusetts, lawyers for a brother and sister planned to petition the U.S. Supreme Court to review the case of the two siblings. The Massachusetts Supreme Court had ruled that a 6-year-old girl would remain in Boston with her foster mother, who

FIGURE 6.16

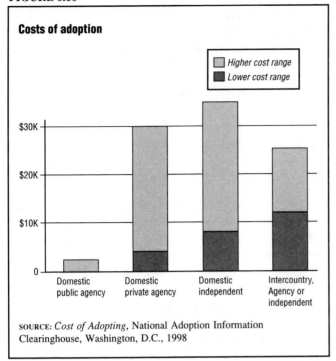

Costs of adoption

SOURCE: *Cost of Adopting*, National Adoption Information Clearinghouse, Washington, D.C., 1998

TABLE 6.8

Representative adoption benefit plans

Wendy's International, headquartered in Dublin, Ohio, covers eligible adoption expenses up to a maximum of $4,000 per adoption for employees who have completed one year of service and participate in the company's Group Insurance Program. For the adoption of a child with special needs, Wendy's will reimburse up to $6,000 per adoption. Financial assistance will cover specific adoption-related expenses. A paid leave of absence is available upon assuming custody of the child, with the amount of leave determined by the employee's length of service.

The Campbell Soup Company of Camden, New Jersey, offers salaried employees financial reimbursement of up to $2,000 for adoption-related expenses, payable when the adoption is finalized. In addition, the company may give some paid leave to adoptive parent employees based on their length of service. Additional unpaid leave is available for up to 60 days with the approval of the employee's supervisor. This plan is available to both male and female regular salaried employees.

The Procter & Gamble Company of Cincinnati, Ohio, reimburses employees for up to $2,000 of eligible expenses at any time after the child is placed in the family's home and considers each child separately in the case of multiple adoptions, permitting a maximum of $6,000 payable to any one family within a one-year period. Employees with at least 6 months of continuous regular employment may be reimbursed, up to the $1,000 maximum, for recognized adoption agency fees, placement fees, maternity fees for the birth mother, temporary foster care fees, and legal fees.

Xerox Corporation of Stamford, Connecticut, acknowledges that because adoption costs vary "depending on such factors as geographic location, the nature of the adoption agency, and income of the prospective parents (or parent), the intent of the program is to provide some level of assistance to employees who wish to adopt." Xerox reimburses regular full-time or part-time employees who adopt with up to $3,000 in expenses such as: public and private agency fees, legal and court fees, medical expenses (including physical examinations for adopting parents and maternity expenses for birth mothers), foreign adoption fees, and temporary foster care charges.

SOURCE: *Adoption Benefits*, National Adoption Information Clearinghouse, Washington, D.C., August, 2000

had adopted her three years earlier, while her 4-year-old brother, who was adopted by an aunt, would move to New Jersey. Over the years, although some courts have considered the problem of sibling adoption, there has been no ruling that adoptive siblings have the same constitutional right to be together as do parents and children.

Employers Offer Adoption Benefits

The National Adoption Information Clearinghouse (NAIC) reports that an adoption can be far more expensive (up to $30,000) than a birth (average cost of $6,430). The domestic adoption of a healthy infant through a private or independent agency can cost anywhere from $4,000 to $30,000. The costs of foreign adoptions can run between $12,000 and $25,000, not including travel and living expenses to visit the child's home country. (See Figure 6.16.)

A growing number of employers have begun offering employment and/or medical benefits to adoptive parents. These companies recognize that employees who choose to build their families through adoption should receive the same benefits as biological parents. According to the Philadelphia, Pennsylvania–based National Adoption Center, which helps companies put together adoption benefits plans, such plans do not cost employers much, since fewer than 1 percent of workers use adoption benefits when they are available.

The National Adoption Center reports that, in the 1980s, only about 40 companies in the United States had adoption benefits plans. By the 1990s, 450 companies, including 65 percent of Fortune 500 firms, offered such benefit plans. (See Table 6.8 for examples.)

Single-Parent Adoption

During the 1980s and 1990s the fastest-growing trend in adoption was single-parent adoption. According to the National Adoption Center, about 25 percent of all "special needs" adoptions were by single people. An estimated 5 percent of all other adoptions were also by single men and women.

Changing Concept of Adoptive Parents

As late as the 1960s, single-parent adoptions were not only discouraged but also banned by states. Such adoptions have become more widely accepted. There is now less stigma attached to single-parent families, and the child welfare system and adoption agencies are more open to consider single people as potential adoptive parents. They now believe it better for a child to have a single parent than no family at all.

Some women who have pursued a career and have not married realize later in life that they want to have a child. Some single men also wish to raise adoptive children. Other single people, many of them professionals in the "helping" professions—teachers, nurses, psychologists— want to help improve the lives of children such as those in foster care and in developing countries. A number of foreign countries, including Bolivia, Brazil, El Salvador,

Honduras, and Peru, are willing to consider single adoptive parents. Some researchers believe that single-parent families might prove especially suited for older foster children who may need a very close relationship with a single parent in order to develop.

ISSUES AFFECTING GAYS AND LESBIANS

Marriage

The issue of same-sex marriage continues to be hotly debated as more gay couples demand legal recognition of their unions. In 2000 Vermont became the first state to officially sanction same-sex marriages; in the November 1998 election, voters in Hawaii and Alaska approved a constitutional amendment to ban gay couples from civil marriages. In the meantime, gay and lesbian couples continue to go to court for the right to get married.

Workers' Benefits for Domestic Partners

Many local governments have begun to provide benefits to domestic partners of gay and lesbian employees. Also, a number of private companies offer the same medical and other benefits to same-sex partners of employees that they provide to spouses and live-in partners of heterosexual employees. In 1997, in the first state law of its kind, the Hawaii Legislature gave gay and lesbian couples the right to participate in their partners' medical insurance and state pensions. Lesbian and gay couples were also granted inheritance rights, joint property ownership rights, and the right to sue for wrongful death.

In December 1998, in the first judicial decision of its kind, the Oregon State Court of Appeals ruled that the denial of insurance benefits to the domestic partners of lesbian or gay government employees violated the Oregon Constitution. Article I, Section 20 of the state Constitution provides that "No law shall be passed granting to any citizen or class of citizens privileges or immunities, which, upon the same terms, shall not equally belong to all citizens."

Adoption

The National Adoption Information Clearinghouse (NAIC) reports that gays and lesbians have always adopted children, but that the number of adoptive parents is unknown. The last several years saw more gay and lesbian individuals and/or couples raising children, and many more interested in adoption.

The NAIC, in *Working with Gay and Lesbian Adoptive Parents* (Gloria Hochman, Mady Prowler, and Anna Huston, Washington, D.C., 1995), noted that American people generally continue to have differing views about same-sex parenting. Some people opposing same-sex parent adoption believe that children raised in those households will become gay. Those in favor claim that much of the evidence available shows that children raised by gays/lesbians are no more prone to become gay or lesbian themselves

than children raised by heterosexuals. A number of studies of offspring of gay fathers have found the majority of these children to be heterosexual, with the percentage of gay children similar to that of the general population.

Some courts are concerned that children adopted by lesbian or gay parents may develop psychological problems. Researchers have shown these children are no different in their psychological development than their counterparts in heterosexual families. These studies show that parenting skills in supporting and nurturing a child far outweigh the influence of the parents' sexual preference.

THE LAW AND ADOPTION BY GAYS AND LESBIANS. Ten states (California, Massachusetts, New Jersey, New Hampshire, New Mexico, New York, Ohio, Vermont, Washington, and Wisconsin), as well as the District of Columbia, have allowed openly gay and lesbian individuals or couples to adopt. Although some joint adoptions have been successful, the most common practice is for a single person to apply as the legal adoptive parent of the child. Couples who both want custody usually apply for a second parent, or coparent, adoption.

In 2000 Florida and Utah were joined by Mississippi as the only states banning lesbians and gays from adopting children. The American Civil Liberties Union is challenging the constitutionality of the Florida legislation and is planning on doing the same in Mississippi. (New Hampshire also prohibited lesbian or gay adoption until 1999.) Some states, however, have strict regulations about adoptive parents. For instance North Dakota considers only married couples as prospective adopters of foster children, while Massachusetts requires adoption applicants to reveal their sexual orientation. Each state decides its own adoption cases, with the courts making the final decisions.

SECOND-PARENT ADOPTION. In the past, if a gay or lesbian couple adopted a child, only one parent was recognized as that child's legal guardian. However, some jurisdictions now allow second-parent adoption. In second-parent adoption, a child's nonbiological parent is permitted to adopt the child without severing the rights of the biological parent. According to the National Adoption Information Clearinghouse, as of 2000, Alaska, California, Colorado, Connecticut, the District of Columbia, Illinois, Indiana, Iowa, Maryland, Massachusetts, Minnesota, Michigan, Nevada, New Jersey, New York, Ohio, Oregon, Pennsylvania, Rhode Island, Texas, Vermont, and Washington allowed second-parent adoptions for same-sex couples. These decisions apply to intercountry adoption, as well.

In the landmark 1993 case *In re: Adoption of B.L.V.B. and E.L.V.B.* (628 A.2d 1271, 160 Vt. 369) the Vermont Supreme Court became the first state Supreme Court to recognize gay coparent adoption. Through anonymous donor insemination, Jane Van Buren gave birth to two boys. The Vermont law at the time recognized Van

Buren—but not her lesbian partner, Deborah Lashman—as the sole legal parent. If the mother died, the boys would be considered orphans and Lashman could not step in as the boys' guardian. If the couple separated, Lashman would have no further relationship with the boys. Nor would Lashman be bound by law to provide for the children.

Lashman petitioned the court to allow her second-parent adoption of her partner's children while leaving the mother's parental rights intact. The lower court denied the petition, stating that Lashman was not married to the boys' mother. (State law does not recognize couples who cannot legally marry.) The couple appealed to the Vermont Supreme Court arguing that the second-parent adoption was in the best interests of the children. The court agreed ruling that "To deny the child of same-sex partners, as a class, the security of a legally recognized relationship with their second parent serves no legitimate state interest."

On the other hand, the State Court of Appeals in Akron, Ohio, in *In re: Adoption of Jane Doe* (No. 19017), ruled that such adoptions were not possible for gay or lesbian parents under Ohio law. "Trish Smith" and "Marcia Jones" had been together since 1981. The child, "Jane Doe," was conceived through artificial insemination in 1990. While Marcia was the biological mother, both women had raised the child from birth.

In 1996 the women filed a petition for Trish to adopt the child while Marcia retained her parental status. A lower court ruled that the Ohio Adoption Act required that Marcia give up her status as a parent before Trish could adopt. The case was appealed, and a unanimous state court of appeals in Akron observed that

Although we are mindful of the dilemma facing the parties and are sympathetic to their plight, it is not within the constitutional scope of judicial power to change the face and effect of the plain meaning of [the Ohio Adoption Act].

A class action lawsuit filed by the American Civil Liberties Union in 1998 on behalf of lesbian or gay partners made great strides in giving them equal status with married heterosexuals in adoptions. Michael Galluccio and Jon Holden became the first gay couple to file jointly for adoption. They successfully gained legal custody of their 2-year-old foster child. Similar cases around the country, however, have had different outcomes.

This is a growing new area of law, and case findings will likely continue to differ greatly as various states determine if second-parent adoption by gays and lesbians is legal.

CHILDLESS WOMEN

In "Education First, Children Next?" (*Census and You*, Washington, D.C., 1998) the Census Bureau reported that, in 1995, 41.8 percent of women ages 15–44 were childless. The District of Columbia (55.4 percent) and Massachusetts (51 percent) had the largest percentages of childless women. Arkansas, at 34.8 percent, had the lowest proportion of childless women. (See Figure 6.17.)

According to the Census Bureau's report, the childless rate increases as the level of education increases. Women with a bachelor's, graduate, or some type of professional degree were more likely to have no children than women who had not completed high school. This difference was most prominent among women ages 25–34. In 1995, 15 percent of women in this age group who had no high school diploma were childless, compared with 57 percent of women with a bachelor's degree and 63 percent of those with an advanced degree.

Women of this age group who lived in central cities (39 percent) were far more likely to be childless than their counterparts in nonmetropolitan areas (22 percent), and employed women were more likely to be childless than those unemployed or out of the labor force. Among working women the most likely to be childless were in managerial and professional occupations while the least likely to be childless were employed as operators, fabricators, or laborers.

In 1960 approximately one-half (47.5 percent) of women ages 20–24 had not had at least one live birth. In 1980 a larger proportion (two-thirds, or 66.2 percent) of women in this age group had not had at least one live birth. This pattern of postponing childbearing continued in 1998, with still two-thirds (65.1 percent) of women not having had at least one live birth. Among older women, the levels of childlessness in 1998 were also higher than in 1960: 43 percent for those 25–29 years old; 26.1 percent for women 30–34 years old; 18.3 percent for women 35–39 years old; and 16.5 percent for those 40–44 years old. (See Table 6.9.)

MULTIPLE BIRTHS

Each year in the United States the number of triplets and other higher-order births continue to rise. Increases in triplet births averaged about 2 percent a year for the 1970s, approximately 7 percent a year for the early 1980s, and around 11 percent a year from 1985 to 1989. During the early 1990s, despite a decline in single births, multiple births rose rapidly. More multiple births occurred during the first half of the 1990s than during the entire 1980s. (See Table 6.10.)

In 1997, 104,137 twins, 6,148 triplets, 510 quadruplets, and 79 quintuplets and other higher-order multiple births occurred. Triplet births continue to comprise the overwhelming majority of all higher-order multiple births (91 percent for 1997). (See Table 6.11.)

More twins were born to women in their 40s during 1997 than during the entire decade of the 1980s. The

FIGURE 6.17

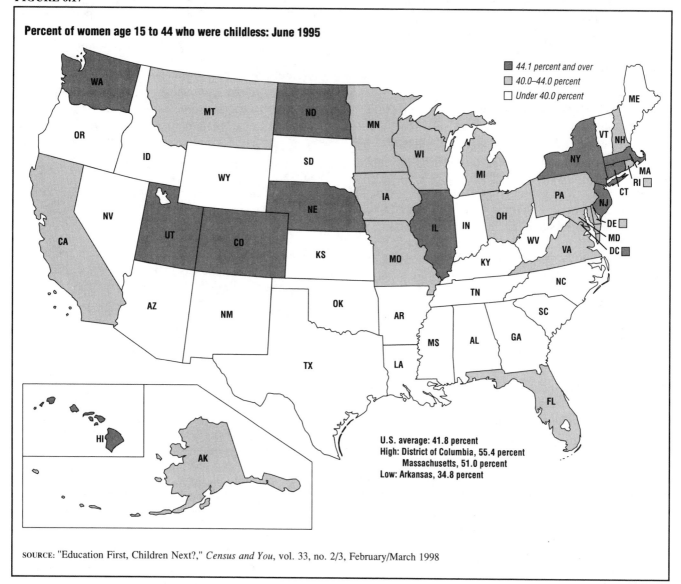

Percent of women age 15 to 44 who were childless: June 1995

■ 44.1 percent and over
░ 40.0–44.0 percent
□ Under 40.0 percent

U.S. average: 41.8 percent
High: District of Columbia, 55.4 percent
       Massachusetts, 51.0 percent
Low: Arkansas, 34.8 percent

SOURCE: "Education First, Children Next?," *Census and You*, vol. 33, no. 2/3, February/March 1998

numbers of multiple births (triplets or more) also increased—by 400 percent for women in their 30s and an astounding 1,000 percent for women in their 40s.

Race-Specific Ratios

Historically, differences in twin birth rates have been most noticeable between white and black mothers (in 1980, 18.1 and 24.0 per 1,000 births, respectively.) That difference is now virtually gone. In 1996 twin birth rates for non-Hispanic whites and blacks were 27.8 and 29.1, respectively, and, by 1997, 28.8 and 30.0, respectively. Women of Hispanic origin continue to be substantially less likely than white or black mothers to have a twin birth (19.1 in 1996). Non-Hispanic whites (207.1) were more than twice as likely to have higher-order multiple births than were black (73.8) and Hispanic women (58.3). (See Table 6.12 and Figure 6.18.) Many of these phenomena are attributable to fertility treatments.

Patterns of Childbearing and Multiple Births

According to the CDC, about one-third of the increase in multiple births can be attributed to the changing patterns of childbirth. Many women have postponed childbearing in favor of a higher education and a career. By the time an older woman is ready to start a family it may be more difficult for her to conceive. About 15 percent of all American women of childbearing age have received an infertility service of some type. Of the approximately 60 million women of reproductive age in 1995, about 1.2 million, or 2 percent, had an infertility-related medical appointment within the previous year, and an additional 13 percent had received infertility services at some time in their lives. (Infertility services include medical tests to diagnose infertility, medical advice, and treatments to help a woman become pregnant, and services other than routine prenatal care to prevent miscarriage.) Of married couples, 7 percent (2.1 million) in which the woman was of reproductive age reported they

TABLE 6.9

Women 15–44 years of age who have not had at least 1 live birth, by age: selected years 1960–98

[Data are based on the national vital statistics system]

Year[1]	15–19 years	20–24 years	25–29 years	30–34 years	35–39 years	40–44 years
			Percent of women			
1960	91.4	47.5	20.0	14.2	12.0	15.1
1965	92.7	51.4	19.7	11.7	11.4	11.0
1970	93.0	57.0	24.4	11.8	9.4	10.6
1975	92.6	62.5	31.1	15.2	9.6	8.8
1980	93.4	66.2	38.9	19.7	12.5	9.0
1985	93.7	67.7	41.5	24.6	15.4	11.7
1986	93.8	68.0	42.0	25.1	16.1	12.2
1987	93.8	68.2	42.5	25.5	16.9	12.6
1988	93.8	68.4	43.0	25.7	17.7	13.0
1989	93.7	68.4	43.3	25.9	18.2	13.5
1990	93.3	68.3	43.5	25.9	18.5	13.9
1991	93.0	67.9	43.6	26.0	18.7	14.5
1992	92.7	67.3	43.7	26.0	18.8	15.2
1993	92.6	66.7	43.8	26.1	18.8	15.8
1994	92.6	66.1	43.9	26.2	18.7	16.2
1995	92.5	65.5	44.0	26.2	18.6	16.5
1996	92.5	65.0	43.8	26.2	18.5	16.6
1997	92.8	64.9	43.5	26.2	18.4	16.6
1998	93.1	65.1	43.0	26.1	18.3	16.5

[1] As of January 1.

Notes: Data are based on cohort fertility. Percents are derived from the cumulative childbearing experience of cohorts of women, up to the ages specified. Data on births are adjusted for underregistration and population estimates are corrected for underregistration and misstatement of age. Beginning in 1970, births to persons who were not residents of the 50 States and the District of Columbia are excluded.

SOURCE: *Health, United States, 2000*, National Center for Health Statistics, Hyattsville, MD, 2000

had not used contraception for 12 months and had not become pregnant.

The introduction of the fertility drug Clomid in the 1970s and of assisted reproductive technology (ART) in 1981 has accounted for the increasing number of multiple births. Of all ART cycles performed in 1997, 29.5 percent resulted in pregnancy. Of those pregnancies, 14.8 percent were single births and 9.2 percent multiple births. (See Figure 6.19.) Of the multiple births, 25.9 percent were triplets or higher order, and 25.9 percent were twins. (See Figure 6.20.)

Seventy-eight percent of these mothers had no previous births; however, they may have had a pregnancy that resulted in a miscarriage or a therapeutic abortion. Sixteen percent reported one previous birth, and 6 percent reported two or more. However, the CDC does not know how many of these children were conceived naturally and how many by an ART procedure. These data point out that women who have previously had children can still face infertility problems, including infertility of a new partner.

Artificial Reproduction and the Family

In the late 1980s and early 1990s, when an estimated 4,000 women became surrogate mothers by being artificially inseminated with sperm from men whose wives were infertile, many people were concerned that surrogate motherhood might threaten family stability. Who would be considered the child's mother? Also, some surrogate mothers refused to relinquish the child after delivery resulting in long, bitter fights for custody of the child.

Rapid advances in fertility technology have made such family matters even more complicated. Using donor sperm and/or eggs could mean a child may have three or four parents—the donor or donors, the mother who carries the transplanted embryo in her uterus, and her spouse. The federal funding of human embryo research has been banned since the Reagan Administration. Private fertility enterprises, however, continue to be unregulated in this country and each fertility clinic has its own guidelines. Critics fear that fertility patients as well as donors may fall victims to unscrupulous clinics and doctors who may not have to answer to scientific and ethical review boards.

PROTECTING THE FAMILY. In 1998 the New York State Task Force on Life and the Law, a 24-member panel of doctors, lawyers, ethicists, and clergy members, urged the formulation of more rigid standards to monitor reproductive technology. The task force was especially concerned about the wellbeing of children born using such technology, especially those who are siblings in multiple births. These infants are at a high risk of prematurity, low birth weight, long-term disabilities, and death. The task force believes children born through assisted reproduction have the right

TABLE 6.10

Number and rate of twin and triplet/+ births by race and Hispanic origin of mother, 1980–97

Race, Hispanic origin, and year	Total births	Twin	Triplet/+[1]	Twin	Triplet/+[1]
		Number		Rate per 1,000 live births	Rate per 100,000 live births
All races[2]					
1997	3,880,894	104,137	6,737	26.8	173.6
1996	3,891,494	100,750	5,939	25.9	152.6
1995	3,899,589	96,736	4,973	24.8	127.5
1994	3,952,767	97,064	4,594	24.6	116.2
1993	4,000,240	96,445	4,168	24.1	104.2
1992	4,065,014	95,372	3,883	23.5	95.5
1991	4,110,907	94,779	3,346	23.1	81.4
1990	4,158,212	93,865	3,028	22.6	72.8
1989	4,040,958	90,118	2,798	22.3	69.2
1988	3,909,510	85,315	2,385	21.8	61.0
1987	3,809,394	81,778	2,139	21.5	56.2
1986	3,756,547	79,485	1,814	21.2	48.3
1985	3,760,561	77,102	1,925	20.5	51.2
1984	3,669,141	72,949	1,653	19.9	45.1
1983	3,638,933	72,287	1,575	19.9	43.3
1982	3,680,537	71,631	1,484	19.5	40.3
1981	3,629,238	70,049	1,385	19.3	38.2
1980	3,612,258	68,339	1,337	18.9	37.0
White, total[3]					
1997	3,072,640	82,090	6,018	26.7	195.9
1996	3,093,057	79,677	5,383	25.8	174.0
1995	3,098,885	76,196	4,505	24.6	145.4
1994	3,121,004	75,318	4,127	24.1	132.2
1993	3,149,833	74,643	3,748	23.7	119.0
1992	3,201,678	73,547	3,444	23.0	107.6
1991	3,241,273	73,045	2,905	22.5	89.6
1990	3,290,273	72,617	2,639	22.1	80.2
1989	3,192,355	69,373	2,483	21.7	77.8
1988	3,102,083	66,383	2,048	21.4	66.0
1987	3,043,828	64,005	1,821	21.0	59.8
1986	3,019,175	62,396	1,585	20.7	52.5
1985	3,037,913	60,351	1,648	19.9	54.2
1984	2,967,100	57,274	1,416	19.3	47.7
1983	2,946,468	56,604	1,319	19.2	44.8
1982	2,984,817	56,035	1,199	18.8	40.2
1981	2,947,679	54,341	1,188	18.4	40.3
1980	2,936,351	53,104	1,104	18.1	37.6
Non-Hispanic white					
1997	2,333,363	67,191	5,386	28.8	230.8
1996	2,358,989	65,523	4,885	27.8	207.1
1995	2,382,638	62,370	4,050	26.2	170.0
1994	2,438,855	62,476	3,721	25.6	152.6
1993	2,472,031	61,525	3,360	24.9	135.9
1992[4]	2,527,207	60,640	3,115	24.0	123.3
1991[4]	2,589,878	60,904	2,612	23.5	100.9
1990[5]	2,626,500	60,210	2,358	22.9	89.8
1989[6]	2,526,367	56,798	2,172	22.5	86.0
Black, total[3]					
1997	599,913	17,989	530	30.0	88.3
1996	594,781	17,285	439	29.1	73.8
1995	603,139	17,000	352	28.2	58.4
1994	617,689	18,344	358	28.8	56.3
1993	658,875	18,551	327	28.2	49.6
1992	673,633	18,619	361	27.6	53.6
1991	682,602	18,593	368	27.2	53.9
1990	684,336	18,164	321	26.5	46.9
1989	673,124	17,844	262	26.5	38.9
1988	638,562	16,334	286	25.6	44.8
1987	611,173	15,450	246	25.3	40.3
1986	592,910	14,662	199	24.7	33.6
1985	581,824	14,646	240	25.2	41.2
1984	568,138	13,616	195	24.0	34.3
1983	562,624	13,711	216	24.4	38.4
1982	568,506	13,592	240	23.9	42.2
1981	564,955	13,928	172	24.7	30.4
1980	568,080	13,638	211	24.0	37.1

TABLE 6.10

Number and rate of twin and triplet/+ births by race and Hispanic origin of mother, 1980–97 [CONTINUED]

Race, Hispanic origin, and year	Total births	Twin	Triplet/+[1]	Twin	Triplet/+[1]
		Number		**Rate per 1,000 live births**	**Rate per 100,000 live births**
Non-Hispanic black					
1997	581,431	17,472	523	30.0	90.0
1996	578,099	16,873	425	29.2	73.5
1995	587,781	16,622	340	28.3	57.8
1994	619,198	17,934	357	29.0	57.7
1993	641,273	18,115	314	28.2	49.0
1992[4]	657,450	18,294	346	27.8	52.6
1991[4]	666,758	18,243	367	27.4	55.0
1990[5]	661,701	17,646	306	26.7	46.2
1989[6]	611,269	16,266	246	26.6	40.2
Hispanic					
1997	709,767	13,821	516	19.5	72.7
1996	701,339	13,014	409	18.6	58.3
1995	679,768	12,685	355	18.7	52.2
1994	665,026	12,206	348	18.4	52.3
1993	654,418	12,294	321	18.8	49.1
1992[4]	643,271	11,932	239	18.5	37.2
1991[4]	623,085	11,356	235	18.2	37.7
1990[5]	595,073	10,713	235	18.0	39.5
1989[6]	532,249	9,701	189	18.2	35.5

[1] Includes quadruplets and other higher order multiple births.
[2] Includes races other than white and black and origin not stated.
[3] Includes births to women of Hispanic origin.
[4] Excludes data for New Hampshire, which did not report Hispanic origin.
[5] Excludes data for New Hampshire and Oklahoma, which did not report Hispanic origin.
[6] Excludes data for Louisiana, New Hampshire, and Oklahoma, which did not report Hispanic origin.

Notes: Race and Hispanic origin are reported separately on birth certificates. Persons of Hispanic origin may be of any race.

SOURCE: Joyce A. Martin and Melissa M. Park, "Trends in Twin and Triplet Births: 1980–97," *National Vital Statistics Reports*, vol. 47, no. 24, National Center for Health Statistics, 1999

to know the donors' medical and family histories. These experts recommend that doctors require genetic testing to detect any harmful conditions the children could inherit and that donors be particularly screened for the AIDS virus.

This panel of experts was the first public group in the United States to address the many implications of ART on families and society. Past recommendations by this same panel have been included in U.S. Supreme Court rulings and state laws on issues in medical ethics, such as the definition of death and organ transplantation. Some of the task force's recommendations in regulating reproductive medicine include:

- Doctors cannot make embryos from donor sperm and eggs without permission from the donors who had intended those embryos for their own use.

- The birth mother should be considered the child's legal mother, even if a donor egg was used.

- There should be no discrimination in fertility technology when it comes to unmarried couples, including lesbians.

- The odds of consanguinity (blood relationship) should be studied. The task force believes children have the right to know of their genetic origin to avoid future mating with a blood relative from the same donors.

TABLE 6.11

Numbers of twin, triplet, quadruplet, and quintuplet and other higher order multiple births: 1989–97

Year	Twin	Triplet	Quadruplet	Quintuplet and other higher order multiple[1]
1997	104,137	6,148	510	79
1996	100,750	5,298	560	81
1995	96,736	4,551	365	57
1994	97,064	4,233	315	46
1993	96,445	3,834	277	57
1992	95,372	3,547	310	26
1991	94,779	3,121	203	22
1990	93,865	2,830	185	13
1989	90,118	2,529	229	40

[1] Quintuplets, sextuplets, and higher order multiple births are not differentiated in the national data set.

SOURCE: Joyce A. Martin and Melissa M. Park, "Trends in Twin and Triplet Births: 1980–97," *National Vital Statistics Reports*, vol. 47, no. 24, National Center for Health Statistics, 1999

- Retrieval of gametes (sperm and eggs) from the dead should be banned.

MONITORING FERTILITY TECHNOLOGY. In December 1998 Nkem Chukwu, who had been taking fertility drugs, delivered the first surviving octuplets in the world. As with the birth of septuplets to Bobbi McCaughey in

TABLE 6.12

Live births by plurality of birth and ratios, by age and race and Hispanic origin of mother: 1996

Plurality and race and Hispanic origin of mother	All ages	Under 15 years	Age of mother								
			15-19 years			20-24 years	25-29 years	30-34 years	35-39 years	40-44 years	45-49 years
			Total	15-17 years	18-19 years						
						Number					
All live births											
All races[1]	3,891,494	11,148	491,577	185,721	305,856	945,210	1,071,287	897,913	399,510	71,804	3,045
White, total	3,093,057	5,526	344,685	123,376	221,309	726,669	878,449	747,436	329,782	58,062	2,448
White, non-Hispanic	2,358,989	2,532	225,197	75,069	150,128	508,056	683,376	616,224	274,431	47,215	1,958
Black, total	594,781	5,193	130,596	56,026	74,570	179,361	133,204	94,295	43,718	8,124	292
Black non-Hispanic	578,099	5,084	127,616	54,802	72,814	174,958	129,002	91,050	42,279	7,835	275
Hispanic[2]	701,339	3,056	118,878	48,344	70,534	214,173	185,478	119,690	49,812	9,819	433
Live births in single deliveries											
All races[1]	3,784,805	11,006	484,339	183,342	300,997	925,704	1,042,220	866,404	383,310	69,127	2,695
White, total	3,007,997	5,463	340,201	122,001	218,200	712,980	855.027	720,655	315,836	55,712	2,123
White, non-Hispanic	2,288,581	2,498	222,149	74,189	147,960	497,986	663,952	592,987	262,206	45,149	1,654
Black, total	577,057	5,122	128,049	55,087	72,962	174,193	128,606	90,800	42,106	7,900	281
Black, non-Hispanic	560,801	5,014	125,124	53,886	71,238	169,877	124,519	87,676	40,708	7,619	264
Hispanic[2]	687,916	3,026	117,436	47,839	69,597	210,682	181,786	116,603	48,354	9,603	426
Live births in twin deliveries											
All races[1]	100,750	139	7,161	2,359	4,802	19,134	27,612	28,963	14,958	2,467	316
White, total	79,677	63	4,448	1,363	3,085	13,400	22,120	24,390	12,813	2,152	291
White, non-Hispanic	65,523	34	3,029	880	2,149	9,824	18,260	21,031	11,185	1,890	270
Black, total	17,285	68	2,510	931	1,579	5,088	4,470	3,388	1,538	212	11
Black, non-Hispanic	16,873	67	2,458	908	1,550	5,002	4,355	3,268	1,508	204	11
Hispanic[2]	13,014	30	1,422	493	929	3,451	3,572	2,950	1,377	205	7
Live births in higher-order multiple deliveries[3]											
All races[1]	5,939	3	77	20	57	372	1,455	2,546	1,242	210	34
White, total	5,383	-	36	12	24	289	1,302	2,391	1,133	198	34
White, non-Hispanic	4,885	-	19	-	19	246	1,164	2,206	1,040	176	34
Black, total	439	3	37	8	29	80	128	107	72	12	-
Black, non-Hispanic	425	3	34	8	26	79	128	106	63	12	-
Hispanic[2]	409	-	20	12	8	40	120	137	81	11	-
						Ratio per 1,000 live births					
All multiple births											
All races[1]	27.4	12.7	14.7	12.8	15.9	20,6	27.1	35.1	40.5	37.3	114.9
White, total	27.5	11.4	13.0	11.1	14.0	18.8	26.7	35.8	42.3	40.5	132.8
White, non-Hispanic	29.8	13.4	13.5	11.7	14.4	19.8	28.4	37.7	44.5	43.8	155.3
Black, total	29.8	13.7	19.5	16.8	21.6	28.8	34.5	37.1	36.8	27.6	*
Black, non-Hispanic	29.9	13.8	19.5	16.7	21.6	29.0	34.8	37.1	37.2	27.6	*
Hispanic[2]	19.1	9.8	12.1	10.4	13.3	16.3	19.9	25.8	29.3	22.0	*
Twin births											
All races[1]	25.9	12.5	14.6	12.7	15.7	20.2	25.8	32.3	37.4	34.4	103.8
White, total	25.8	11.4	12.9	11.0	13.9	18.4	25.2	32.6	38.9	37.1	118.9
White, non-Hispanic	27.8	13.4	13.5	11.7	14.3	19.3	26.7	34.1	40.8	40.0	137.9
Black, total	29.1	13.1	19.2	16.6	21.2	28.4	33.6	35.9	35.2	26.1	*
Black, non-Hispanic	29.2	13.2	19.3	16.6	21.3	28.6	33.8	35.9	35.7	26.0	*
Hispanic[2]	18.6	9.8	12.0	10.2	13.2	16.1	19.3	24.6	27.6	20.9	*
						Ratio per 100,000 live births					
Higher-order multiple births[3]											
All races[1]	152.6	*	15.7	10.8	18.6	39.4	135.8	283.5	310.9	292.5	1116.6
White, total	174.0	*	10.4	*	10.8	39.6	148.2	319.9	343.6	341.0	1388.9
White, non-Hispanic	207.1	*	*	*	*	48.4	170.3	358.0	379.0	372.8	1736.5
Black, total	73.8	*	28.3	*	38.9	44.6	96.1	113.5	164.7	*	*
Black, non-Hispanic	73.5	*	26.6	*	35.7	45.2	99.2	116.4	149.0	*	*
Hispanic[2]	58.3	*	16.8	*	*	18.7	64.7	114.5	162.6	*	*

- Quantity zero.

* Figure does not meet standards of reliability or precision.

[1] Includes races other than white and black and origin not stated.
[2] Persons of Hispanic origin may be of any race.
[3] Births in greater than twin deliveries.

SOURCE: *Monthly Vital Statistics Report*, vol. 46, no. 11(S), June 30, 1998

FIGURE 6.18

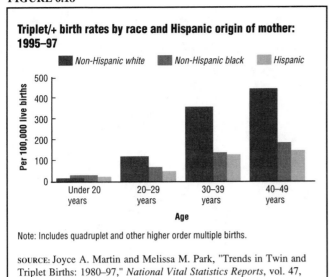

Triplet/+ birth rates by race and Hispanic origin of mother: 1995–97

Non-Hispanic white Non-Hispanic black Hispanic

Note: Includes quadruplet and other higher order multiple births.

SOURCE: Joyce A. Martin and Melissa M. Park, "Trends in Twin and Triplet Births: 1980–97," *National Vital Statistics Reports*, vol. 47, no. 24, National Center for Health Statistics, 1999

FIGURE 6.20

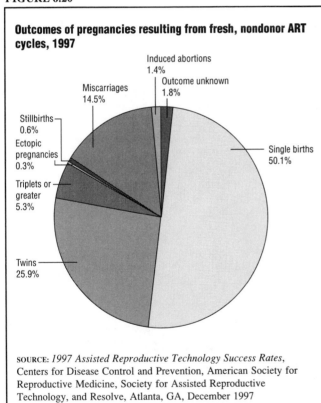

Outcomes of pregnancies resulting from fresh, nondonor ART cycles, 1997

SOURCE: *1997 Assisted Reproductive Technology Success Rates*, Centers for Disease Control and Prevention, American Society for Reproductive Medicine, Society for Assisted Reproductive Technology, and Resolve, Atlanta, GA, December 1997

FIGURE 6.19

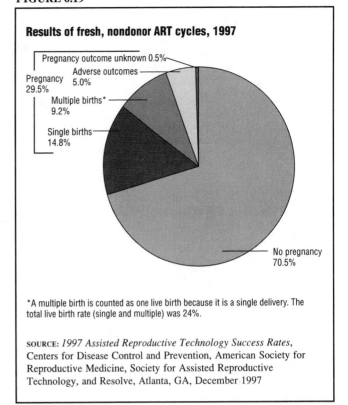

Results of fresh, nondonor ART cycles, 1997

*A multiple birth is counted as one live birth because it is a single delivery. The total live birth rate (single and multiple) was 24%.

SOURCE: *1997 Assisted Reproductive Technology Success Rates*, Centers for Disease Control and Prevention, American Society for Reproductive Medicine, Society for Assisted Reproductive Technology, and Resolve, Atlanta, GA, December 1997

tive clients. Therefore, some fertility doctors may tend to be more aggressive in transferring more fertilized eggs to the uterus to ensure a higher probability of success.

Because of the expense (about $8,000 for each attempt) of fertility treatments, couples want to ensure a successful pregnancy. In most cases the procedure must be repeated several times. Therefore, close monitoring by Health Maintenance Organizations (HMOs) also plays a role in the development of multiple births. Through ultrasound imaging doctors can keep track of the number of maturing eggs. If too many eggs have matured the doctor typically advises discontinuing the treatment. This means the next step in the treatment, introducing the husband's sperm, is canceled. However, since ultrasound imaging is quite expensive, HMOs may limit the number of times doctors can use it on certain patients. Doctors who comply with the HMOs' decision may be unable to diligently monitor egg maturation.

In cases in which it can be determined that a higher-order multiple birth will likely occur, many doctors consider destroying some of the embryos in order to improve viability of the pregnancy. Generally, this may not be done without the permission of the parents. Some parents, such as the Chukwus, consider this act an abortion and refuse to permit it, a stance that often leads to a much higher level of multiple births.

1997, some critics have faulted the mothers' fertility doctors for not closely monitoring the number of maturing eggs prior to fertilization. It is believed that, in the competitive field of fertility medicine, clinics vying for more patients use their high pregnancy rates to attract prospec-

CHAPTER 7

PUBLIC OPINION ON THE FAMILY

MOST AMERICANS HAPPY WITH THEIR MARRIAGES

Society often has expectations which people think they should meet. Certainly many of these expectations concern the family. In such situations, it is not unusual for a survey respondent to give the answer that he or she thinks is expected. Therefore, while such surveys may be used as indicators, they must be used with care. For example, you will notice that almost everyone indicates complete happiness with their marriage. If this were true, it would be unlikely there would be such a high rate of divorce.

The Gallup Poll, in a 1996 survey, found that the overwhelming majority of Americans claimed to be happy with their marriages. When asked to grade their marriages on a scale of A to F, almost all rated their marriage either A (59 percent) or B (29 percent). Only 1 in 9 rated his or her marriage a C (10 percent) or D (1 percent). Almost no one gave his or her marriage a failing grade. (See Table 7.1.)

This should not be surprising since, when asked to grade themselves as husbands or wives in a 1997 Gallup survey, 81 percent of both husbands and wives graded their performance as a spouse with an A or B. Almost none looked upon themselves as failures. (See Table 7.2.)

Asked by the Gallup researchers in 1996 if they would do it over again with the same person, the overwhelming majority (91 percent) indicated they would. (See Table 7.3.) Gallup asked a similar question the following year, "Knowing what you do now, if you had to do it over, is there a chance you might not marry the same person, or do you think you probably would, or are you certain you would?" Almost all said they would either certainly or probably marry the same person again. (See Table 7.4.)

A higher percentage of married people would remarry their spouse in 1997 than would have in 1948. (See Table 7.4.) This is probably because in 1948 many couples had just gotten back into their marriages as their spouses returned from World War II. In many instances they had married in haste and hardly knew each other. Others had been separated for many years. For some the experience of war had changed one or both partners. Even when a 1996 Gallup Poll asked, "If it were legal to marry more than one person, would you want to do so, or not?" almost

TABLE 7.1

Using an A, B, C, D and F grading scale like they do in school, what grade would you give your marriage today?

A	59%
B	29
C	10
D	1
F	*
No opinion	*
	100%

*Less than 0.5%

SOURCE: *The Gallup Poll Monthly*, September 1996

TABLE 7.2

Using an A, B, C, D and F grading scale like they do in school, what grade would you give to yourself as a [husband/wife]?*

	Total	Husbands	Wives
A	30%	26%	34%
B	51	55	46
C	16	16	17
D	1	2	1
F	1	0	1
No opinion	1	1	1
	100%	100%	100%

*Based on those who are married, 592 respondents, ±4%

SOURCE: *The Gallup Poll Monthly*, March 1997

TABLE 7.3

If you had it to do over again, would you marry the person to whom you are currently married, or not?

Yes	91%
No	6
No opinion	3
	100%

SOURCE: *The Gallup Poll Monthly*, September 1996

TABLE 7.5

Have you and your [husband/wife] ever talked to a marriage counselor or therapist together?

	Marriage counselor? —Trend		
	Yes	No	No opinion
1997			
Total	**14%**	**85**	**1**
Husbands	14 %	85	1
Wives	15%	85	0
1996	**14%**	**86**	*
1988	**9%**	**90**	**1**

* Less than 0.5%
(Based on 592 married respondents, ±4%)

SOURCE: *The Gallup Poll Monthly*, March 1997

all (94 percent) said no. Five percent thought they would. (One percent had no opinion.)

Marital happiness is apparently reflected in the finding that so few had ever visited a marriage counselor or therapist. Some 85 percent claimed they had never gone with their spouse to a therapist. (See Table 7.5.)

When asked what was most fulfilling in their lives male respondents answered that the family provided the most fulfillment. On a scale of 1 to 10 the respondent's relationship with his spouse and young children brought, by far, the most satisfaction. Very few felt unfulfilled with these relationships. (See Table 7.6.)

Perhaps so many couples were happy because they had dated for a long time and gotten to know each other very well before they married. When asked how long they had dated before marriage, only 21 percent had dated for less than a year. Very few (9 percent) had a whirlwind courtship (less than 6 months). Far more (29 percent) had dated for more than three years. (See Table 7.7.)

The respondents to the National Opinion Research Center's 1999 survey on marital satisfaction also seemed happy with their family lives. Sixty-two percent stated they were "very happy" in their marriage, but only 40 percent said they were very happy with their lives as a whole.

TABLE 7.4

Would you marry the same person?—Trend
Knowing what you do now, if you had to do it over, is there a chance you might not marry the same person, or do you think you probably would, or are you certain you would?

	Might not	Probably would	Certainly would	No opinion
1997				
Total	**6%**	**28**	**62**	**1**
Husbands	7%	29	63	1
Wives	10%	26	65	1
1948				
Total	**10%**	**28**	**49**	**13**
Husbands	8%	27	52	13
Wives	11 %	29	47	13

(Based on 592 married respondents, ±4%)

SOURCE: *The Gallup Poll Monthly*, March 1997

What Do You Like or Dislike About Your Spouse?

There were many things spouses told the Gallup Poll that they liked about each other. Most liked their spouse's caring and compassion (14 percent) and honesty (11 percent). Being a family person (6 percent), having a sense of humor (5 percent), a good personality, patience, being a hard worker, and intelligence (4 percent each) were also important. (See Table 7.8.)

But there were some things about their spouse that made them unhappy. Some were concerned that their spouse worked too much (4 percent), spent too much or too little money (4 percent), or was messy, grouchy, or stubborn (3 percent each).

AMERICANS' OPINIONS ON MARRIAGE-RELATED ISSUES

Living Together Before Marriage

During the 1990s the amount of cohabitation before marriage increased. In 1988, 19 percent of the respondents indicated they had lived together before they married. In 1996, 31 percent said they had lived together before marriage. (See Table 7.9.)

This increase reflects a change in attitude in the United States towards sex before marriage. In 1969 the Gallup researchers asked, "Do you think it is wrong for a man and a woman to have sexual relations before marriage, or not?" More than 2 out of 3 (68 percent) responding thought it was wrong. By 1973 that proportion had dropped to 48 percent. In 1996 only 39 percent believed it was wrong, while more than one-half (55 percent) thought it was not. (See Table 7.10.) This is a major change in opinion and social mores in just one generation.

In 1994 the National Opinion Research Center asked respondents whether "it's a good idea for a couple who

TABLE 7.6

What is most fulfilling in your life?
Next, I'd like to ask you about some different aspects of your life. As I read the following list please tell me how important each aspect is to your personal happiness and fulfillment using a scale from zero to ten, where ten means very important and zero means not important at all. First, . . . Next, . . . (Random order, as appropriate)**

	Degree of fulfillment											
	Zero	1	2	3	4	5	6	7	8	9	10	No opinion
(Asked of all) Your relationship with friends	1%	1	1	*	2	7	6	11	25	13	32	1
(Asked of all) The things you do in your free time	*	*	1	1	2	8	8	13	25	13	28	1
(Asked of those employed, 337, ±6%) Your job or career	*	0	1	1	2	7	5	15	29	9	30	1
(Asked of those with living mother, 307, ±6%) Your relationship with your mother	*	*	*	1	0	2	2	7	12	12	64	0
(Asked of those married or with partners, 284, ±7%) Your relationship with your [wife/partner]	0%	*	0	0	0	0	1	1	6	10	81	1
(Asked of those with living father, 229, ±,7%) Your relationship with your father	1%	1	3	1	3	6	4	11	16	9	45	0
(Asked of fathers with children under 18, 177, ±8%) Your relationship with your [child/children] under 18	*	0	0	0	0	1	1	3	4	8	83	0
(Asked of fathers with adult children, 172, ±8%) Your relationship with your adult [child/children]	1%	0	1	1	2	2	1	4	12	13	61	2

* Less than 0.5%
** Each respondent was asked as many of the six sub-questions as was appropriate: that is, when he belonged to the qualifying subgroup for that question.
(Asked of men**, 449 respondents, ±5%)

SOURCE: *The Gallup Poll Monthly*, June 1997

TABLE 7.7

How long did you date your [husband/wife] before you got married?

	Dated before married—Trend	
	Dec 27–29 1988	Sep 3–5 1996
Less than six months	10%	9%
Six months to 1 year	14	12
1 year	22	15
Between 1 and 2 years	NR	11
2 years	21	14
Between 2 and 3 years	NR	8
3–5 years	24	20
More than 5 years	7	9
No opinion	2	2
	100%	100%

SOURCE: *The Gallup Poll Monthly*, September 1996

intend to get married to live together first." About 10 percent strongly agreed, 23 percent agreed, and 23 percent neither agreed nor disagreed, while 26.5 percent disagreed and 15 percent strongly disagreed. (Three percent had no opinion.)

Single-Parent Families

Most Americans believe that it is better to grow up in a two-parent than a one-parent family. When asked, "Do you think that children who grow up in one-parent families are just as well-off as children who grow up in two-

---

TABLE 7.8

What would you say is the best quality in your [husband/wife]?

Caring/compassionate/kind/empathy	14%
Honesty	11
Family person/good wife-mother/ good husband-father/good provider	6
Sense of humor	5
Personality	4
Patience	4
Hard worker	4
Intelligence/uses his-her mind	4
Good person/good to me	3
Understanding	3
Loving/love for me	3
Good natured/even temperment/ easy to get along with	3
Loyalty/dedication/faithful	2
Generous	2
Friend/best friend	1
Christian/love of God	1
Sensitive/thoughtful	1
Dependable/reliable	1
Good cook	1
Considerate	*
Communication	*
Organized	*
Nothing	*
Everything	4
Other	16
No opinion	7
	100%

* Less than 0.5%

SOURCE: *The Gallup Poll Monthly*, September 1996

TABLE 7.9

Did you and your [husband/wife] live together before you got married or not?

Co-habit before marriage? — Trend

	Yes	No	No opinion
1996 Sep 3-5	31%	69	*
1988 Dec 27-29	19	81	0

*Less than 0.5%

SOURCE: *The Gallup Poll Monthly*, September 1996

FIGURE 7.1

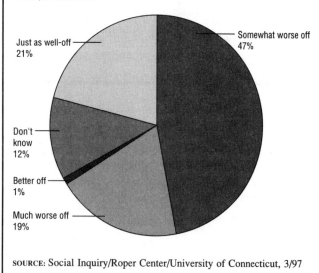

The family: people's chief concerns
Most Americans say children who grow up in single-parent families are worse off
Do you think that children who grow up in one-parent families are just as well-off as children who grow up in two-parent families, somewhat worse off than children who grow up in two-parent families, or much worse off than children who grow up in two-parent families?

Somewhat worse off 47%

Just as well-off 21%

Don't know 12%

Better off 1%

Much worse off 19%

SOURCE: Social Inquiry/Roper Center/University of Connecticut, 3/97

TABLE 7.10

Do you think it is wrong for a man and a woman to have sexual relations before marriage, or not?

Sex before marriage? — Trend

	Wrong	Not wrong	No opinion
1996 May 28-29	39%	55	6
1991	40%	54	6
1985	39%	52	9
1973	48%	43	9
1969	68%	21	11

SOURCE: *The Gallup Poll Monthly*, June 1996

TABLE 7.11

Questions about adultery

What proportion of married men in this country do you think have ever committed adultery: most married men; more than half; about half; less than half; very few married men?

	Total	Men	Women
More than half	33%	30%	36%
About half	31	33	29
Less than half	16	19	14
Most	15	14	16
Very few	2	2	1
No opinion	3	2	4
	100%	100%	100%

What proportion of married women in this country do you think have ever committed adultery: most married women; more than half; about half; less than half; very few married women?

	Total	Men	Women
About half	34%	31%	37%
Less than half	32	35	30
More than half	19	17	20
Most	7	8	5
Very few	5	8	3
No opinion	3	1	5
	100%	100%	100%

Do you personally have a close friend or close family member who you know has had an extramarital affair?

	Total	Men	Women
Yes	52%	52%	53%
No	47	47	46
No opinion	1	1	1
	100%	100%	100%

SOURCE: *The Gallup Poll Monthly*, June 1997

parent families, somewhat worse off than children who grow up in two-parent families, or much worse off than children who grow up in two-parent families?" most thought the children somewhat worse off (47 percent) or much worse off (19 percent). About 21 percent thought the children were just as well off, and 1 percent thought them better off. (See Figure 7.1.)

Adultery

Many spouses violate their marriage vow "to forsake all others." Most Americans think adultery is rather common, although they believe men are more likely than women to commit adultery. When asked what proportion of married men have ever committed adultery, 15 percent of respondents thought most had, one-third (33 percent) thought more than one-half had, while one-third (31 percent) believed one-half had done so.

When asked the same question about women 7 percent said most had and 34 percent thought that one-half had. Only 2 percent of respondents thought very few men committed adultery while just 5 percent believed very few women did. (See Table 7.11.) (This finding does not indicate how frequently adultery actually occurs, only what people perceive regarding its frequency.)

The Gallup surveyors also asked respondents, "Do you personally have a close friend or close family member who you know has had an extramarital affair?" Equally about one-half of the men (52 percent) and women (53 percent) claimed they knew someone who had done so. (See Table 7.11.)

About 4 out of 5 (79 percent) Americans surveyed said that they believed adultery is always wrong. Barely 1 in 10 believed it is only wrong sometimes (6 percent) or not wrong at all (3 percent). A high percentage of both men (76 percent) and women (81 percent) agreed that adultery is unacceptable. (See Table 7.12.)

A September 1997 CBS News poll found similar attitudes. About 89 percent of the respondents thought adultery is "always wrong" and 8 percent believed adultery is "okay some of the time." (Three percent said they "did not know.")

DIVORCE

Should Adultery Always Lead to Divorce?

Although most people believe that adultery is always wrong, they do not necessarily think it should lead to divorce. A poll conducted by CBS News in September 1997 asked, "If you had a spouse who committed adultery, do you think you would get a divorce, or would you stay together and work things out?" More than one-half of respondents (54 percent) indicated they would try to work things out. Another 8 percent answered "it depends." On the other hand almost one-third (31 percent) said they would get a divorce. (Seven percent said they "did not know.")

Is Divorce Too Easy to Get?

In 1996 the Gallup Poll asked whether a number of issues were serious problems facing the United States. Concerning the number of divorces involving parents with young children, some 37 percent of respondents thought it was a critical problem and 44 percent considered it a very serious problem, while 16 percent believed it not too serious and 2 percent thought it was no problem. (One percent had no opinion.)

A May 1997 Yankelovich Partners survey, prepared for *Time*/CNN, asked, "Should it be harder than it is now for married couples with young children to get a divorce?" Most respondents (61 percent) said yes while 35 percent indicated no. (Four percent were not sure.)

A March 1998 Hart & Teeter survey for NBC and the *Wall Street Journal* asked respondents, "Should divorce in

TABLE 7.12

Adulterous behavior—is it wrong?

What is your opinion about a married person having sexual relations with someone other than their marriage partner – is it always wrong, almost always wrong, wrong only sometimes, or not wrong at all?

	Total	Men	Women
Always	79%	76%	81%
Almost always	11	12	10
Only sometimes	6	7	6
Not at all	3	4	2
No opinion	1	1	1
	100%	100%	100%

SOURCE: *The Gallup Poll Monthly*, June 1997

this country be easier or more difficult to obtain than it is now?" Most (62 percent) thought it should be harder while 20 percent believed it should be easier. (Eighteen percent were not sure.)

Should a Couple Stay Together?

In 1994 the National Opinion Research Center asked people if "divorce is usually the best solution when a couple can't seem to work out their marriage problems." The majority of respondents thought divorce was an acceptable solution to an unworkable marriage. Nine percent of the respondents said they strongly agreed and 38 percent agreed. Nineteen percent neither agreed nor disagreed. Twenty-three percent disagreed and 8 percent strongly disagreed. (Four percent had no opinion.)

In the same survey, the researchers stated, "When there are children in the family, parents should stay together even if they don't get along." The respondents strongly indicated that an incompatible couple should not stay together "for the sake of the children." Only 2.5 percent strongly agreed and 12 percent agreed that the couple should stay together for the children. Sixteen percent neither agreed nor disagreed. Almost one-half (46 percent) disagreed, and another 17 percent strongly disagreed, that such a couple should stay together. (Seven percent had no opinion.)

The researchers then stated, "Even when there are no children, a married couple should stay together even if they don't get along." In response the overwhelming majority said they did not believe that in these circumstances a couple should stay together. Only 2 percent strongly agreed and 6 percent agreed. Ten percent neither agreed nor disagreed. One-half (50 percent) disagreed and 28 percent strongly disagreed. (Six percent had no opinion.)

A survey prepared in 1997 for the Institute for Social Inquiry by the Roper Center at the University of Connecticut asked 950 adults, "Do you think divorce is always wrong, sometimes wrong, rarely wrong, or never wrong?" Most (85 percent) thought divorce was sometimes (80 percent) or always (5 percent) wrong. Only 9

FIGURE 7.2

Divorce—is it wrong?

Do you think that divorce is always wrong, sometimes wrong, rarely wrong, or never wrong?

Sometimes wrong
80%

Always wrong
5%

Rarely wrong
5%

Never wrong
4%

Don't know
6%

SOURCE: Social Inquiry/Roper Center/University of Connecticut., Women, Men and Media, 3/97

FIGURE 7.3

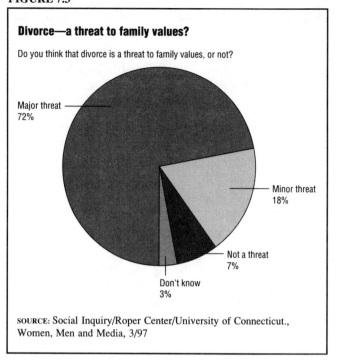

Divorce—a threat to family values?

Do you think that divorce is a threat to family values, or not?

Major threat
72%

Minor threat
18%

Not a threat
7%

Don't know
3%

SOURCE: Social Inquiry/Roper Center/University of Connecticut., Women, Men and Media, 3/97

TABLE 7.13

Comparison of women's and men's definitions of "family values"

Definition	Women	Men
Base	**1502**	**460**
Loving/Taking care of/ Supporting each other	52%	42%
Knowing right from wrong/ Having good values	38	35
Spending time with each other	18	6
God/Bible/Religious	5	1
Respecting your family as well as others	3	2
Family comes first	2	N/A
Traditional nuclear family	2	1
Political rhetoric	1	2
Other	7	4
No sure/refused	6	6

SOURCE: *Women: The New Providers*, Whirlpool Foundation, Families and Work Institute, Louis and Harris Associates, 1995

percent thought it was either rarely (5 percent) or never (4 percent) wrong. (See Figure 7.2.)

When asked, "Do you think divorce is a threat to family values, or not?" most thought divorce was either a major (72 percent) or a minor (18 percent) threat to family values. Just 7 percent did not think it was a threat. (See Figure 7.3.)

FAMILY VALUES

In 1998 Louis Harris and Associates prepared a survey on family values for the Families and Work Institute

and the Whirlpool Foundation. About one-half (52 percent) of women and 42 percent of men thought family values meant "loving, taking care of, and supporting each other." An almost equal proportion of women (38 percent) and men (35 percent) defined family values as "knowing right from wrong and having good values." Only 2 percent of women and 1 percent of men defined family values in terms of the traditional nuclear family. (See Table 7.13.)

Family Values and Structure

Questions about family values generally imply issues concerning the current diverse compositions of families. The same Harris Poll asked women, "Do you think that society should value only certain types of families, like those with two parents, or should society value all types of families?" More than 9 of 10 (93 percent) respondents thought that society should value all types of families. Only 5 percent indicated that society should value certain types of families, such as those with two parents. Almost all women ages 18–24 years (98 percent) felt that society should value all types of families, compared to 92 percent of the older age groups of women. Across different educational levels a large majority (91–95 percent) agreed with this consensus. (See Table 7.14.)

The Class of 2001

In 1997 Northwestern Mutual Life sponsored a survey conducted by Louis Harris and Associates which questioned incoming college freshmen on a variety of subjects, some of which focused on family values. Most

TABLE 7.14

Types of families that society should value according to women

	Total	Age groups				Education			
		18–24	25–34	35–44	45–55	Less than high school	High school	Some college	B.A./post grad
Base	1502	224	448	460	361	100	432	485	485
Certain types	5%	2%	6%	7%	6%	3%	4%	8%	6%
All types	93	98	92	91	92	95	93	91	93
Not sure/refused	2	*	2	2	2	2	3	2	1

* Indicates less than one-half of one percent

SOURCE: *Women: The New Providers*, Whirlpool Foundation, Families and Work Institute, Louis and Harris Associates, 1995

TABLE 7.15

For you personally, do you think it is necessary or not necessary to have a child at some point in your life in order to feel fulfilled?

	Yes	No
Hungary	94%	6
India	93%	6
Taiwan	87%	3
Iceland	85%	13
Thailand	85%	13
Lithuania	82%	10
Singapore	81%	7
Guatemala	74%	23
France	73%	26
Colombia	72%	26
Mexico	61%	38
Spain	60%	35
Canada	59%	37
Great Britain	57%	41
Germany	49%	45
United States	46%	51

Note: "No opinion" omitted.

SOURCE: *The Gallup Poll Monthly*, November 1997

TABLE 7.16

What do you think is the ideal number of children for a family to have?

	0-2	3 or more
Iceland	26%	69
Guatemala	35%	61
Taiwan	41%	52
United States	50%	41
France	51%	49
Singapore	53%	47
Mexico	56%	42
Canada	61%	33
Lithuania	63%	33
Great Britain	67%	24
Thailand	69%	30
Hungary	73%	24
Colombia	77%	23
Germany	77%	17
Spain	77%	18
India	87%	12

Note: "No opinion" omitted.

SOURCE: *The Gallup Poll Monthly*, November 1997

(94 percent) of the students in the Class of 2001 planned to be married by the time they were 26 years old, with 89 percent intending to have children. Most of these future parents favored three children. Some 90 percent felt that "marriage is a cornerstone of societal values." More than 60 percent thought that living together as a couple before marriage was a good idea, and nearly 70 percent felt that premarital sex is all right when two people love each other. On the other hand only 2 of 10 respondents believed that divorce was an acceptable solution if two people were unhappy in their marriage.

Family Values Around the World

Family values differ around the world. The Gallup Organization also surveyed people in a number of countries about certain values. The researchers asked, "Do you think it is necessary or not necessary to have a child at some point in your life in order to feel fulfilled?" In many countries, including Hungary, India, Taiwan, Iceland, and Thailand, most people thought it was absolutely necessary to have a child in order to be fulfilled. In Germany, the United States, and Great Britain, having a child was not considered as necessary to personal happiness. (See Table 7.15.)

When asked, "Do you think it is, or is not, morally wrong for a couple to have a baby if they are not married?" most respondents in India and Singapore thought it was morally wrong to have a child out of wedlock. In contrast most of those surveyed in Germany, France, and Iceland did not consider out-of-wedlock childbirth as morally wrong. (See Table 7.16.)

While most people in India, Spain, Germany, and Colombia considered 0-2 children the ideal number of children, respondents in Iceland and Guatemala preferred larger families. (See Table 7.17.)

TABLE 7.17

Do you think it is, or is not, morally wrong for a couple to have a baby if they are not married?

	Wrong	Not wrong
India	84%	14
Singapore	69%	11
Taiwan	55%	26
United States	47%	50
Guatemala	38%	56
Thailand	37%	57
Mexico	31%	67
Canada	25%	72
Great Britain	25%	73
Spain	21%	73
Lithuania	16%	75
Hungary	16%	81
Colombia	10%	87
Germany	9%	90
France	8%	91
Iceland	3%	95

Note: "No opinion" omitted.

SOURCE: *The Gallup Poll Monthly*, November 1997

FIGURE 7.4

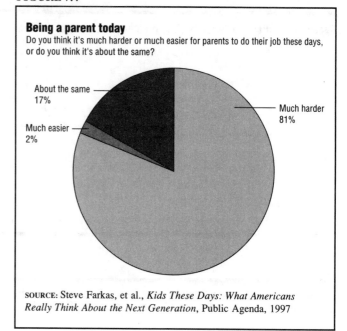

Being a parent today
Do you think it's much harder or much easier for parents to do their job these days, or do you think it's about the same?

About the same 17%

Much harder 81%

Much easier 2%

SOURCE: Steve Farkas, et al., *Kids These Days: What Americans Really Think About the Next Generation*, Public Agenda, 1997

PARENTS AND PARENTING

The Public Agenda survey, *Kids These Days: What Americans Really Think About the Next Generation* (New York, 1998), found that most people are not satisfied with today's parents and believe they are responsible for what they consider to be the disturbing state of today's youth. Only 1 of 5 (22 percent) felt it was very common to find parents who are good role models and teach their children right from wrong. (See Table 7.18.)

One-half of survey respondents thought parents do not know how to communicate with their children (51 percent) or believe buying things for their children means the same thing as caring for them (50 percent). Half of the public also believed it is very common these days to find parents who fail to discipline their children (50 percent) or parents who spoil their children (49 percent). (See Table 7.18.)

Even parents indict themselves and their peers, tending to blame other parents for young people's problems. Two-thirds (65 percent) thought it is very common for people to have children before they are ready to take responsibility for them. Four of 10 (41 percent) young people surveyed also agreed. While only 19 percent of parents thought other parents provide good role models and teach their children right from wrong, 39 percent of the young people thought they do. (See Table 7.18.)

Harder to Raise a Child

The Public Agenda survey found that most Americans (81 percent) believed it is harder for parents to raise a child today, while only 1 of 5 felt it is much easier or about the same as in the past. (See Figure 7.4.)

Mothers Under Pressure

According to the Public Agenda survey people think parents—especially mothers—are working harder than ever to fulfill their responsibilities. Only one-quarter (27 percent) believed it very common for mothers to give up time with their children and go to work to gain personal satisfaction. Most (75 percent) thought it very common for mothers to give up time with their kids to work in order to make ends meet. (See Table 7.18.)

MOST AMERICANS THINK IT BETTER FOR MOTHER TO STAY HOME. Both an August-September 1997 *Washington Post* survey prepared for the Kaiser Family Foundation, and a December 1997 *Washington Post* survey, found that most Americans believe that, if possible, the mother should stay home with the children. Respondents were asked if they agreed or disagreed that "It may be necessary for mothers to be working because the family needs the money, but would it be better if she could stay at home and just take care of the house and children?" Two-thirds of both the men and women either strongly or somewhat agreed. (See Table 7.19.)

Similarly, when asked, "All things being equal, do you think it is better if the mother or the father stays home and takes care of the house and children?" 69 percent thought it better that the mother stays home and only 2 percent thought the father should. (See Figure 7.5.)

YET MOST AMERICANS BELIEVE WORKING MOTHERS ARE GOOD PARENTS. Nonetheless, when the September 1997 survey prepared by the *Washington Post* for the

TABLE 7.18

Views on parents

"Now I'm going to describe different types of parents and ask if you think they are common or not. How about parents who [insert them]? Are they very common, somewhat common, not too common, or not common at all?"

% saying "very common"	General public	Parents	African American parents	Hispanic parents	White parents	Youth (12-17 years old)
Mothers who have to give up time with their kids to work so their families can make ends meet	75%	78%	83%	76%	79%	NA
People who have children before they are ready to take responsibility for them	63	65	72	69	63	41
Parents who break up too easily instead of trying to stay together for the sake of their kids	55	57	56	57	58	31
Parents who sacrifice and work hard so that their kids can have a better life	51	54	65	58	52	50
Parents who do not know how to communicate with their kids	51	52	54	56	51	32
Parents who think buying things for their kids means the same thing as caring for them	50	51	53	52	51	29
Parents who fail to discipline their children	50	50	58	49	50	33
Parents who spoil their kids	49	50	56	46	50	43
Parents who resent advice about their kids even when it comes from people who mean well	43	42	48	44	40	NA
Fathers who act like their careers are more important than their kids	35	35	47	39	33	NA
Parents who care more about their jobs than their kids	NA	NA	NA	NA	NA	11
Parents who abuse welfare and teach their kids to depend on handouts	32	31	41	43	29	NA
Mothers who give up time with their kids and go to work to gain personal satisfaction	27	29	32	33	26	NA
People who are failures as parents and should never have had kids to begin with	22	21	31	29	17	12
Fathers who are affectionate and loving toward their kids[1]	22	20	24	20	20	35
Parents who are good role models and teach their kids right from wrong	22	19	32	25	18	39

[1] Wording for Youth: "Fathers who are warm and loving toward their kids"

SOURCE: Steve Farkas, et al., *Kids These Days: What Americans Really Think About the Next Generation*, Public Agenda, 1997

Kaiser Family Foundation asked whether "A woman can have a successful career and be a good mother or a woman must decide between having a successful career and being a good mother?" a large majority thought that women could have both. Among working women 82 percent thought they could have both career and motherhood. Among all women 74 percent thought they could have both while 68 percent of the men thought this was possible.

When a September 1997 CBS News poll asked, "Would you say the working women you know make better or worse mothers than women you know who don't work outside the home?" most thought that working mothers were either better (36 percent) or the same (26 percent). Some 25 percent believed they made worse mothers. (Thirteen percent said they "did not know.")

Similarly, when a 1994 National Opinion Research Survey asked whether respondents agreed or disagreed that "A working mother can establish just as warm and secure a relationship with her children as a mother who does not work," 29 percent strongly agreed and 41 percent agreed. On the other hand 19 percent disagreed and 5 percent strongly disagreed. (Five percent neither agreed nor disagreed and 1.5 percent could not choose.)

WORKING MOTHERS THINK THEIR WORKING BENE-FITS CHILDREN. In *Report Card on the New Providers:*

TABLE 7.19

Do you agree or disagree with the following statements: It may be necessary for mothers to be working because the family needs the money, but would it be better if she could stay at home and just take care of the house and children?

	Men	Women
Strongly agree	43%	46%
Somewhat agree	26%	22%
Somewhat disagree	17%	15%
Strongly disagree	12%	16%
No opinion	2%	2%

SOURCE: Washington Post, 1997

Kids and Moms Speak (Irene Natividad, National Commission on Working Women, Benton Harbor, Michigan, 1998), Roper Starch Worldwide surveyed school-age children and their mothers for the Whirlpool Foundation. The study found that "Children [continue to be] the key to women's choices." Women's lives have dramatically changed but their children are as important to them as they were to women 50 years ago. More than 9 of 10 (92 percent) working mothers believed that their job allowed them to provide better opportunities for their children. At the same time these women (83 percent) reported that they got personal fulfillment from working. (See Table 7.20.)

Many of these working mothers enjoyed the social life that was part of their workplace. Eighty-one percent thought that the people they worked with were "fun" and 56 percent considered their coworkers as friends. Forty percent considered their job a refuge from the demands of home and 40 percent sought advice from fellow employees. (See Table 7.20.)

More than two-thirds of both stay-at-home and working mothers recommended that good parenting should involve spending lots of time with the children (69 percent). (See Table 7.21.) This advice coincided with the children's response that their favorite activity with their moms was "just being together"—such things as having dinner together, sitting and talking, shopping, and vacation. (See Table 7.22.) A similar proportion (68 percent) of mothers believed that providing financial security was a component of good parenting. (See Table 7.21.) According to the researchers mothers including "provider" in their present-day roles "underscores their practical recognition of the evolving role of motherhood." In fact 8 of 10 (79 percent) stay-at-home mothers said that if they ever did go to work for pay, the foremost reason would be "because of a need for money."

Family Structure

FAMILY LEADERSHIP. Most Americans say they believe that the leadership of the family and the care of the children should be shared equally between the mother

FIGURE 7.5

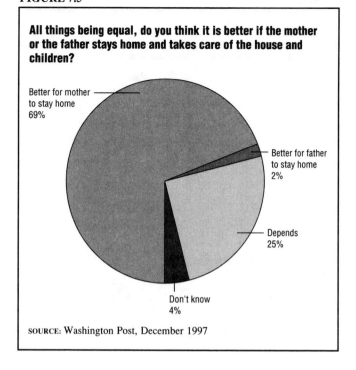

All things being equal, do you think it is better if the mother or the father stays home and takes care of the house and children?

Better for mother to stay home 69%

Better for father to stay home 2%

Depends 25%

Don't know 4%

SOURCE: Washington Post, December 1997

and the father. An October 1997 Opinion Dynamics poll prepared by Fox News asked, "Do you think the man should be the family leader, the woman should be the family leader, or should they share family leadership equally?" A large majority (84 percent) indicated they both should lead, while 15 percent thought the man and just 1 percent believed the woman should lead.

Similarly, when the September 1997 Kaiser Family Foundation survey, prepared by the *Washington Post*, asked, "Do you agree or disagree that everything about the care of children should be shared equally by both parents?" 91 percent of the men and 94 percent of the women agreed.

In 1997 the Gallup Poll asked, "In general, do you think American women dominate their husbands—or do you think husbands dominate their wives?" About 26 percent indicated "wives" dominate, 39 percent thought "husbands," and 26 percent said "equally or no difference." Those who were older, and presumably married the longest, were most likely to indicate "equally or no difference." Those with the most education and those 18-29 years old were most likely to see the husband as the dominating spouse. Surprisingly, in 1952, almost half (45 percent) thought the spouses were equally dominant; by 1997, only 26 percent thought so. (See Table 7.23.)

HOUSEHOLD CHORES. Although more mothers than ever are working outside the home, the division of household labor tends to continue along gender lines. According to the Whirlpool Foundation study *Report Card on the New Providers: Kids and Moms Speak* (see above), "Women's changed lives, that now includes paid employment for the majority of mothers, have not been met with

TABLE 7.20

Statements about work

Here are some statements people have made about their work and their work environment. For each one, I'd like you to tell me if you strongly agree with the statement, somewhat agree, somewhat disagree, or strongly disagree with the statement.

| | Employed mothers | | | | | |
| | | | | Household income | | |
Base: % strongly/somewhat agree	Total (664) %	Full- time (504) %	Part- time (160) %	Under $20K (133) %	$20K- $49K (275) %	$50K+ (227) %
Work allows me to provide better opportunities for my children	92	93	89	90	94	91
I get a sense of personal fulfillment at work	83	83	83	73	81	90
The people I work with are fun	81	81	81	73	82	84
Work is a part of my life that I can keep separate from my family life	71	72	69	67	69	75
Work to me is just something I have to do to pay the bills	56	57	52	73	60	44
Some of my closest friends are co-workers	56	60	41	56	47	63
I've always wanted to work outside the home	55	56	55	50	49	64
I often think of work as a refuge away from all the demands of my home and family	40	40	40	43	41	38
I seek advice from the people at work how to integrate home and family life	40	42	33	35	40	42

SOURCE: Irene Natividad, *Report Card on the New Providers: Kids and Moms Speak,* Whirlpool Foundation, 1998

commensurate changes in the home, in the workplace, or in society as a whole."

In the Whirlpool Foundation survey most women claimed that motherhood is better than they imagined it could be (87 percent) while saying at the same time that it is harder than they imagined it to be (82 percent). Children who were surveyed reported that mothers remain the primary caregivers to children whether they work or not. (See Table 7.24). According to the children mothers continue to do the major share of housework, while the fathers usually mow the lawn (37 percent) and take care of the trash (29 percent). (See Table 7.25.)

Another 1997 Gallup Poll found that the world had changed considerably during the second half of the twentieth century. In 1949, when married couples were asked whether husbands helped with the housework, 62 percent said yes. By 1997 that percentage had increased to 85 percent. There was some difference, however, between the husband's and the wife's perceptions. While 97 percent of the husbands claimed they helped, only 75 percent of the wives agreed. (See Table 7.26.) These proportions generally applied to helping with cooking and the dishes.

TEENS' OPINIONS OF FATHERS

A Gallup Youth Survey (*YOUTHviews,* vol. 5, no. 9, May 1998) of teenagers ages 13–17 years found that nearly two-thirds (63 percent) of teens thought it harder to be

TABLE 7.21

What makes a good parent

Here is a list of things that other people we've talked to say help to make a good parent. For each one I'd like you to tell me how important you think each one is to making a person a good parent - whether it is very important, somewhat important, not too important, or not at all important.

| | | Mothers employment | |
Base % saying "very important"	Total (1005) %	Works for pay (664) %	Does not work for pay (341) %
Being able to spend lots of time with the children	69	69	70
Having money to support family and pay the bills	68	67	69
Having a support system of friends/relatives/ neighbors who help out	57	61	49
Having a spouse or partner who helps out with household chores	54	57	48
Being satisfied with a job and your job outside the home	44	50	32
Being able to stay home and not have to work outside the home	32	24	49
Having regular breaks from the children	27	28	26
Having enough time to pursue your own interests	25	26	22

SOURCE: Irene Natividad , *Report Card on the New Providers: Kids and Moms Speak,* Whirlpool Foundation, 1998

TABLE 7.22

Favorite things to do with mother

Now I'd like you to think about all the things we just talked about and choose the top three favorite things to do with mother?

		Children 6–17							
		Age of child		Gender		Mother's employment		Employed mother	
	Total	6–12	13–17	M	F	Works for pay	Does not work for pay	Mother only household	Both parent household
Base:	(1005)	(600)	(405)	(299)	(301)	(664)	(341)	(311)	(694)
% of total children respondents saying...	%	%	%	%	%	%	%	%	%
Have dinner together	39	37	41	38	40	38	41	39	38
Go out to eat	38	34	45	41	36	40	35	39	40
Go shopping	38	38	38	26	51	39	35	35	41
Sit and talk	35	31	42	32	39	33	39	40	31
Take a vacation	34	32	37	38	31	37	28	30	39
Watch TV	32	34	29	36	28	30	36	33	30
Go to the movies	28	32	22	29	26	29	25	31	29
Work on projects around the house	15	16	14	16	15	14	16	15	14
Go to religious services/church	13	14	12	15	11	13	14	10	14
Read	12	18	4	13	12	11	15	9	12
Use computer	6	6	6	6	7	7	3	6	8

SOURCE: Irene Natividad, *Report Card on the New Providers: Kids and Moms Speak*, Whirlpool Foundation, 1998

a father today than it was 20 or 30 years ago. Most (71 percent) thought their fathers were doing the same or better job as parents than their own fathers did a generation before. On the other hand nearly 3 in 10 teens believed their fathers were doing a worse job than their grandfathers did two or three decades ago. (See Table 7.27.)

Fathering Skills

The Gallup Youth Survey also asked teenagers what characteristics make for a good father. While a majority thought a good father shows respect and caring for his children's mother (91 percent) and teaches his children politeness toward others (90 percent), just three-quarters reported their own father doing so (75 and 79 percent, respectively).

Teens believed their fathers needed to demonstrate and tell their children about their affection for them. According to most teens (85 percent) a good father tells his kids he loves them at least once a week, but only two-thirds said their fathers did so. Three-quarters felt a good father also hugs his kids at least once a week; however, just slightly over half (55 percent) indicated their fathers did so. (See Table 7.28.)

Teenagers reported that fathers could be more involved with their school life. Seven in 10 (71 percent) teens thought a good father definitely helps his children with homework, but less than half (45 percent) said their fathers did. Despite the belief of 4 in 10 teens (41 percent) that good fathers talked to their children's teacher

regularly, only 2 in 10 (19 percent) reported their fathers doing so. (See Table 7.28.)

Many teenagers thought their fathers were doing a good job when it came to disciplining them at home (61 percent) or punishing them for misbehaving in school (59 percent). About as many teens believed a good father teaches his child how to ride a bike or play a sport (81 percent) as those who indicated their own fathers having done so (76 percent). (See Table 7.28.)

PUBLIC OPINIONS ON RELIGION IN AMERICAN LIFE

Among Adults

Periodically, the Gallup Poll interviews Americans on the role of religion in their lives. In 2000 the Poll found that 68 percent of Americans claimed to be members of a church or synagogue, a percentage that has changed little over the past 60 years. (See Table 7.29.) Forty-three percent indicated they had attended a church or synagogue in the past week. (See Table 7.30.) About one-third of Americans claimed they went to church or synagogue either at least once a week (35 percent) or almost every week (11 percent). On the other hand a slightly smaller proportion either seldom (27 percent) or never (11 percent) attended religious services. (See Table 7.31.) A majority of Americans (63 percent) believed that "religion can answer all or most of today's problems," while only 17 percent thought it is "old-fashioned." (See Table 7.32.)

TABLE 7.23

Who dominates: husbands or wives?

Question: In general, do you think American women dominate their husbands - or do you think husbands dominate their wives?

	Wives	Husbands	Equally/no difference (vol.)	No opinion	No. of interviews
National	26%	39	26	9	1036
Sex					
Male	27%	39	25	9	519
Female	25%	40	26	9	517
Age					
18–29 years	20%	53	23	4	199
30–49 years	27%	43	23	7	432
50–64 years	30%	33	26	11	215
65 & older	28%	22	36	14	177
Region					
East	28%	7	26	9	228
Midwest	27%	40	24	9	251
South	26%	40	24	10	336
West	23%	40	29	8	221
Community					
Urban	28%	42	22	8	344
Suburban	26%	38	28	8	462
Rural	24%	37	26	13	230
Race					
White	26%	39	26	9	835
Non-white	30%	43	22	5	189
Education					
College postgraduate	25%	47	21	7	149
Bachelor's degree only	23%	50	20	7	170
Some college	26%	36	28	10	298
High school or less	27%	38	27	8	411
Politics					
Republicans	28%	39	24	9	328
Democrats	27%	40	26	7	341
Independents	24%	39	27	10	367
Ideology					
Liberal	22%	46	24	6	168
Moderate	26%	42	23	9	416
Conservative	28%	36	27	9	409
Income					
$75,000 & over	26%	39	24	11	123
$50,000 & over	23%	41	27	9	284
$30,000-49,999	31%	42	22	5	268
$20,000-29;999	26%	42	23	9	210
Under $20,000	24%	38	32	6	199

Who dominates?- Trend

	Wives	Husbands	Equally/no difference (vol.)	No opinion
1997				
Total	26%	39	26	9
Husbands	26%	37	27	10
Wives	27%	37	28	8
1952				
Total	32%	19	45	5
Husbands	34%	16	45	5
Wives	26%	22	49	3

SOURCE: *The Gallup Poll Monthly*, March 1997

In August 2000 the overwhelming majority of Americans thought religion was either very important (57 percent) or fairly important (31 percent) in their lives. Only 12 percent considered religion not very important in their lives. (See Table 7.33.) While there were small differences in the characteristics of respondents to the survey concerning the importance of religion in their lives, in no instance did the proportion of those who answered "not very important" exceed 18 percent. (See Table 7.34.)

On the other hand most Americans believe that the influence of religion is decreasing. In August 2000 more than one-half (58 percent) of the respondents thought the influence of religion was dropping. This number, however, has been going up and down over the past 40 years. (See Table 7.35.)

TABLE 7.24

Who takes care of children

Now I have a list of things that parents or other people do for young people and children. The first one is (read first item). Is that something you usually do in your home, something your mother usually does, something your father usually does, something your brother or sister usually does, or something somebody else usually does?

	Children 6-17		
	Mother usually does	Mother's employment	
		Works for pay	Does not work for pay
Base:	(1005)	(664)	(341)
% of children saying	%	%	%
Take you to doctor/dentist appointments	76	76	78
Take care of you when you're sick	71	69	78
Take you/pick you up from weekend activities (clubs, sports, parties, etc.)	51	49	56
Take you/pick you up from after school activities	48	46	53
Take you/pick you up from school	46	43	52
Help you with homework	45	41	54
Get you ready for school in the morning	43	40	48

SOURCE: Irene Natividad, *Report Card on the New Providers: Kids and Moms Speak*, Whirlpool Foundation, 1998

TABLE 7.25

Who usually does household chores

I'm going to read you a list of jobs and chores that need to be done in most homes. First, who usually (read first item)? Is that a job that you usually do in your home, a job your mother usually does, a job your father usually does, a job your brother or sister usually does, or a job somebody else usually does? (ask about each item)

	Children aged 6–17			
	Mother usually does	Father usually does	Brother or sister usually does	You usually do
BASE:	(1005)	(1005)	(1005)	(1005)
% of children saying...	%	%	%	%
Prepares meals	80	7	2	4
Shops for groceries	75	9	2	8
Does the laundry	74	5	3	8
Does the dishes	62	6	7	15
Pays the bills*	59	18	1	1
Vacuums or sweeps	56	5	7	21
Cleans your room	21	1	3	72
Takes care of trash/garbage	21	29	13	30
Takes care of pets	21	9	8	29
Mows the lawn	9	37	9	15

* Asked of teens only Base: 405

SOURCE: Irene Natividad, *Report Card on the New Providers: Kids and Moms Speak*, Whirlpool Foundation, 1998

TABLE 7.26

Do husbands help with housework?

[Male] Do you help with the housework in your home? [Female] Does your husband help with the housework in your home?

	Husbands do housework? — Trend		
	Yes	No	No opinion
Total			
1997	85%	14	1
1949	62%	38	0

	1997, by Gender		
	Yes	No	No opinion
Husbands	97%	3	*
Wives	75%	24	1

* Less than 0.5%

(Asked of 592 married respondents, ±4%)

SOURCE: *The Gallup Poll Monthly*, March 1997

TABLE 7.27

How are fathers doing?

Generally speaking, do you think it is easier to be a father today than it was twenty or thirty years ago, more difficult, or about the same?
All in all, do you think that fathers today are doing a better job as parents than their own fathers did twenty or thirty years ago, a worse job, or about the same?

	All teens
Generally speaking . . .	
Easier to be a father today	7%
Same	53
More difficult than twenty or thirty years ago	63
Fathers today . . .	
Are doing a better job	18%
Same	53
Worse than twenty or thirty years ago	29

SOURCE: *YOUTHviews*, The George H. Gallup International Institute, Princeton, NJ, vol. 5, no. 9, May 1998

Among Young People

Public Agenda, in *Kids These Days: What Americans Really Think About the Next Generation,* found that, in 1997, two-thirds (66 percent) of teens said, "faith in God is an important part of my life." A 1998 Gallup International poll found that 49 percent of teens believe their life belongs to God or another high power. Approximately two-thirds (64 percent) of teenagers ages 13–17 years surveyed belonged to a church, synagogue, mosque, or some other organized religious group, and 42 percent of teens reported that they had attended religious worship services in the week prior to the survey.

More recent data from the 2000 Barna Research Organization shows that 56 percent believed their religious faith was very important in their lives and about 34 percent believed they had been born again. American teens also perceive themselves as deeply spiritual. Over one-quarter of respondents (28 percent) felt a personal responsibility to tell others about their religious beliefs,

TABLE 7.28

What makes a good father?

For each [statement I read to you about fathers], I'd like you to tell me whether a good father definitely does this, might do this, or probably doesn't do this.
I'm going to read to you the same statements. This time, I would like you to tell me, for each statement, whether your father definitely does this, sometimes does this, or usually doesn't do this.

	A good father definitely does this	My own father definitely does this
Affection and caring:		
A good father...		
Shows respect and caring for his child's mother	91%	75%
Teaches his children to be polite to neighbors and older people	90%	79%
Tells his children he loves them at least once a week	85%	66%
Hugs his children at least once a week	75%	55%
Asks his children how their day went	70%	62%
Teaches his children they are loved by God	65%	49%
Tells them the dreams and desires he has for their future	59%	49%
School life:		
A good father...		
Helps his children with their homework	71%	45%
Talks to his children's teachers regularly	41%	19%
Discipline:		
A good father...		
Punishes them when they have broken a rule at home	71%	61%
Punishes them when they have gotten in trouble at school	68%	59%
Other:		
A good father...		
Teaches his children how to ride a bike or pay a sport	81%	76%
Takes them shopping to buy the things they need	67%	46%
Takes his children on hikes and trips to camp, fish, or enjoy nature	55%	43%
Goes to church or other places of worship with them	52%	37%

SOURCE: *YOUTHviews,* The George H. Gallup International Institute, Princeton, NJ, vol. 5, no. 9, May 1998

TABLE 7.29

Do you happen to be a member of a church or synagogue?

Membership in church — Trend
(percent saying "yes")

2000 Aug 24-27	68%
2000 Mar 17-19	68%
1999 Dec 9-12	68%
1999 Apr 9-12	71%
1998 Jun 22-23	70%
1998 Jan 16-18	67%
1997 Aug 12-13	68%
1997 Mar 24-26	67%
1996 Nov 21-24	66%
1996 Sep 3-5	65%
1996 Jun 27-30	64%
1995 Dec 15-18	71%
1995 Sep 22-24	66%
1995 Aug 28-30	69%
1995 May 11-14	69%
1994 Dec 16-18	67%
1994 Jun 25-28	68%
1994 Mar 28-30	70%
1993 Jun	65%
1993 Mar	71%
1992 Nov	70%
1992 Apr	71%
1991 Nov	69%
1991 May	69%
1991 Mar	66%
1991 Feb	67%
1990 Jun	69%
1989	68%
1988	65%
1987	69%
1985	71%
1983	69%
1982	67%
1979	68%
1976	71%
1965	73%
1952	73%
1947	76%
1944	75%
1940	72%
1937	73%

SOURCE: *The Gallup Poll Monthly*, December 2000

64 percent consider themselves religious, and 60 percent say they are spiritual. Nearly 9 of 10 (89 percent) teens say that they pray at least weekly, and 56 percent said they had attended church or synagogue in the last week. (See Table 7.36.)

TABLE 7.30

Did you, yourself, happen to attend church or synagogue in the last seven days, or not?

Church attendance — Trend
(percent saying "yes")

2000 Aug 24-27	43%
2000 Mar 17-19	44%
1999 Dec 9-12	45%
1999 Apr 30-May 2	40%
1998 Jun 22-23	40%
1998 Jan 16-18	39%
1997 Aug 12-13	35%
1997 Mar 24-26	43%
1996 Nov 21-24	39%
1996 Sep 3-5	37%
1996 Jun 27-30	38%
1995 Dec 15-18	44%
1995 Aug 28-30	42%
1995 May 11-14	41%
1994 Dec 16-18	38%
1994 Jun 25-28	40%
1994 Mar 28-30*	48%
1993 Jun	38%
1993 Mar	41%
1992 Nov	40%
1992 Apr	41%
1991 Nov	41%
1991 May	43%
1991 Mar	43%
1990 Jun	40%
1989	43%
1988	42%
1987	40%
1985	42%
1983	40%
1982	41%
1981	41%
1979	40%
1972	40%
1969	42%
1967	43%
1962	46%
1958	49%
1957	47%
1955	49%
1954	46%
1950	39%
1940	37%
1939	41%

* conducted between Palm Sunday and Easter

SOURCE: *The Gallup Poll Monthly*, December 2000

TABLE 7.31

How often do you attend church or synagogue – at least once a week, almost every week, about once a month, seldom or never?

	Regularity of church attendance – Trend					
	At least once a week	Almost every week	About once a month	Seldom	Never	No opinion
2000 Aug 24-27	35%	11	15	27	11	1
2000 Mar 17-19	36%	11	13	30	10	*
2000 Jan 7-10	32%	12	13	29	13	1
1999 Dec 9-12	36%	12	16	28	8	*
1999 Sep 23-26	30%	9	13	28	19	1
1999 Sep 10-14	31%	13	14	26	14	1
1999 Apr 30-May 2	30%	14	18	28	9	1
1998 Jun 22-23	32%	13	19	26	9	1
1998 Jan 16-18	32%	12	15	30	10	1
1997 Aug 12-13	29%	12	17	29	12	1
1997 Mar 24-26	30%	13	17	30	9	1
1996 Nov 21-24	28%	11	17	33	10	1
1996 Sep 3-5	29%	12	16	32	10	1
1996 Jun 27-30	27%	13	13	34	13	*
1996 Jan 12-15	33%	12	15	28	11	1
1995 Dec 15-18	34%	11	16	28	10	1
1995 Sept 22-24	31%	13	14	31	11	*
1995 Aug 28-30	30%	13	17	31	8	1
1995 May 11-14	30%	12	17	31	10	*
1994 Dec 16-18	30%	12	16	31	11	*
1994 Jun 25-28	32%	14	17	27	10	*
1994 Mar 28-30	35%	15	16	25	9	*
1992 Sep 11-15	34%	10	15	26	14	1
1992 Jan 3-6	31%	9	15	29	16	1

* Less than 0.5%

SOURCE: *The Gallup Poll Monthly*, December 2000

TABLE 7.32

Do you believe that religion can answer all or most of today's problems, or that religion is largely old-fashioned and out of date?

	Religion's usefulness – Trend		
	Can answer problems	Old-fashioned	No opinion
2000 Aug 24-27	63%	17	20
2000 Mar 17-19	66%	21	13
1999 Dec 9-12	68%	19	13
1999 Apr 30-May 2	66%	21	11
1998 Jun 22-23	63%	20	17
1998 Jan 16-18	67%	20	13
1997 Aug 12-13	66%	20	14
1997 Mar 24-26	61%	20	19
1995 Dec 15-18	61%	21	18
1994 Jun 25-28	59%	23	18
1994 Mar 28-30	64%	20	16
1991 Feb	61%	25	14
1991 May	59%	23	19
1991 Mar	60%	22	17
1990 Jun	63%	18	19
1989 Apr	61%	18	22
1988 May	57%	29	23
1986 Sep	58%	23	20
1985 Nov	58%	24	18
1985 Mar	61%	22	17
1984 Jun	56%	21	23
1982 Dec	60%	22	18
1981 Jan	65%	15	20
1974 Dec	62%	20	18
1957 Mar	82%	7	11

SOURCE: *The Gallup Poll Monthly*, December 2000

TABLE 7.33

How important would you say religion is in your own life – very important, fairly important, or not very important?

	Importance of religion -Trend			
	Very important	Fairly important	Not very important	No opinion
2000 Aug 24-27	57%	31	12	*
2000 Mar 17-19	61%	27	12	*
1999 Dec 9-12	61%	27	11	1
1999 Apr 30-May 2	58%	30	11	1
1998 Jun 22-23	62%	25	12	1
1998 Jan 16-18	59%	29	12	*
1997 Nov 6-9	58%	28	13	1
1997 Aug 12-13	62%	27	11	*
1997 Mar 24-26	61%	27	11	1
1996 Nov 21-24	58%	27	14	1
1996 Sep 3-5	55%	31	13	1
1996 Jun 27-30	57%	26	17	*
1995 Dec 15-18	60%	28	12	*
1995 Aug 28-30	58%	30	11	1
1995 May 11-14	56%	30	13	1
1994 Dec 16-18	60%	28	11	1
1994 Jun 25-28	55%	30	14	1
1994 Mar 28-30	59%	29	11	1
1993 Mar 12-14	59%	32	9	*
1992 Nov 20-22	59%	28	12	1
1992 Apr	58%	29	13	*
1991 Nov	55%	29	15	1
1991 May	57%	30	13	*
1991 Mar	55%	29	16	*
1991 Feb 7-10	60%	29	11	*
1991 Jan 30-Feb 2	63%	28	9	1
1990 Jun	58%	29	13	*
1989	55%	30	14	1
1988	54%	31	14	1
1987	53%	32	14	1
1986	55%	30	14	1
1985	55%	31	13	1
1984	56%	30	13	1
1983	56%	30	13	1
1982	56%	30	13	1
1981	56%	29	14	1
1980	55%	31	13	1
1978	52%	32	14	2
1965	70%	22	7	1
1952†	75%	20	5	*

† Ben Gaffin and Associates

* Less than 0.5%

SOURCE: *The Gallup Poll Monthly*, December 2000

TABLE 7.34

How important would you say religion is in your own life – very important, fairly important, or not very important?
(By social characteristics)

	Very important	Fairly important	Not very important	No opinion	No. of interviews
National	61%	27	11	1	1009
Sex					
Male	52%	31	15	2	488
Female	70%	23	17	*	521
Age					
18-29 years	53%	29	16	2	208
30-49 years	59%	30	11	*	457
50-64 years	61%	27	10	2	198
65 & older	79%	15	6	*	138
Region					
East	55%	31	14	*	230
Midwest	59%	32	8	1	208
South	74%	20	6	*	348
West	53%	27	18	2	223
Community					
Urban	62%	23	13	2	345
Suburban	60%	30	10	*	489
Rural	63%	26	10	1	175
Race					
White	59%	29	12	*	826
Non-white	80%	13	7	*	174
Education					
College postgraduate	50%	30	18	2	189
Bachelor's degree only	55%	31	12	2	149
Some college	58%	27	14	1	282
High school or less	69%	25	6	*	385
Politics					
Republicans	68%	25	7	*	310
Democrats	64%	23	12	1	354
Independents	53%	32	14	1	345
Ideology					
Liberal	54%	28	18	*	215
Moderate	58%	27	14	1	408
Conservative	69%	26	5	*	353
Income					
$75,000 & over	46%	36	17	1	139
$50,000 & over	51%	33	15	1	315
$30,000-49,999	62%	26	11	1	258
$20,000-29,999	56%	29	13	2	172
Under $20,000	76%	18	6	*	201
Religion					
All Protestants	69%	25	6	*	578
White Protestants	65%	28	7	*	478
Catholics	58%	29	13	0	260

* Less than one percent

SOURCE: *The Gallup Poll Monthly*, March 1997

TABLE 7.35

At the present time, do you think religion as a whole is increasing its influence on American life or losing its influence?

Religion's influence on American life – Trend

	Increasing	Losing	Same (vol)	No opinion
2000 Aug 24-27	35%	58	4	3
2000 Mar 17-19	37%	58	—	5
1999 Dec 9-12	40%	54	3	3
1999 Apr 30-May 2	32%	62	3	3
1998 June 22-23	37%	56	4	3
1998 Jan 16-18	48%	48	1	3
1997 Aug 12-13	36%	60	1	3
1997 Mar 24-26	36%	57	3	4
1995 Dec 15-18	38%	57	2	3
1995 May 11-14	36%	58	3	3
1994 Jun 25-28	28%	67	2	3
1994 Mar 28-30	27%	69	2	2
1992 Nov	27%	63	4	5
1991 Nov	27%	66	3	4
1991 May	34%	57	—	9
1990 Jun	33%	48	8	11
1989 Apr	33%	49	9	9
1988 Mar	36%	49	6	9
1986 Sep	48%	38	6	7
1985 Nov	45%	41	—	14
1985 Mar	48%	39	10	3
1984 Jun	42%	39	14	6
1983 Oct	44%	42	9	5
1983 Jan	44%	42	9	5
1982 Dec	41%	45	9	5
1981 Dec	38%	47	10	6
1980 Apr	35%	46	11	8
1978 Dec	37%	48	10	5
1977 Dec	37%	45	10	9
1976 Dec	44%	45	8	3
1975 Dec	39%	51	7	3
1974 Dec	31%	56	8	5
1970 Jan	14%	75	7	4
1969 May	14%	71	11	5
1968 Apr	19%	67	8	7
1967 Mar	23%	57	14	6
1965 Feb	33%	45	13	8
1962 Feb	45%	32	17	7
1957 Mar	69%	14	10	6

SOURCE: *The Gallup Poll Monthly*, December 2000

TABLE 7.36

Teen beliefs and behavior regarding spirituality/religious faith

	Yes	No
Classified as "born again?"	34%	66%
Self-identified Christian	82%	18%
Absolutely committed to the Christian faith (among self-identified Christians.)	26%	74%
Moderately committed to the Christian faith (among self-identified Christians.).	57%	43%

	Strongly Agree
Is the Bible totally accurate in all of its teachings?	39%
Self-identified as "religious."	64%
Self-identified as "spiritual."	60%
Do you feel a personal responsibility to tell others about your religious beliefs?	28%
Is your religious faith very important in your life?	56%
The Devil, or Satan, is not a living being but is a symbol of evil.	37%
If a person is generally good or does enough good things for others during their life, they will earn a place in heaven.	37%
Jesus Christ, when he lived on earth, committed sins like other people.	22%
Muslims, Buddhists, Christians, Jews and all other people pray to the same God, even though they use different names for their God.	30%

	Yes
Have you prayed to God in the past seven days?	89%
Have you attended church or synagogue in the last seven days?	56%
Have you donated some of your own money to a church in the last seven days?	38%
Have you read the Bible outside of church or synagogue in the last seven days?	35%
Have you attended youth group in the last seven days?	32%
Have you participated in small group for Bible study or prayer (not including Sunday school or 12-step groups) in the last seven days?	29%
Have you read from a sacred text other than the Bible during the last seven days?	18%

SOURCE: Barna Research, October 23, 2000

IMPORTANT NAMES AND ADDRESSES

Administration for Children and Families
U.S. Department of Health and Human Services
200 Independence Ave. SW
Washington, D.C. 20201
(202) 619-0257
Toll-free: (877) 696-6775
E-mail: hhsmail@os.dhhs.gov
URL: http://www.hhs.gov

The Annie E. Casey Foundation
701 St. Paul St.
Baltimore, MD 21202
(410) 547-6600
FAX (410) 547-6624
E-mail: webmail@aecf.org
URL: http://www.aecf.org

Barna Research
5528 Everglades St.
Ventura, CA 93003
(805) 658-8885
FAX: (805) 658-7298
E-mail: mwells@barna.org
URL: http://www.barna.org

Bureau of the Census
U.S. Department of Commerce
Washington, D.C. 20233-0001
(301) 457-4608
FAX: (301) 457-4714
E-mail: webmaster@census.gov
URL: http://www.census.gov

Centers for Disease Control and Prevention
1600 Clifton Road
Atlanta, GA 30333
(404) 639-3311
Toll-free: (800) 311-3435
URL: http://www.cdc.gov

Center for Nutrition Policy and Promotion
U.S. Department of Agriculture
1120 20th St. NW

Suite 200, North Lobby
Washington, D.C. 20036
(202) 418-2312
E-mail: cnpp-web@www.usda.gov
URL: http://www.usda.gov/cnpp

Center for Research for Mothers and Children
National Institute of Child Health and Human Development
Bldg 31, Room 2A32, MSC 2425
31 Center Drive
Bethesda, MD 20892-2425
(301) 496-5097
FAX: (301) 402-2085
E-mail: NICHDClearinghouse@mail.nih.gov
URL: http://www.nichd.nih.gov/

Center on Budget and Policy Priorities
820 1st St. NE, # 510
Washington, D.C. 20002
(202) 408-1080
FAX: (202) 408-1056
E-mail: bazie@cbpp.org
URL: http://www.cbpp.org

Child Care Bureau
Administration on Children, Youth, and Families
U.S. Department of Health and Human Services
200 Independence Ave. SW
Washington, D.C. 20201
(202) 619-0257
Toll-free: (877) 696-6775
E-mail: hhsmail@os.dhhs.gov
URL: http://www.hhs.gov

Child Trends, Inc.
4301 Connecticut Ave. NW, # 100
Washington, D.C. 20008
(202) 362-5580
FAX: (202) 362-5533
E-mail: webmaster@childtrends.org
URL: http://www.childtrends.org

Children's Defense Fund
25 E St. NW
Washington, D.C. 20001
(202) 662-3520
URL: http://www.childrensdefense.org

Families and Work Institute
330 Seventh Ave., 14th Floor
New York, NY 10001
(212) 465-2044
FAX: (212) 465-8637
E-mail: ebrownfield@familiesandwork.org
URL: http://www.familiesandwork.org

The Gallup Organization
The Gallup Building
47 Hulfish StreetPrinceton, NJ 08524
(609) 924-9600
FAX: (609)924-0228
E-mail: sarah_van_allen@gallup.com
URL: http://www.gallup.com

Head Start
U.S. Department of Health and Human Services
Administration for Children and Families
330 C Street, SW
Washington, D.C. 20447
(202) 205-8572
E-mail: hhsmail@os.dhhs.gov
URL: http://www2.acf.dhhs.gov/programs/hsb/

The Joint Center for Poverty Research
Institute for Policy Research
Northwestern University
2046 Sheridan RoadEvanston, IL 60208
(847) 491-4145
FAX: (847) 467-2459
E-mail: povcen@northwestern.edu

Lambda Legal Defense and Education Fund
120 Wall St., # 1500
New York, NY 10005-3904
(212) 809-8585
FAX: (212) 809-0055
E-mail: lambdalegal@lambdalegal.org
URL: http://www.lambdalegal.org

National Adoption Information Clearinghouse
330 C St. SW
Washington, D.C. 20447
(703) 352-3488
FAX: (703) 385-3206
Toll-free: (888) 251-0075
E-mail: naic@calib.com.
URL: http://www.calib.com/naic

National Alliance for Caregiving
4720 Montgomery Lane, # 642
Bethesda, MD 20814
(301) 718-8444
FAX: (301) 652-7711
E-mail: gailhunt.nac@erols.com
URL: http://www.caregiving.org

National Campaign to Prevent Teen Pregnancy
1776 Massachusetts Avenue NW, Suite 200
Washington, D.C. 20036
(202) 478-8500
E-mail: campaign@teenpregnancy.org
URL: http://www.teenpregnancy.org

National Center for Children in Poverty
The Joseph L. Mailman School of Public Health of Columbia University
154 Haven Ave.New York, NY 10032-1180
(212) 304-7100
FAX: (212) 544-4200
URL: http://cpmcnet.columbia.edu/dept/nccp/

National Center for Education Statistics
1990 K Street, NW
Washington, D.C. 20006
(202) 502-7300
E-mail: NCESWebMaster@ed.gov
URL: http://www.nces.ed.gov

National Clearinghouse on Child Abuse and Neglect Information
330 C St. SW
Washington, D.C. 20447
(703) 385-7565
FAX: (703) 385-3206
Toll-free: (800) 394-3366
E-mail: nccanch@calib.com
URL: http://www.calib.com/nccanch/

National Fatherhood Initiative
101 Lake Forest Boulevard, # 360
Gaithersburg, MD 20877
(301) 948-0599
FAX: (301) 948-4325
E-mail: nfi1995@aol.com
URL: http://www.fatherhood.org

National Low Income Housing Coalition
1012 14th St. NW, # 610
Washington, D.C. 20005
(202) 662-1530
FAX: (202) 393-1973
E-mail: info@nlihc.org
URL: http://www.nlihc.org

Public Agenda
6 E. 39th St.

New York, NY 10016
(212) 686-6610
FAX: (212) 889-3461
URL: http://www.publicagenda.org

United States General Accounting Office
441 G Street, NW
Washington, D.C. 20548
(202) 512-4800
E-mail: webmaster@gao.gov
URL: http://www.gao.gov

The Urban Institute
2100 M St. NW
Washington, D.C. 20037
(202) 833-7200
FAX: (202) 223-3043
E-mail: webmaster@ui.urban.org
URL: http://www.urban.org

U.S. Conference of Mayors
1620 I St. NW
Washington, D.C. 20006
(202) 293-7330
FAX: (202) 293-2352
E-mail: info@usmayors.org
URL: http://www.usmayors.org/uscm/

Women's Bureau
U.S. Department of Labor
200 Constitution Ave. NW
Room S-3002
Washington, D.C. 20210
FAX: (202) 219-5529
Toll-free: (800) 827-5335
URL: http://www.dol.gov/dol/wb

RESOURCES

The Bureau of the Census of the U.S. Department of Commerce is probably the single most important collection point for demographic information about American life. Many of its publications were essential for the preparation of this book, including *Marital Status and Living Arrangements: 1998* (1999), *Household and Family Characteristics: 1998* (1999), *Projections of the Number of Households and Families in the United States: 1995 to 2010* (1996), *Population Projections of the United States by Age, Sex, Race, and Hispanic Origin: 1995 to 2050* (1996), *Coresident Grandparents and Their Grandchildren: Grandparent Maintained Families* (1999), *Money Income in the United States: 1999* (2000), *Poverty in the United States: 1999* (2000), *Child Support for Custodial Mothers and Fathers: 1995* (1999), *Non-Custodial Parents' Participation in Their Children's Lives: Evidence from the Survey of Income and Program Participation, My Daddy Takes Care of Me! Fathers as Care Providers* (1997), *Health Insurance Coverage: 1999* (2000), and *Who Can Afford to Buy a House in 1993?* (1997).

Along with the Census Bureau the U.S. Department of Housing and Urban Development (HUD) produces *The State of the Cities 2000* which we also used in preparing this book.

The different agencies of the U.S. Department of Health and Human Services (HHS) produce important publications on a wide variety of statistical data. Its Substance Abuse and Mental Health Service Administration (SAMHSA) published *The Relationship Between Family Structure and Adolescent Substance Abuse* (1996). The Department's Maternal and Child Health Bureau published the annual *Child Health USA 2000* (2000), which reported on the health status and service needs of America's children, as well as disseminating data collected through the Adoption and Foster Care Analysis and Reporting System (AFCARS). The Federal Interagency Forum on Child and Family Statistics presented an overview of the wellbeing of the nation's children in *America's Children: Key National Indicators of Well-Being* (1998). The National Child Abuse and Neglect Data System (NCANDS) of the HHS reported on child abuse and neglect statistics submitted by state child protective services agencies in *Child Maltreatment 1998: Reports From the States to the National Child Abuse and Neglect Data System* (2000).

Another agency of the HHS, the Centers for Disease Control and Prevention (CDC), provided sobering data on young adults who had died of AIDS in its publication *HIV/AIDS Surveillance Report* (2000). The CDC's *Morbidity and Mortality Weekly Report* discussed the "Trends in Sexual Risk Behaviors Among High School Students—United States, 1991–1997" (1998), and youth risk behaviors were studied in *Youth Risk Behavior Surveillance—United States, 1999* (2000). The CDC's National Center for Health Statistics (NCHS) is another valuable resource. Its annual *Health, United States, 2000* (2000) provided a statistical overview of the nation's fertility. The NCHS periodical *National Vital Statistics Report*, formerly called the *Monthly Vital Statistics Report*, supplied data on marriage, divorce, and births. Additionally, some data was gleaned from *Provisional Vital Statistics for the United States, Births, Marriages, Divorces, and Deaths: Provisional Data for November 1999* (2000), *Births: Preliminary Data for 1999* (2000) and *Highlights of Trends in Pregnancies and Pregnancy Rates by Outcome: Estimates for the United States, 1976–96* (1999) and (2000).

Trends in multiple births were researched using data from the CDC's report *Trends in Twin and Triplet Births: 1980–97* (1999), as well as *1997 Assisted Reproductive Technology Success Rates, National Summary and Fertility Clinic Reports* (1999) released by the U.S. Department of Health and Human Services.

The U.S. Department of Labor (DOL) was also a vital source for this work. The Department's *Pilot Survey on* the Incidence of Child Care Resource and Referral Services in June 2000 (2000), released through the Bureau of Labor Statistics, was very helpful. The DOL's Women's Bureau reported on the growing importance of child care during nonstandard hours in *Care Around the Clock: Developing Child Care Resources Before 9 and After 5* (1995). The Bureau also provided a historical analysis of the economic trends affecting female workers from the years leading to the Equal Pay Act to the present in *Equal Pay: A Thirty-five Year Perspective* (1998) and *Women's Jobs 1964–1999: More Than 30 Years of Progress* (2000). The Bureau of Labor Statistics of the DOL published information on "Employer-sponsored Childcare Benefits" (*Issues in Labor Statistics*, 1998) and the *Employment Characteristics of Families: 1999* (2000).

We are also grateful for the in-depth research of the U.S. Department of Agriculture's (USDA) Center for Nutrition Policy and Promotion, which annually releases the report *Expenditures on Children by Families*, which helps quantify how much it costs to raise a child in today's economy.

The National Center for Education Statistics (NCES) of the U.S. Department of Education published the *Characteristics of Children's Early Care and Education Programs: Data from the 1995 National Household Education Survey* (1998), which examined the care and education of preschoolers in nonparental child care settings. In *Fathers' Involvement in Their Children's Schools* (1997), the NCES analyzed the influence of fathers' involvement on their children's performance in school. *Gender Differences in Earnings Among Young Adults Entering the Labor Market* (1998) examined the work consistency of women as it related to family formation.

The U.S. Government Accounting Office (GAO), the investigative arm of Congress, reported on *Teen Mothers-Selected Socio-Demographic Characteristics and Risk Factors* (1998) and *Health Insurance for Children— Private Insurance Continues to Deteriorate* (1996).

The Gale Group thanks the Department for Professional Employees of AFL-CIO for permission to reprint graphics from *Salaried and Professional Women, Relevant Statistics: 1997 Edition* (1997). The United States Conference of Mayors graciously granted permission to reproduce graphics and use information from *A Status Report on Hunger and Homelessness in America's Cities, 1999: A 26 City Survey* (1999).

The Gale Group is also grateful to the National Alliance for Caregiving and the American Association of Retired Persons (AARP) for permission to reproduce graphics from *Family Caregiving in the U.S.: Findings from a National Survey* (1997). Appreciation is also due to the National Adoption Information Clearinghouse for its in-depth information and statistics on adoption and foster care in America.

Our thanks also go to the National Low Income Housing Coalition for permission to use figures from *Out of Reach: The Growing Gap Between Housing Costs and Income of Poor People in the United States*, September 2000 and to the Center on Budget and Policy Priorities for allowing us to reproduce graphics from *In Search of Shelter: The Growing Shortage of Affordable Rental Housing* (1998).

The National Campaign to Prevent Teen Pregnancy very kindly granted permission to reprint figures from *Whatever Happened to Childhood? The Problem of Teen Pregnancy in the United States* (1997) and *Not Just For Girls: The Roles of Boys and Men in Teen Pregnancy Prevention* (1997). We also thank The Urban Institute for the use of figures from *Involving Men in Preventing Teen Pregnancy: A Guide for Program Planners* (1997).

The Gale Group extends a special thanks to the Gallup Organization for permission to use their opinion polls. The George H. Gallup International Institute graciously granted permission to publish its survey on "Teens Say It's Harder to be a Father Today" (*YOUTHviews*, May 1998). Additionally, we are grateful to Barna Research for use of their extensive surveys on teens' views on religion and spirituality. We also express our gratitude to the Whirlpool Foundation, Public Agenda, and the National Opinion Research Center at the University of Chicago for permission to use their opinion polls.

INDEX